Spiritualism in Antebellum America

RELIGION IN NORTH AMERICA
Catherine L. Albanese and Stephen J. Stein, editors

William L. Andrews, editor.
Sisters of the Spirit: Three Black Women's Autobiographies of the Nineteenth Century

Mary Farrell Bednarowski.
New Religions and the Theological Imagination in America

David Chidester.
Salvation and Suicide: An Interpretation of Jim Jones, the Peoples Temple, and Jonestown

David Chidester and
Edward T. Linenthal, editors.
American Sacred Space

Thomas D. Hamm.
God's Government Begun: The Society for Universal Inquiry and Reform, 1842–1846

Thomas D. Hamm.
The Transformation of American Quakerism: Orthodox Friends, 1800–1907

Jean M. Humez, editor.
Mother's First-Born Daughters: Early Shaker Writings on Women and Religion

Carl T. Jackson.
Vedanta for the West: The Ramakrishna Movement in the United States

David Kuebrich.
Minor Prophecy: Walt Whitman's New American Religion

John D. Loftin.
Religion and Hopi Life in the Twentieth Century

Colleen McDannell.
The Christian Home in Victorian America, 1840–1900

Ronald L. Numbers and
Jonathan M. Butler, editors.
The Disappointed: Millerism and Millenarianism in the Nineteenth Century

Richard W. Pointer.
Protestant Pluralism and the New York Experience: A Study of Eighteenth-Century Religious Diversity

Sally M. Promey.
Spiritual Spectacles: Vision and Image in Mid-Nineteenth-Century Shakerism

Stephen Prothero.
The White Buddhist: Henry Steel Olcott and the Nineteenth-Century American Encounter with Asian Religions

Russell E. Richey.
Early American Methodism

A. Gregory Schneider.
The Way of the Cross Leads Home: The Domestication of American Methodism

Richard Hughes Seager.
The World's Parliament of Religions: The East/West Encounter, Chicago, 1893

Ann Taves, editor.
Religion and Domestic Violence in Early New England: The Memoirs of Abigail Abbot Bailey

Thomas A. Tweed.
The American Encounter with Buddhism, 1844–1912: Victorian Culture and the Limits of Dissent

Valarie H. Ziegler.
The Advocates of Peace in Antebellum America

ILLUSTRATIONS

CONTENTS

For Iris, Judith, and Gilbert

The paper used in this publication meets the minimum requirements of American National Standard for Information Sciences—Permanence of Paper for Printed Library Materials, ANSI Z39.48–1984.

Manufactured in the United States of America

Library of Congress Cataloging-in-Publication Data

Carroll, Bret E., date
Spiritualism in antebellum America / Bret E. Carroll.
p.   cm. — (Religion in North America)
Includes bibliographical references and index.
ISBN 0-253-33315-6 (cloth : alk. paper)
1. Spiritualism—United States. 2. United States—Religion—19th century.
I. Title. II. Series.
BF1242.U6C37   1997
133.9'0973'09034—dc21   97-7354

1   2   3   4   5   02   01   00   99   98   97

Title page illustration: "Invitation to the Spirit Land."
Frontispiece of John W. Edmonds and George T. Dexter,
SPIRITUALISM, volume 1 (New York: Partridge and Brittan, 1853).

Spiritualism in Antebellum America

BRET E. CARROLL

INDIANA UNIVERSITY PRESS
Bloomington & Indianapolis

FOREWORD

❧

This volume by Bret E. Carroll takes its place alongside a significant and growing historical literature engaged with nineteenth-century spiritualism. By contrast with those who once regarded mediums and instruments, seances and other spiritualist phenomena as subjects for comic relief, pioneering studies by R. Laurence Moore and Ann Braude focused serious attention on this religious movement for all scholars working in social and women's history. Now Carroll moves beyond those instructive studies by analyzing nineteenth-century spiritualism in its early decades as a religious ideology. In fact, he does more than simply add to our understanding: he corrects the standard and conventional reading of spiritualism as an individualistic religious movement that fragmented hopelessly because of its thoroughgoing antistructuralism. In place of that interpretation Carroll argues persuasively for a "spiritualist republicanism" in which the search for order existed in successful tension with spiritualism's individualistic impulse.

Carroll's use of the rubric of "republicanism" allows him to encompass and reconcile the values of freedom and order within spiritualism. These values, he demonstrates, were a central concern of the American culture of the era. In effect, then, overall he succeeds in treating spiritualism as a religion, which is his religious-studies goal, and in contextualizing it in the nineteenth century, which is his historical goal. In this Carroll is strongly and creatively revisionist. Earlier interpreters of spiritualism have paid close attention to its freedom-loving antinomianism, but they have failed to notice its search for and expressions of cosmic and social order. Carroll makes a coherent and effective argument for his case.

In the course of his revisionism Carroll enriches our understanding of both religion and culture. He situates spiritualism in nineteenth-century America within a Swedenborgian subculture that embraced both New England Transcendentalism on the left and the Swedenborgian Church of the New Jerusalem on the right, with the former oriented to freedom and the latter to order. The message is that, by contrast, spiritualists searched for both. Moreover, Carroll's analysis joins another significant historiographical tradition in contemporary scholarship, that represented by the work of Nathan O. Hatch who has underscored the democratizing impulse in antebellum religion. Carroll rereads spiritualist independence and individualism in terms of the democratic ideology of the American Revolution and the American

Enlightenment. From this, he argues, emerged a sharp spiritualist critique of traditional religious affiliation and of conventional religious institutions—a critique spiritualists shared with other "come-outers" in the period.

Carroll's description of the spiritualist cosmology breaks new ground in a richly textured account of the structure of the spirit world. The spiritualists' social construction of the spirit world combined symbols of universal and enduring quality—the circle and the sphere—with powerful contemporary images of science, the telegraph, and electricity, in their effort to conceptualize and explain an imagined and experienced spiritual reality. Similarly, Carroll explores the "ministry" of the spirits, demonstrating the ways in which their activities mirrored activities in the regular world. The spirits functioned as parents and caretakers, thereby playing significant roles in human life. Inevitably, therefore, the spirits affected spiritualist attitudes toward the limits of both self-reliance and external authority—two additional manifestations of freedom and order.

But the "circle" was more than simply a powerful cosmological metaphor for spiritualists. It also became the name of the functioning institutional and structural unit that members of this religious movement established to bring spiritual harmony to the earthly plane. Carroll shows how the spiritualist circle, comprised of a handful of believers, was the site where they developed seance rituals, where the medium presided, and where the movement attempted to organize itself. In these face-to-face small groups the spiritualists found both freedom and order, both individualism and community. Here in this volume for the first time we have an extended discussion of the institutional context through which most serious spiritualists sought to participate in the world of the spirits. Thus Carroll carries the reader beyond the sensationalism of public performances that were often more for entertainment than religious edification. Meanwhile, the impulse to institutionalize spiritualism in communal structures reached its fullest expression in the short-lived Mountain Cove Community in what is now West Virginia. In Carroll's examination of this ultimately unsuccessful attempt to communalize spiritualist ideals, we see in striking relief the ideological tensions that fragmented the entire movement.

Carroll carries the study of nineteenth-century spiritualism to a new level in this volume. He refuses to dismiss the belief in spirits that forms the core of the movement, or to reduce that fundamental religious commitment to some socio-psychological phenomenon. He takes seriously the complexity of the religious belief in spirits and yet also demonstrates the integral relationship between that belief and the world of nineteenth-century American religion and culture.

CATHERINE L. ALBANESE
STEPHEN J. STEIN
SERIES EDITORS

ACKNOWLEDGMENTS

The people whose religion I propose to explore in the pages that follow would say that this book is as much the product of the minds of departed spirits as it is of my own, and that I ought to call attention to the fact. I must indeed acknowledge that I owe many debts, intellectual and otherwise, to minds other than my own. Many people have helped shape and make possible this study as it developed from seminar paper to doctoral dissertation to its current form.

Perhaps the most important of these debts is to R. Laurence Moore. Not only did his own groundbreaking study of Spiritualism pave the way for this one and many others and have an enormous influence on all of them, but his insightful critical comments as one of my dissertation advisers have undoubtedly made this a far better work than it otherwise would have been. He was openminded and encouraging when faced with a student whose slant on the topic differed in many respects from his own and who was sometimes less than subtle in pointing that out. My other dissertation advisers, Stuart Blumin and L. Pearce Williams, also provided helpful comments and were instrumental in leading me into the line of research of which this book is the culmination.

Other readers too offered valuable commentary. Catherine L. Albanese and Stephen J. Stein, the editors of Indiana University Press's Religion in North America Series, were thoughtful readers whose suggestions have undoubtedly improved this book. Robert C. Fuller and Mary Farrell Bednarowski also provided helpful suggestions. Vicki Eaklor, a dear friend and esteemed colleague, read an early draft of what is now a portion of chapter 7 as I prepared to publish it in article form; that article was originally published in *Communal Societies,* the journal of the Communal Studies Association. This book has benefited too from countless casual conversations over the past several years with friends and colleagues too numerous to name here; I trust that they will know who they are, and am grateful to them all. Finally, Ann Braude, another one of the very few people who have made Spiritualism the topic of close study, was quite helpful during the early stages of this project, generously providing me with a copy of her bibliography when access to it was not otherwise possible.

Considerable portions of the research and writing were made possible through funding provided by Cornell University. A summer fellowship at the Smithsonian Institution was important during the incipient stages of this project. I drew on the resources of many libraries and archives as the research proceeded, most notably Cornell University, the American Antiquarian Society, the Library of Congress, the New York Public Library, and the State Historical Society of Wisconsin. I would like to thank the staffs of all these places. The importance of the interlibrary loan system to my work can hardly be overestimated; I am especially indebted to the interlibrary loan staffs at Cornell University, Alfred University, and the University of Texas at Arlington, whose efforts in locating hard-to-find sources have been invaluable as the life of a "gypsy professor" has whisked me from place to place.

My most profound debt is to my family, whose emotional support has been valuable beyond measure. The three people mentioned in the dedication are especially important to me. The memory of my father Gilbert, who died before he could write the book he had always wanted to write, surely provided some of the inspiration that made mine possible. My mother Judith, who is coming to appreciate the nature of my work and what it means to me, merits special mention. Above all, my wife and best friend Iris has been there to share my trials and triumphs from the beginning of this project and has patiently put up with being awakened by my 4:00 A.M. brainstorms. This book is for the three of them.

ABBREVIATIONS

•┼•

AC	Emanuel Swedenborg, *Arcana Coelestia* (New York: Swedenborg Foundation, 1963)
AE	Emanuel Swedenborg, *Apocalypse Explained* (New York: Swedenborg Foundation, 1968)
AP	*Age of Progress*
BJM	*Buchanan's Journal of Man*
BL	*Banner of Light*
CFWP	Report on Spiritualist Meetings, Charlotte Fowler Wells Papers, Cornell University Special Collections
HH	Emanuel Swedenborg, *Heaven and Its Wonders and Hell* (New York: Swedenborg Foundation, 1944)
JSW	John Shoebridge Williams Manuscripts on Spiritualism, State Historical Society of Wisconsin
JSWP	John Shoebridge Williams Miscellaneous Papers, State Historical Society of Wisconsin
MCJ	*Mountain Cove Journal and Spiritual Harbinger*
NE	*New Era*
NI	*Nichols' Journal*
NJ	Emanuel Swedenborg, *The New Jerusalem and Its Heavenly Doctrine* (London: Swedenborg Society, 1938)
NJM	*New Jerusalem Magazine*
PC	*Practical Christian*
SA	*The Spiritual Age*
SC	*Sacred Circle*
SD	*Emanuel Swedenborg, Spiritual Diary* (London: Swedenborg Society, 1981)
SH	*Shekinah*

SM   *The Spirit Messenger*

ST   *The Spiritual Telegraph*

SW   *Spirit World*

USP   *The Univercoelum and Spiritual Philosopher*

Spiritualism in
Antebellum America

1

Introduction

SPIRITUALIST RELIGION
AND THE SEARCH FOR ORDER

The desire to establish contact with a spirit world is as old as humanity. A belief in the possibility and fact of spirit communication has figured prominently in the historical traditions of both Western and non-Western religions. But the need to experience a close relationship with spirits became particularly intensified and culturally salient in the United States, especially in the Northeast and Midwest, during the 1840s and 1850s. The result was the emergence of Spiritualism, one of the most peculiar, fascinating, and colorful "isms" in a culture bursting with innovative and experimental new movements in religion, social reform, and science. Many devotees of Spiritualism made a belief in communion with departed spirits the basis for a distinct and thoroughly spirit-centered system of religious belief and practice—involving not simply spirit communication but also, in the words of one of its early publicists and historians, a belief in "the direct agency and immediate presence of bright ministering spirits"—that would provide an alternative to traditional Protestantism.[1]

The emergence of Spiritualism evoked expressions of wonder from contemporaries, who were unable to explain what seemed to them a bizarre cultural aberration. New York lawyer and classical scholar George Templeton Strong, for example, pondered it with a mixture of disdain and puzzlement. "What would I have said six years ago," he asked in his diary in 1855, "to anybody who predicted that before the enlightened nineteenth century was ended hundreds of thousands of people in this country would believe themselves able to communicate with the ghosts of their grandfathers?" The purpose of this book is to make sense of Spiritualism as Strong could not. Doing so requires something of an anthropological approach. That is, one must take seriously what Spiritualists believed, said, and did, attempt to understand what their religion meant to them, and try to understand the internal logic of their belief and practice. To succeed is to show that Spiritualism constituted not an aberration in antebellum American life but an understandable and even logical historical and cultural phenomenon. It is also to show that Spiritualists were rational people in search of a religion that answered their religious questions and satisfied their spiritual needs. As with other "emergent" (as opposed to "established") religions, the advent of Spiritualism was not an improbable development but was "there all the time" and "understandable in terms of known logic or processes." It is no longer possible to share Strong's assessment of Spiritualism as a cultural anomaly.[2]

Although attempted contact with spirits reflects a deeply rooted human need for cosmic connectedness, American Spiritualism was a response to its specific historical setting. It therefore tells us much about the shape and texture of the society and culture that produced it. In particular, it was a response to a multifaceted spiritual crisis that had developed by the late 1840s in those places where the movement was strongest. The changes that precipitated it were in large part religious and were produced by the successive impact first of Enlightenment religious thinking, which encouraged a rational and scientific approach to deity, and then of Romanticism, which called for greater attention to subjective religious insight and feeling. These two often opposing currents, both incorporated into Spiritualist religion, generated transformations that included the increasing cultural authority of science and the corresponding growth of a scientific materialism that denied the existence, or at least the knowability, of spirit; a shift in emphasis from external and empirical to internal and intuitive sources of religious experience and epistemological authority; an uneasy coexistence of personal conceptions of God with abstract and impersonal ideas of a deity who operated through natural law; a transformation from an older religious (and social) order based on deference and hierarchy to a newer one which emphasized personal experience, spiritual equality, and self-reliant individualism; and the emergence of a pluralistic religious culture in which a bewildering array of ideologies and sects competed for support and religious truth seemed increasingly uncertain and relativistic. Furthermore, many Spiritualists had rebelliously repudiated the professionalizing clergy of their society as too mechanical and too influenced by powerful social interests to exercise effective religious and moral authority. Insofar as these developments encouraged people to explore their personal spirituality, they seemed immensely liberating and commensurate with the nation's cultural commitment to personal freedom. Yet they also generated intense anxiety.

The troubling effects of these religious developments were reinforced by related changes in American social, economic, and political life—also simultaneously liberating and unsettling—that reshaped the Northeast and Midwest during the early to mid-nineteenth century. Industrialization, urbanization, and the growth of commercial capitalism were rapidly altering the nation by the 1830s, and growing immigration added to the social flux by the late 1840s. The growth of population, the development of a mass society and culture, and the reality of cultural, ethnic, and religious pluralism encouraged among many middle-class Protestants a sense that social order was threatened and that their control over it was lost. The rise of a market economy, meanwhile, meant increasing economic uncertainty and insecurity, placed a premium on individual acquisitiveness and competitive values, and undermined older value systems that emphasized community and social hierarchy. The changing economy seemed to some to have fostered materialism and sapped Americans' commitment to things spiritual. Technology, too, was transforming American life. The proliferation of factories, railroads, and telegraph lines in particular fostered a sense that America's potential for expansive growth was only beginning to be developed, and that anything was possible. Politically, these decades witnessed the emergence of a mass democratic political culture and, along with it, new political rules and the rise of a new generation of political leaders whose methods and priorities seemed to undermine or ignore older moral standards. Meanwhile, the Revolutionary generation which had governed the nation for its first half century was dying off, leaving many with the sense that their heroes were disappearing, that republican values were waning in strength, and that they were losing their connectedness to the past. Indeed, it is not entirely coincidental that the year 1848, when Margaret and Kate Fox first heard spirit rapping in upstate New York and sparked the emergence of Spiritualism, also saw the death of John Quincy Adams, considered by many Americans of the period as the last major representative of the founding generation.[3] Finally, the attempt by antebellum reformers to shape the social structure and moral values of the new republic seemed to be losing its steam at about this time without having succeeded in its goals. The result was a sense of disappointment and despair. The fabric of American life seemed to be unraveling, stretched and torn by forces which promoted selfishness, materialism, fragmentation, and atomization as Americans drifted away from the past and toward modernity.

These unsettling developments combined to produce spiritual malaise, discomfort, discontent, and above all a search for order among many Americans.[4] Most of those attracted to Spiritualism found their deities distant, their cultural and social surroundings disturbing, and their ministers and churches ineffectual in addressing the resulting uneasiness. Fearing that spiritual values and religious institutions were losing their influence on American society, they experimented with new religious ideas and practices and joined their contemporaries in a variety of cultural, social, moral, and scientific (or quasi-scientific) reform movements. They hoped to find more satisfying forms of religious belief and expression and, like many religious Americans before and after them, to resacralize a society and a cosmos that they feared was spiritually empty. This restless searching, resulting in what Jon Butler has called an "antebellum spiritual hothouse," was a major theme of nineteenth-century American culture.[5] Those who embraced Spiritualist religion often had backgrounds suggesting a restless disapproval of the status quo and an openness to new and progressive philosophies. They usually came from such liberal religions as Swedenborgianism, Universalism, Quakerism, and, to a lesser extent, Unitarianism, Transcendentalism, and rationalism, each of which contributed not only members to the Spiritualist movement but also ideas to its religious ideology. They often moved through more than one of these belief systems before drifting into Spiritualism. They also tended to be committed to one or more of such causes as temperance, women's rights, abolitionism, communitarianism, phrenology, and mesmerism, as well as dietary, dress, marriage, and medical reform. Their desire for order and spiritual fulfillment eventually led them to seek communion with spirits and to create their new religion.

They were not alone in their anguish. Indeed, one of the defining dramas in the cultural life of the early republic was the attempt by American reformers, troubled by national development and the questioning of traditional authorities and restraints, to counteract perceived social and cultural chaos with new structures of authority. Carroll Smith-Rosenberg has suggested that people feeling "powerless in the face of massive and unremitting social transformation" respond by "attempting to capture and encapsulate such change within a new and ordered symbolic universe." Through imagery and myth, they bring change "within the control of the imagination." The result was a "host of religious and ideological revolts against bourgeois ideology" (including Spiritualism) during the antebellum decades. Robert A. Abzug similarly suggests that American reformers of the period used their religious imaginations to create a new ideology and restore sacred order to their society, adding that they used the persuasive and reassuring languages of republicanism, Christianity, and science. Recent sociological and psychological research on Spiritualism supports these views. Psychohistorian Shomer Zwelling has interpreted Spiritualism as a "historical group-fantasy" created in response not only to a yearning for freedom but also to a sense of fragmentation and social chaos in the antebellum North. Sociologist William L. MacDonald has similarly suggested that historical cultural surges in such paranormal beliefs as perceived encounters with spirits are fairly common responses to existential problems and rapid social change. Sensing that conventional science and traditional religious institutions have failed to address their needs, many people turn to paranormal experiences for "understanding, meaning, and control." Spiritualists consulted spirits and developed their ideology with this end consistently in mind.[6]

Their efforts confronted them with the classic problem of balancing freedom and order, not to mention the host of other familiar dyadic pairings that have characterized American religious discourse: spirit and matter, individual and community, spontaneity and discipline, self-realization and conformity, free will and determinism, subject and object, and equality and hierarchy. In each case they sought equilibrium and therefore developed ideologically complex positions. They and other antebellum reformers and religious seekers embraced the expansive possibilities of freedom, democracy, individualism, and economic liberalism only so far as these values were compatible with the social and moral stability and the religious and republican principles of virtue once maintained by the now weakening communal values and restraints of an idealized past. They therefore urged social coherence and moral conformity, usually in accordance with a perceived model of divine order, while encouraging the personal liberty and individual agency that were emerging as paramount values in the new republic. Anxious to free themselves only from those traditions they considered outmoded, they and others combined an experimental approach to new ideas with an unmistakable nostalgia for disappearing sources of authority and security. Reaching out for what George Templeton Strong derisively called "the ghosts of their grandfathers," they exalted the ideals of their heroic past in their new religious ideology. They constructed a cosmos at once personal and communal, liberating and ordered.

Their search for order and security located them squarely within a broad cultural transformation "from boundlessness to consolidation," whereby Americans sought to stabilize their malleable society. Like the Republican party, another product of the late antebellum period, Spiritualism fused opposing ideological currents, combining "the crusading idealism of an older America with a rising conservatism that looked forward to a more stable and cohesive society." They "stood at one and the same time for the assertion of freedom and the acceptance of limits." They reflected the growing mid-century "respect for institutions, for discipline, for the principles of loyalty and authority." They wanted to ensure that what Robert H. Wiebe has called the "opening of American society"—the shift from a deferential social order toward a more democratic society that seemed to offer unlimited opportunity for free white males—take place within a well-defined spiritual and moral framework. If they were "radical spirits" articulating a "middle-class radicalism" that challenged the conventions of the status quo in the name of liberty and envisioned an alternative social structure, they also displayed a profoundly conservative middle-class concern for order. As these free spirits rebelled against authority, they fashioned their new religion with the goal of achieving a thoroughly ordered and disciplined freedom.[7]

Insofar as Spiritualists designed their religion to counter social and religious tendencies they considered degenerative, their movement can be understood as part of a larger antebellum American process of what anthropologist Anthony F. C. Wallace has called religious and cultural "revitalization." According to Wallace, enormous social and cultural change can elicit attempts to energize society through the restoration of an older, purer, and disappearing state.[8] Sharing Spiritualists' concern with the apparently amoral direction in which American society seemed to be moving, the spirit voices they heard reassured them in a form of wish-fulfillment that human society was being controlled from above and molded into conformity with a spiritual reality that resembled a comfortably familiar but disappearing past. Such assurances helped them both to resist and to accommodate to disorienting developments on earth.

In their creative religious activity, as in their pursuit of both freedom and order, Spiritualists participated in the cultural life of antebellum America. According to Mary Farrell Bednarowski, the various new religious groups that emerged in the early republic located and defined themselves with reference to the larger religious culture through their exercise of "theological imagination." That is, they used their "creative human capacity to formulate meaning systems, models of the universe, by which men and women are able to orient and interpret their lives." According to Bednarowski, advocates of new religions in America, especially those who like Spiritualists put new emphases and twists on traditional religious ideas in a new cultural setting, "must be seen as participants" in ongoing theological conversations that involve all groups in the religious culture. The various interlocutors "understand themselves as having new revelations to offer, new models of the universe that will address the inadequacies of those meaning systems, religious and secular, that are presently available." Spiritualists joined the cultural conversation to convince antebellum Americans that their religion offered a feeling of security and order that others lacked.[9]

The product of their efforts was a new expression of what Sydney Ahlstrom has called American "harmonial religion." Religious systems in this tradition, which took shape in the mid-nineteenth century, assume that "spiritual composure, physical health, and even economic well-being . . . flow from a person's rapport with the cosmos. Human beatitude and immortality are believed to depend to a great degree on one's being 'in tune with the infinite.'" Spiritualists developed a distinctive and coherent religious "ideology," a "system of interlinked ideas, symbols, and beliefs by which a culture . . . seeks to justify and perpetuate itself; the web of rhetoric, ritual, and assumption through which [a] society coerces, persuades, and coheres."[10] Encompassing ideas and practices, this ideology was constructed around well-defined symbols and rituals that fostered a sense of Spiritualist identity and became the basis of a distinct and loosely unified Spiritualist religious subculture.[11]

Like the larger religious culture, Spiritualist religion involved a complex and tension-filled blend of the modes of religious behavior termed "structure" and "antistructure" by anthropologist Victor Turner.[12] Scholars have thus far emphasized Spiritualism's individualistic, antiauthoritarian, and antistructural features, or what Stephen J. Stein has called "the deconstructive aspect of the populist vision" in American religious culture.[13] But Stein's work on the Shakers suggests that "the process of cultural change *inevitably* moves from separation to reaggregation, from structure back to structure, from deconstruction to reconstruction." While some Spiritualists displayed an "antistructural" resistance to the formation of large-scale organizations during the antebellum period, most exhibited decidedly structural tendencies—called by Stein "the stuff of religious life"—which have been slighted in previous treatments of the movement.[14] They developed well structured religious practices and used structural metaphors in justifying their moments of antistructural behavior. They remind us that religions seek to provide structures of meaning in belief and practice for their adherents. To concentrate primarily on their "deconstructive" aspects is to disregard their very substance.

However puzzling Spiritualists were to the likes of George Templeton Strong, their strategy of constructing a religious belief system around spirits made theological sense. If they felt uncomfortably alone as their God seemed to fade into abstractness and adrift in a new world that required them to rely on themselves and other human beings, if they sought spiritual meaning as theocentric notions of religious authority were gradually giving way to anthropocentric ones, what more appropriate religious response than an ideology focusing specifically on the semidivine human spirit midway between humanity and deity? This unique theological strategy grounded Spiritualism firmly in antebellum religious culture even as it distinguished the new religion from the variety of competitors being produced in the free religious marketplace of the antebellum spiritual hothouse.

While the Spiritualist strategy was distinctive, the practice of spirit communication hardly burst onto the antebellum religious scene as an unprecedented novelty. It is as old as religion itself, characterizes a wide variety of religious traditions, figures prominently in the history of Judeo-Christian religiosity, and, most immediately, appeared in many of the new religions that predated Spiritualism on the antebellum scene. American culture was pervaded by the belief that the birth of the republic had been a religiously significant event heralding a new dispensation, and a corresponding impulse toward religious democratization encouraged an explosion of claims to personal religious experience and spiritual power.[15] A wave of revival activity and emotional conversions during the early nineteenth century was the most culturally salient expression of this trend. It was in this environment that claims and reports of spirit communication became increasingly widespread during the decades preceding the advent of Spiritualism.

These claims came mostly from people who were trying to replace or modify traditional Protestantism through the development of alternative religious ideologies. Joseph Smith, the founder of Mormonism, claimed to have been visited by an angel in 1820, and his leadership of the new religion was based in large part on his ongoing function as a perceived link between his followers and the unseen world.[16] In the late 1830s and early 1840s, the Shakers had experienced a shower of spiritualistic activity, and some flirted with Spiritualism after its emergence a short time later. Indeed, some of them later claimed to have initiated modern Spiritualism, and even Emma Hardinge, a Spiritualist medium and one of the movement's earliest historians and most popular lecturers, considered the Shakers as Spiritualism's "John the Baptists."[17] Finally, in the mid-to-late 1840s, some renegade members of the Church of the New Jerusalem, a religious sect based on Emanuel Swedenborg's interpretation of the Scriptures, claimed to have replicated Swedenborg's practice of spirit communication and showed a strong interest in Spiritualism.[18] Each of these groups shared with Spiritualists a belief in the possibility of modern-day revelations; in each case, as in the case of Spiritualism, spirit communion was accompanied by a sense of spiritual dissatisfaction and confusion; and in each case such communication became the basis for expressions of religious rebelliousness and the creation of new religious structures. Clearly, Spiritualism bloomed in a cultural soil that had been prepared for it.

Only the Spiritualists, however, built an entire religious system around a belief in spirit activity and the practice of spirit communication.[19] In the process, they highlighted the place of spirit contact on the cultural map of American religion. A fully elaborated religion of the spirits was their distinctive contribution to the history of American religious culture. It is this aspect of antebellum Spiritualism that leads me to call it a "new religion" despite its being only a new emphasis in an American setting on a familiar religious practice.

Spiritualism's unique aspects should not obscure its close connections to the Christian traditions which defined much of antebellum religious life and which most Americans instinctively associated with divine order. As many Spiritualists insisted and Jon Butler has emphasized, American Spiritualism remained within the broad spectrum of Christian belief. It is true that the movement was divided into self-conscious, outspoken, and often mutually hostile Christian and rationalistic wings. Some Spiritualists defended what they called "Christian Spiritualism" and felt that spirit communication would revivify the faith and support the authenticity of the Bible. Others subjected the Bible to severe criticism, rejected its claims to authority, welcomed latter-day spirit inspiration as a supplement or even replacement for it, and attempted to present the new religion as a rational and post-Christian alternative to conventional religious life. But those on both sides defended their beliefs and practices by attempting to locate them squarely within the Christian tradition as they understood it. Almost all Spiritualists, whether "Christian" or not, agreed that spirit activity in the world was central to the early history of Christianity but had not ended in antiquity. They also agreed that communion between the earth and the spiritual world had been stifled by organized Christianity, in which they saw more oppression than freedom, more of the earthly than of the spiritual, and more fear and moral tepidity than love and moral force. Finally, even outspokenly "anti-Christian" Spiritualists frankly admired, even revered, Christ and the fundamental moral tenets he articulated, and consistently numbered him among the most significant figures in the history of religion. Andrew Jackson Davis, one of the movement's more outspokenly rationalistic figures and one of its severest critics of the authority of the Bible (he led an "anti-Bible convention" in Hartford in 1853), spoke of love and justice as the "CHRIST-PRINCIPLE" and often quoted Scripture. And Spiritualist editor Samuel Bryan Brittan, who shared Davis's leanings, depicted Christ on the frontispiece of the first volume of his monthly journal *Shekinah*,[20] a title derived from the Hebrew term for "divine presence" and itself suggestive of Spiritualism's Judeo-Christian sources.

Indeed, Spiritualism was an expression of a powerful restorationist or primitivist impulse by which many American Protestants of the early nineteenth century tried to revitalize Christianity by restoring what they considered its original purity and eliminating perceived institutional and doctrinal incrustations. Like contemporary Mormons, Shakers, Oneidans, Baptists, and Disciples of Christ, not to mention the Puritans of early New England, Spiritualists trying to achieve a new religious order looked to early Christianity for standards of faith and practice and tried "to live ancient lives." Early Mormons in particular shared their belief that new revelations from the spiritual world constituted a needed restoration of early Christians' interaction between humanity and spiritual powers, and early Disciples shared their aversion to organizational and doctrinal rigidity as fetters on the genuine religiosity that Christ had promoted. To be sure, Spiritualist primitivism, like antebellum Protestant primitivism generally, combined its Christian dimension with a rationalistic one that incorporated the eighteenth-century Enlightenment tendency to look back to a primeval and pristine nature and to ancient pre-Christian republics as models for a golden age. Antebellum Americans, including Spiritualists, interpreted the American Revolution as the harbinger of a "new order of the ages" that would restore ancient republicanism and the rule of natural law and "nature's God." Both dimensions of the primitivist impulse became essential elements of the American national identity that gelled during the antebellum period, and both tied Spiritualism to the wider American culture. But the point to be emphasized here is that Spiritualists' persistent comparisons of their practices to those of early Christians and their insistence that they were simply restoring something very old underscored their self-consciously Christian pedigree.[21]

But however important the Christian elements in Spiritualism, Butler may deny too strongly that Spiritualism constituted a religious "alternative" to Christianity. Spiritualists not only rejected existing Christian institutions but made substantial departures from conventional Christian belief and practice. They were, to quote one recent commentator, part of an "alternative, mystically inclined tradition" that in many ways "challenged traditional Protestant interpretations" of spiritual life. This distinct tradition emerged around the middle of the nineteenth century and rejected key tenets of orthodox Christian theology. Expressed in Transcendentalism and Spiritualism before the Civil War and, later in the nineteenth century, in Christian Science, Theosophy, and New Thought, this group of religions emphasized an impersonal divine principle over a personal God, focused on the individual's inner life, denied or played down the existence of evil, emphasized self-realization through union with or perfect apprehension of the divine, and postulated continuing spiritual progression, even after death, eventuating in salvation. The case of Spiritualism suggests that the distinction between Christian religious culture and the "alternatives" to it is sometimes hazy but real nonetheless.[22]

Certainly religious Spiritualists incorporated both Christian and "alternative" elements into the experiential dimension of their religion. Indeed, their experiences in many ways fit the descriptions of "encounters with the sacred" and contact with something "wholly other" offered by Rudolf Otto and Mircea Eliade in their classic analyses of religious experience. When Andrew Jackson Davis, for example, described a vision of spirits "[s]erene and high, . . . surrounded with a glory altogether inexpressible," he perfectly illustrated Otto's point that an experience of the sacred evokes "a beatitude beyond compare" whose "real nature [one] can neither proclaim in speech nor conceive in thought." In another religious vision, Davis beheld "a great multitude of spirits and angels" who "neither fly nor walk; but they *ride* upon a magnificent Shining River" which flowed "from the hidden fountain in infinitude toward all the planets and constellations in our department of the material universe!" Again, Otto's comments surely apply to Davis's encounter and to Spiritualist religion more generally:

> It is one thing merely to believe in a reality beyond the senses and another to have experience of it also; it is one thing to have ideas of "the

holy" and another to become consciously aware of it as an operative reality, intervening actively in the phenomenal world. Now it is a funda- mental conviction of all religions, of religion as such, we may say, that this latter is possible as well as the former. Religion is convinced not only that the holy and sacred reality is attested by the inward voice of con- science and the religious consciousness . . . but also that it may be di- rectly encountered in particular occurrences and events.

I am not suggesting that Spiritualist religion never deviated from such mod- els; as we will see, cultural circumstances dictated certain departures. But like all "religion as such," it involved a belief in palpable manifestations, external and internal, by which the spiritual realm manifested itself in the material world, and a prescribed set of rituals by which its adherents sought mystical contact with it.[23]

Although Spiritualism was above all a religion, its religious dimension has been neglected by scholars despite their increasing attention to the move- ment over the past two decades and their willingness to consider it as an integral part of American cultural history.[24] R. Laurence Moore's pathbreak- ing study interpreted Spiritualism as an attempt by nineteenth-century Ameri- cans to establish empirical grounds for religious belief amid the growing cul- tural authority of science. In particular, he emphasizes its appeal to those who feared a lost interest by science in spirit or had recently suffered the loss of a loved one. This interpretation is correct but incomplete, for it does not explain the many Spiritualists who established or maintained contact with spirits long after convinced of their reality and independently of the experi- ence of bereavement. Indeed, many Spiritualists considered scientific proof as merely the starting point of their religiosity and devoted much more at- tention to the theological and metaphysical functions of spirits. Far from seriously analyzing Spiritualist religion, furthermore, Moore criticizes the movement for debasing spirituality by focusing almost pathetically on the materiality of spirit and on sensational séance phenomena in an attempt to achieve scientific legitimacy. Spiritualists were often guilty of his charges, but he neglected much of Spiritualism's ideological content and therefore missed an opportunity to explain what it meant religiously to its adherents.[25]

Janet Oppenheim considered Spiritualism in a British context and, like Moore, offered an extended treatment of psychical research in the late nine- teenth and early twentieth centuries. But her recognition that Spiritualists "were articulating a fundamentally religious point of view" and creating "a surrogate faith" in "proclaiming the existence and activity of spirit agencies throughout the universe" is unaccompanied by an exploration of Spiritualist religion. And Ann Braude and Alex Owen have alluded only briefly to the religion of Spiritualism, concentrating far more on its important connection to the women's rights movement and its effect on existing gender roles.

Finally, Logie Barrow analyzed the relationship between English Spiritualism and working-class radicalism but had little to say about the movement's religious content.[26]

Nor have attempts to explain Spiritualism in terms of the social and economic dislocations of the period been entirely satisfactory.[27] These studies have reflected a broader historiographical tendency to explain religious developments in terms of presumably more fundamental material and psychological concerns. Before the 1970s, those few historians who did not more or less ignore the movement tended to depict it as little more than an irrational and unstable product of the wrenching transformation of American social and economic arrangements in the Jacksonian period. These interpretations contain some truth and continue to influence how scholars like Carroll Smith-Rosenberg and Shomer Zwelling understand Spiritualism. Like the many other new forms of religious enthusiasm that emerged in the early and middle decades of the nineteenth century, Spiritualism undoubtedly did help its adherents psychologically anchor themselves in a changing and unsettling social, economic, and cultural setting. But such studies obscure our understanding of Spiritualism in three important ways. First, they perpetuate the notion that Spiritualism was an irrational aberration and therefore effectively reduce it to a culturally marginal status. Second, while such analyses attempt to explain why people have exhibited often experimental religious responses to disorienting social and economic conditions, they sometimes tend toward reductionism. Third, they have not fully or specifically explained the particular forms that such experimentation takes. None of them has offered a specific explanation of how it is that the market revolution drove Americans to seek communication with spirits, or why some Americans chose to respond in other ways.[28]

This is where an interpretation focusing on religious, theological, and ideological content becomes useful. It provides insights about the appeal of Spiritualism that neither social and economic interpretations nor culturally oriented studies have offered. To be sure, this book recognizes the role of social and economic factors and is intended to complement rather than to contradict the studies cited above. But Spiritualists were motivated to seek out the spirits at least as much by religious and theological concerns as by the market revolution. And since Spiritualists were addressing the same religious and theological questions as other Americans, and trying to satisfy the same basic spiritual needs, analyzing Spiritualism as a religious ideology effectively establishes it as a significant phenomenon in American culture.

My argument for Spiritualist religion and the existence of a Spiritualist subculture should not be taken to mean that the participants in this subculture always agreed. Despite their shared belief in spirit communication and spirit agency, and in the symbols and rituals that accompanied that belief, they argued among themselves, and were sometimes uncertain even in their own minds, about the practical implications of their beliefs for the values of freedom that they held dear as Americans. In particular, such issues as the extent of spirit activity and influence in the world and the desirability of creating religious organizations and centralized power structures carried serious implications for the concepts of spontaneity, free will, and equality that figured so prominently in Protestant and republican ideologies. An appreciation of this internal complexity requires close attention to the movement's structural features. It also requires notice of its ideological radicals, that is, those who carried their faith in spirit activity further than others, claimed a privileged contact with spirits, and established a charismatic religious leadership over others (in the name of both freedom and order) that resembled developments in other contemporary religious movements. More scholarly attention has been paid to the moderates (including the movement's earliest chroniclers) who resisted the radicals as threats to both freedom and order and tried to present their own positions as genuine Spiritualism. Tensions between the radicals and the moderates resulted in a Spiritualist press filled with charges and countercharges, denunciations and rebuttals, focusing on the question of who represented Spiritualism's real meaning.[29] But moderates' attempts to marginalize the radicals do not change the reality that the two groups were more alike than different, or that both groups were equally a part of the movement. Exchanges between the radicals who exaggerated Spiritualism's distinctive religious features and the moderates who criticized them lend texture and relief to our portrait of Spiritualist religion and remind us of how misleading it can be to employ such cultural categories as "mainstream" and "fringe."[30]

Another distinction which scholars have drawn within the Spiritualist movement is even more misleading. Following the lead of Andrew Jackson Davis, who lamented the attention being paid to the phenomena of the séance, historians have shown an unfortunate tendency to apply the term "popular" to the movement's sensationalistic side and to distinguish it from the movement's "philosophical" side, thus implying that serious Spiritualist religion was confined to a small elite.[31] But while the Spiritualist movement had a group of leading writers and publicists who explicitly and self-consciously articulated its religious purpose and content, its religious appeal was by no means limited to this group. The producers of published Spiritualist discourse did indeed tend to fit Jon Butler's description of Spiritualists: "white, mostly Anglo-Saxon, middle- and upper-middle class former Protestants."[32] It is also true that this study focuses on these figures, for they provide the most fully developed statements of Spiritualism's religious meaning. But it would be erroneous to assume that Spiritualism's appeal among less articulate Americans was always based more on a thirst for the sensational than on deep religious, spiritual, or philosophical considerations. In fact, Lewis O. Saum, who has attempted to gauge the religious beliefs of "ordinary" Americans during the antebellum period, has argued that Spiritualism was a serious religion for many of the movement's "ordinary" members. Ann Braude, meanwhile, has noted that Spiritualism crossed lines of race, class, and ethnicity.[33] There was, in other words, a truly popular religious interest in the spirit world among antebellum Americans. I cannot and do not claim that religious Spiritualists constituted a majority of what was in its broader aspects a mass movement; whether serious Spiritualist religion (as opposed to the mere curiosity, thrill-seeking, or desire to chat with departed friends and relatives that drove so many Americans to attend séances) ever became a mass movement is indeed debatable. Still, the emergence of Spiritualist religion in the antebellum period is a significant historical and cultural phenomenon that merits close attention and analysis.

I will conduct that analysis in the six chapters that follow. Chapters 2 through 5 focus on the Spiritualist ideology. Chapter 2 traces the defining features of the Spiritualist religion to a unique interpretation and appropriation of the writings and experiences of the eighteenth-century Swedish scientist, mystic, and theologian Emanuel Swedenborg, and locates its particular balance of freedom and order between those of other contemporary American religious groups influenced by Swedenborg. Chapter 3 examines Spiritualists' use of the American ideology of republicanism to defend the individualistic and antistructural features of their religiosity. It analyzes their reasons for rejecting the religious status quo and their use of spirit communication in underwriting their rebellious religious antiformalism. The argument then shifts to Spiritualism's structural features. Chapter 4 outlines the cosmic order of the Spiritualist universe, the place of spirits in it, and the American cultural features that shaped it, highlighting the institutional ways in which Spiritualists conceived of the spirit world. Chapter 5 concerns the ministerial roles which Spiritualists, rejecting the formal ministry, assigned to their spirit contacts in order to fill the resulting insecurity in their religious lives. It notes along the way the influence on their thinking of wider cultural assumptions about the clergy. It also explores the implications of these roles for American concepts of selfhood and individualism. Chapters 6 and 7 concentrate on Spiritualist practice, highlighting its structural features, its ability to provide believers with a feeling of religious community, and its relationship to antebellum American religious culture. Chapter 6 discusses the ways in which Spiritualists institutionalized and structured their religious lives and practices in an attempt to recreate the harmony and order of the spiritual world on an earthly plane. Chapter 7 considers attempts by Spiritualists to organize their religion and analyzes the connection between Spiritualism and communitarianism, focusing in particular on the Mountain Cove community. This short-lived Spiritualist colony was an enlightening episode in Spiritualist communitarian activity, spotlighting the ideological tensions which besieged and rent both it and the larger Spiritualist movement. A brief conclusion looks ahead to the formal organization of Spiritualism during the latter decades of the nineteenth century.

For the purposes of this book, it is pointless to comment on the reality of the phenomena which Spiritualists believed they witnessed. What matters is that they themselves did believe. Our questions are what and why they believed. With this said, we may proceed with our exploration of their peculiarly antebellum American expression of the timeless human need to comprehend, sacralize, and humanize the cosmos through spirit communion.

＋ｌ＋

2

American Spiritualism and the Swedenborgian Order

The Emergence of the Spiritualist Ideology

In August 1847, Andrew Jackson Davis retired to a hilltop near Poughkeep-sie, New York, where he often sought solitude, contact with his spiritual "Guide," and mystical religious experience and insight. His guide, whom he believed to be the spirit of eighteenth-century Swedish scientist, mystic and theologian Emanuel Swedenborg, soon appeared to him. What followed was a dialogue rife with ambivalence concerning the relationship between the youthful religious pilgrim and his spirit mentor. According to Davis's descrip-tion of the experience in his autobiography, *The Magic Staff* (1857), his motherly guide "pillowed my spirit on his beating bosom" and assured him that "the bounty of heaven hath given me wisdom for thee, my son." When Davis offered profuse thanks, however, spirit Swedenborg drew back, asking, "Why callest thou me 'Guide'?" and explaining that "Thy guide is within thee!" This lesson typified the increasing tendency in antebellum America to locate experiential piety, and in some circles of religious thinkers religious authority, within the self. Given Davis's advocacy of spiritual freedom and self-reliance, however, his response might appear surprising. "'Oh, say not so!'" he "exclaimed with great agitation—'do not leave me! My every day's life hangs upon your truth and overruling providence!'" Furthermore, the guide concluded his counsel of spiritual self-reliance with assurances that "as before, I will picture to thee thy works and ways" and that "I will come . . . when thou hast done all thou canst, and yet requirest sight and power."[1]

This episode heralded the advent of a new religious movement and constituted a defining moment in the history of American religious culture.

Inspired by Swedenborg, Davis was instrumental in establishing a new religious ideology postulating the presence and activity of spirits on earth and the ability of human beings to receive religious comfort and guidance through communication with them. Even more, Davis's exchange with his spiritual guide registered the fundamental tension between freedom and authority in American life and in Spiritualist religion in particular. His concern to make his spiritual life an "individual pilgrimage" coexisted with an equally powerful need for spirit Swedenborg's reassuring and authoritative spiritual presence. Davis, in fact, interpreted his whole life up to the time he wrote *The Magic Staff* as a quest for both the spiritual freedom and the religious certainty, security, and authority that he found in this experience and others like it.

Swedenborg's contribution to American Spiritualism, based on the religious writings he produced between the 1740s and his death in 1772, involved not simply the practice of spirit communication but an entire spirit-centered cosmology that promised to Spiritualists both freedom and order. Born in Stockholm, Sweden, in 1688, the son of a Lutheran bishop, he was nurtured in Enlightenment thought and spent the first two-thirds of his life largely in scientific pursuits. But in the mid–1740s he began to undergo a series of profound mystical experiences, including strange dreams, visions, and trances, in which "the world of spirits, hell and heaven, were opened to me with full conviction." From this time forward, he claimed, he could look into "the other world" and "in a state of perfect wakefulness converse with the angels and spirits."[2] His attitude toward these experiences showed that he was still very much the scientist; that is, he claimed simply to be recording what he was permitted to observe. At the same time, however, he emphasized the importance of intuitive as opposed to sensory sources of knowledge and insight, insisting that spiritual truths were not discovered by the intellect alone but rather were revealed by heaven to the inner eye. Whatever the source of his insights, he elaborated from them a metaphysical system in which spirit and matter existed not in a dichotomous relationship of mutual exclusivity but rather as complementary and inseparable dimensions of a single and universal whole.[3]

The foremost product of Swedenborg's experiences was *Heaven and Its Wonders and Hell* (1758). In it he depicted an afterlife more focused on spirits and more earthlike than the theocentric and otherworldly conceptions of heaven which characterized orthodox Christianity.[4] Swedenborg's spirit world was organized into a hierarchy of seven ascending "spheres," populated by seven classes of thoroughly humanized spirits of increasingly exalted spiritual status. It was a socially interactive place in which the seven classes of spirits, who together constituted what he called a "Grand Man," were subdivided into smaller societies or communities based on spiritual similarity and mutual attraction. These spirits were believed to be essential mediators between mortals and God, channels through which the wisdom, love, and spiritual life which radiated outward and downward from a central divine source reached those on earth. Above all, however, Swedenborg's spiritual world was a place of order. He consistently contrasted the increasing order of the upper three spheres or "heavens" with the increasing chaos of the three "hells," poising the fourth sphere, that occupied by spirits in their earthly life, in a delicate balance between them.

The Spiritualists of the following century incorporated important elements of Swedenborg's doctrines and experiences into their religion. They echoed his ideas of interaction and interpenetration between the material and spiritual worlds and an inner core of divinity within each individual. Above all, they combined his spirit-centered cosmic order and his practice of spirit communication to form the heart of their religion. Swedenborg gave to the Spiritualist ideology the bulk of its defining features and was therefore its most important source.

He was not its only source. Of comparable importance was the quasi-scientific and quasi-mystical philosophy of mesmerism, an Enlightenment product which emerged in France in the late eighteenth century and was popularized in America during the 1830s and 1840s. According to the mesmerist ideology, the universe was a harmonious physical and spiritual unity in which an invisible, universal, and all-pervasive fluid acted as the crucial integrating agent. Spiritualists adopted this understanding of the universe, conceiving of it as a spiritual whole bound together by spiritual matter. Mesmerism also contributed to Spiritualism the belief that the body and soul could be affected by means of a magnetic force transmitted from one person to another in the trance state. In this state, the "mesmerized" person was thought to achieve a blissful and passive state of contact with higher spiritual powers. The practice of inducing and entering the mesmeric trance, often for the purpose of physical or spiritual healing, was something of a popular fad in America during the two decades before Spiritualism emerged and became a key element in the Spiritualist religion.[5]

Another important influence on the Spiritualist ideology was the French social theorist Charles Fourier, another Enlightenment product, whose vision of an earthly utopia was based on a doctrine called "Association." His ideas more or less subtly pervaded the writings of many Spiritualists, particularly those who had sympathized with or participated in the Fourierist communitarian impulse of the 1840s. Like Swedenborg's conception of the spirit world, Fourier's conception of human society involved a belief that individuals were parts of a larger socio-spiritual whole; both ideologies combined notions of universal harmony and social wholeness with an emphasis on small cooperative communities; and Fourier, like Swedenborg, presented his worldview as thoroughly scientific. The ideas of Swedenborg, Fourier, and mesmerism were combined in the early to mid-1840s to produce a religious ideology called "harmonialism" by its adherents. Offered as an alternative to traditional Protestantism, this new worldview flowered in the mid-to-late 1840s and attracted small numbers of educated middle-class Americans in the Northeast and Midwest, mostly men. Short-lived as an independent philosophical and religious movement, it constituted the basis of the Spiritualist ideology that absorbed it after 1848.[6]

The Spiritualist ideology also drew on the liberal theologies of the period, which in turn drew on the religious ideas of the Enlightenment and the Romanticism which followed. Like Unitarianism and its offshoot Transcendentalism, it absorbed Romanticism's emphases on a loving deity, the inner divinity and consequent goodness of the individual, and gradual spiritual growth into divine perfection. It shared with Universalism the belief that a loving and merciful God must save everyone, and with its schismatic Restorationist offshoot the qualification that some period of postmortem repentance and punishment would precede redemption. It incorporated the Quaker emphasis on the importance and validity of each individual's "inner light." It derived from deism and the Enlightenment a belief in a "natural" religion that conceived deity in terms of the natural law discovered by science and reason. At the same time, it preserved much of the traditional Christian emphasis on divine sovereignty and theocentrism, human dependence on the divine, the reality of immortality and an afterlife, and a moral obligation to order one's life in conformity with an absolute standard.[7]

Swedenborg's legacy and the larger harmonial philosophy of which it was a part became incorporated into Spiritualist religion largely through the early writings and activities of Andrew Jackson Davis.[8] Born into poverty in Orange County, New York, in 1826, Davis well exemplified broader currents of religious democratization. He portrayed himself in his autobiography as a nervous, sickly, untalented, and insecure child who disliked his ne'er-do-well father and found comfort only in the presence of his mystically inclined mother. He also claimed to have been prone from an early age to unusual visual and auditory experiences, including a vision of heaven at the time of his mother's death early in 1841. His youth was marked by both economic instability, as financial misfortune drove the family from one part of the Hudson valley to another, and a parallel religious restlessness punctuated by unsatisfying exposures to Dutch Reformed Protestantism, Methodism, Episcopalianism, Presbyterianism, and Millerism.

A turning point in Davis's unsettled life came in Poughkeepsie late in 1843, when he met itinerant mesmerist James Stanley Grimes. The youthful Davis discovered that he was a good trance subject and soon began to tour New England as a trance lecturer and clairvoyant healer. In Bridgeport,

Connecticut, he met and attracted a group of Universalists that included Dr. Silas S. Lyon, Rev. Samuel Byron Brittan, and Rev. William Fishbough. All three were interested in mesmerism, clairvoyance, and Swedenborg. By late 1845, Lyon and Davis had opened a clairvoyant medical clinic in New York City, where Davis prescribed cures while in trances induced by Lyon. Convinced that he had become "an appropriate vessel for the influx of truth and wisdom" and had a religious mission to perform, Davis also delivered a systematic series of lectures purporting to come from the spirits of Swedenborg and the ancient physician Galen. He acted as "Seer" while Lyon served as "Operator" and Fishbough as "Scribe" and copy editor. Equally scientific and religious in flavor, Davis's trance talks attracted the interested attention of such contemporaries as Albert Brisbane, America's foremost disciple of Fourier, George Bush, a New York University professor of Hebrew and leading follower of Swedenborg, and poet Edgar Allan Poe, who was fascinated by mesmerism.

The lectures were published in 1847 as *The Principles of Nature, Her Divine Revelations, and a Voice to Mankind*. A standard statement of the harmonial philosophy, this thick volume consisted of a developmental history of a universe conceived in organic terms, an attack on organized religion and especially on the clerical profession, a plan of social reorganization based on the ideas of Fourier, and a Swedenborgian description of the spirit world. Although neither Davis's book nor any other became an authoritative text for the Spiritualist movement, it was very influential and became the fountainhead of the Spiritualist ideology. Its importance as a vehicle for Swedenborg's influence was suggested by George Bush, who had turned to mesmerism as an explanation of the Swedish Seer's experiences. He was so convinced that Davis had contacted Swedenborg that he appended an enthusiastic discussion of "The Revelation of Andrew Jackson Davis" to his 1847 work *Mesmer and Swedenborg*.[9]

The new philosophy was also promoted in the pages of the *Univercoelum*, a New York weekly that first appeared in December 1847. It was edited by Brittan, who had recently arrived in New York from Albany after converting to a belief in spirit communication during a period of illness. He now regarded Davis's trance revelations as "the only unerring source of instruction now accessible" and a "sufficient and reliable ground for the highest and holiest hopes of man."[10] The paper addressed theology, religion, philosophy, psychology ("the science of the Soul"), clairvoyance, medical issues, and social problems, and clearly reflected the views of Universalism, Transcendentalism, mesmerism, Fourier, and, of course, Swedenborg. Its major contributors were for the most part ex-Universalists and followers of Swedenborg who went on to become leading Spiritualists. They included not only Davis, Brittan, and Fishbough, but also Thomas Lake Harris, an English-born aspiring poet who had abandoned Calvinism for Universalism and then, under Davis's inspiration, a strongly Swedenborgian Spiritualism. He was to be one of the movement's most enigmatic figures. Another important contributor was Warren Chase, a reform-minded politician who during the 1840s had begun to investigate mesmerism and the works of Swedenborg and headed a Fourierist communitarian experiment in Wisconsin.[11] The first of what soon became a swelling tide of short-lived Spiritualist periodicals, the *Univercoelum* folded in 1849.

It did last long enough to notice the "Rochester rappings" of the Fox sisters, which the group readily accepted as spiritual in origin and interpreted as the opening of a new era of spirit communication. After investigating their mediumship, Davis explained it in terms of harmonialism in *The Philosophy of Spiritual Intercourse* (1850). As Ann Braude has observed, the sensational rappings aroused much greater public interest than did the harmonial philosophy, which began to find a wider hearing after people turned to it for a philosophical explanation of the mysterious noises. Anxious to promote their new movement, Davis and Fishbough endorsed the Foxes in order to capitalize on the sensation created by "spirit manifestations." Creating what became a tension-filled union between the cause of harmonialism and that of the spirit rappings, the harmonial group set the stage for the growth of a new spirit-centered religion.[12]

The Spiritualist Interpretation of Swedenborg

George Lawton recognized long ago that an ideology involving spirit contact, mediation, activity, and authority was the "great distinguishing mark" of Spiritualist religion. But neither he nor anyone else has emphasized this defining feature of the movement as Swedenborg's most important legacy to it.[13] The emphasis has fallen, rather, on the influence of either Swedenborg's metaphysics or, more especially, his detailed description of heaven.[14] But these elements of his thought appealed just as strongly to many Americans whose search for satisfying alternatives to conventional Christianity did not lead to Spiritualism. What Spiritualists took from Swedenborg that other seekers did not was the spirit-centered religiosity that made theirs a distinctive religious movement.

This is not to deny the importance of Swedenborg's philosophy and his portrayal of the afterlife in Spiritualist religion. Those Spiritualists who described the spirit world usually departed little from his description of heaven, and many of them selectively adopted some of his fundamental theological doctrines and used his phraseology. But many Spiritualist writings lacked a strong Swedenborgian flavor, did not contain "thick" Swedenborg-

ian accounts of the spirit world, repudiated important aspects of Swedenborg's theology (most importantly, the concept of hell), and ignored or
denied Swedenborg's belief that the Bible was the most authoritative source
of religious truth. All religious Spiritualists, on the other hand, echoed his
emphasis on spirits as important agents in religious experience.

Spiritualists did, of course, look to other historical precedents in defense of
their method of seeking religious truth, including not only those of the Bible
but also those of the antebellum period. The early Spiritualist historian Emma
Hardinge, for example, acknowledged the Mormons and Shakers as precur-
sors to Spiritualism.[15] Still, their references to Swedenborg indicate that they
looked primarily to him as an example of using contact with spirits to glimpse
cosmic order. As an inspirational religious practitioner and the source of their
spirit-centered worldview, the Swedish Seer was regarded by Spiritualists as a
forerunner of their religion and became for them a cultural icon. This is why
they, like Andrew Jackson Davis, so often sought communication with his
spirit. This, too, is why they considered Davis "the youthful Swedenborg of
our day" and dubbed him the "Poughkeepsie Seer."[16]

Spiritualist commentaries on Swedenborg's importance almost always
focused more on his claim to communication with spirits than on any other
aspect of his life and work. A biographical sketch in the Spiritualist periodical
Shekinah, for instance, consciously concentrated on Swedenborg "as SEER"
rather than as "theologian" or "philosopher." Even Davis, whose writings
were infused by Swedenborg's cosmology, was attracted more to the Swedish
mystic's example than to his writings. Predicting the advent of a new era of
open spirit intercourse, he advised his readers to study Swedenborg's seership
but cautioned that his theology was in many ways too orthodox to be relevant
to the modern religious world. Other Spiritualists agreed that Swedenborg
was less important as an authoritative theologian than as medium between
mortals and the spirit world. A writer for the Spiritual Telegraph, the longest-
lived and most widely circulated of the antebellum Spiritualist periodicals,
denied the authority of Swedenborg's writings and pointed out that "Spiritualists go directly to the fountain of spiritual wisdom, as Swedenborg did; they
talk with spirits." The "great use of Swedenborg's writings," said John
Shoebridge Williams, whose involvement with Spiritualism was preceded by
stormy affiliations with the Society of Friends and the Swedenborg-based
Church of the New Jerusalem (also called the New Church), was "to show
. . . that we can communicate with spirits" (emphasis added).[17]

Not that Swedenborg would have condoned what Spiritualists were doing
in his name. After all, Spiritualists' understanding of the nature and meaning
of spirit communication was quite different from his own. They and Swedenborg would have agreed, of course, that spirit communication was
possible. They would also have agreed that people on earth were constantly

acted on or influenced by the deity, through a mediating hierarchy of spirits, in a process which Swedenborg called "mediate influx." And Swedenborg's attempt to reconcile individual autonomy with this concept of influx would be echoed by Spiritualists, who were equally concerned to assert independent selfhood. Just as Swedenborg postulated a seat of distinct inner selfhood on which spirits acted but with which they were not to be identified, so Spiritualists insisted on a firm boundary between the activities of one's own spirit and the influences of others on it. But Spiritualists made some crucial departures from Swedenborg's notion of spirit communication and activity.[18]

Swedenborg persistently denied that the spirit roles he described involved any authority. Spirits served only as instruments of the process of "mediate influx," and the process was so gentle "that there is not the least appearance of bondage or authority." Despite his own claim to communication with spirits on religious matters, furthermore, he often asserted their lack of reliability as a source of truth. Spirits' statements, he explained, contained a mixture of truth, divine in origin, and falsehood, originating in the spirits themselves. In conversing with them, he said, he consulted his own reason to evaluate their revelations and to separate wheat from chaff. Spirits were not infallible teachers but impure mediums through which divine truth was taught. In any case, the spirits with whom one was in association were so similar in mind and inclination to oneself that they could do little more than affirm one's previously held beliefs. Since "there is not granted to any spirit nor to any angel leave to instruct any man on this earth in Divine truths," Swedenborg was "not permitted . . . to take any thing whatever from the mouth of any spirit." Nor were angels' writings to be consulted by mortals. A properly interpreted Bible, he insisted, was a sufficient source of religious knowledge.[19]

Having played down the notion of spirits as authorities in moral and spiritual matters, Swedenborg discouraged his readers from attempting them-selves to make open (i.e., conscious) and intentional contact with them. Doing so, he warned, could have a tragic effect on the soul by inducing a dangerous dependence on spirits. "Speaking with spirits on this earth is most perilous, unless one is in true faith. They induce so strong a persuasion that it is the Lord Himself who speaks, and who commands, that a man cannot but believe and obey." To avert moral chaos and a perpetuation of error, Swedenborg urged, people should turn for spiritual authority not to spirits but to the priesthood. "There must be those in authority who shall keep associations of man in order." Priests, "representative of the Lord," would "teach men the way to heaven, and also lead them." The product of a social aristocracy, Swedenborg harbored decidedly undemocratic notions of spirit communication and religious authority.[20]

Despite Swedenborg's disclaimers, however, his presentation of spirits did much to suggest their special status as religious authority figures. His experience indicated that mortals could learn much from communication with the spirits, who in turn received truth through the angels above them. Indeed, his descriptions of his encounters with spirits, the voluminous writings that resulted, and his tendency to introduce doctrinal statements with such phrases as "angels say," could easily belie his numerous warnings. So could his belief that a spirit "loosed from its connection with [the] body . . . no longer thinks naturally, but spiritually" and "becomes wise like an angel." His concept of spirit mediation could easily be taken to mean that spirits derived a representative religious authority from speaking for the angels and ultimately God. If Swedenborg's spirit contacts did not speak pure truth, then, their words nevertheless seemed to command his respect. Finally, his conception of good spirits as authority figures was further suggested by his notion that they exercised a divinely driven influence on mortals. The spirits Swedenborg presented to his readers, then, played important authority-bearing roles in the lives of those on earth.[21]

American Spiritualists therefore deemphasized his warnings and sought spirit communication for themselves. They were clearly anxious to establish contact with the other world, to do as Swedenborg had done rather than as he had said in an effort to connect themselves with the sources of cosmic order and to reinvigorate their religiosity. Spiritualists clearly wanted the channels of communication between the spirit world and themselves to be more open than Swedenborg would have allowed.[22]

Anxious to tailor their religious alternative to their particular circumstances, Spiritualists deviated from Swedenborg in other ways as well. The effect was an expansion of spirit authority, accessibility, and involvement in people's lives. They enhanced the status of spirits as desirable religious teachers by blurring the distinction between angels, who in standard Christian theology had never been human, and spirits, who had passed from an earthly human existence to the afterlife (Spiritualists understood angels simply as purified spirits). They envisioned widespread communication not only between the spirit world and those on earth but among the various levels of the spirit world itself. Above all, however, they democratized spirit communication and access to the religious authority of higher spiritual beings. An awareness of their departure from their exemplar is one reason why Spiritualists so often and self-consciously claimed the Swedish Seer's approval of their activities. Such approval would certainly help make the message of Spiritualism appealing to those who might have found it attractive but were inclined to take Swedenborg's caveats and disclaimers seriously. We shall explore these divergences from Swedenborg more fully in some of the chapters that follow. The point to be emphasized here is that their understanding of Swedenborg's spirits had considerable appeal for them.

Indeed, the American religious culture of the antebellum period provided a particularly hospitable environment for the reception of Swedenborg's ideas of spirit activity, mediation, and communication. According to Nathan O. Hatch, the early republic was characterized by a democratization of religious authority and an "individualization of conscience" which encouraged many demagogues and would-be religious leaders to claim special authority on the basis of personal religious experience. Many emboldened Americans claimed that they were no less spiritually privileged than the religious leaders of the past.[23] Spiritualists participated in this process, finding in spirit communication a basis for a new, alternative, and in many ways democratic structure of religious authority. Spirit communication, they believed, would provide the individual with an immediate and readily accessible source of religious experience and knowledge. It therefore offered an alternative to such conventional conduits of spirituality as established ministers and institutional churches, whose aristocratic pretensions and rigid structures of authority they considered unsuited to the young republic. Spiritualists feared, furthermore, that the God of liberal Protestantism (from which background many of them had come) was less a warm and personal spiritual presence than at best an uncomfortably remote being and at worst a mere impersonal principle. Interaction with an approachable and personal mediating hierarchy of quasi-human spirits therefore seemed especially attractive.[24] Discerning in spirit communication a way to infuse personality into their universe, Spiritualists interpreted Swedenborg and his notion of cosmic order to suit their spiritual needs.

Varieties of Swedenborgian Order

Spiritualists invoked the name of Swedenborg not only because they consciously deviated from his model but also because they were competing with other religious groups who used him to appeal to America's dissatisfied spiritual seekers. In a culture prone to experimentation and attracted to novelty, the figure of Swedenborg became so salient that one scholar has suggested that there was a "Swedenborgian renaissance in the United States" of which Davis's experiences marked the "high point."[25] His influence could be discerned in many antebellum fads and reform movements, including mesmerism, clairvoyant medicine, marriage reform and "free love," and communitarian experimentation. Above all, however, the Swedish mystic was an important symbol on the alternative religious scene. He inspired not only Spiritualism but also Transcendentalism and the New Church, both of which joined it in challenging the mainline Protestant denominations and theological orthodoxies of the period. Set apart from other contemporary religious groups by their shared use of Swedenborg as a religious symbol, these three groups constituted a Swedenborgian religious subculture or counterculture. Within it occurred a trialogue between Spiritualists and their New Church and Transcendentalist rivals about the implications of the Swedish Seer's experiences for American religious life. Religious historian Sydney Ahlstrom was correct when he observed that Swedenborg "meant many things to many minds,"[26] for each group used the Seer's claim to spirit communication and his concept of spirit mediation to develop its own model of religious authority and experience. Convinced that their notion of democratic contact with a hierarchy of spirit mediators permitted an ideal blend of freedom and order, Spiritualists situated themselves between what they considered the anarchy of Transcendentalism and the authoritarianism of the New Church.

That the differences between Spiritualists and Transcendentalists consisted largely of diverging interpretations of Swedenborg and different understandings of the religious order he inspired is evident from the fact that those differences figured so prominently in Ralph Waldo Emerson's critical assessment of "Swedenborg; or, the Mystic." First delivered in 1845, a few years before the advent of the Spiritualist movement, this definitive Transcendentalist commentary on the Swedish Seer may nonetheless be read as a statement on Spiritualism since Emerson attacked precisely the spirit-centered aspects of Swedenborg's worldview that Spiritualists adopted. Indeed, Emerson probably intended that the publication of his essay in 1850, as Spiritualism was beginning to gain widespread attention, serve as a disapproving response.

To be sure, Spiritualists and Transcendentalists alike denied that Swedenborg was an authoritative theologian and rejected substantial components of his religious system. Their respective understandings of Swedenborg's philosophy, moreover, had much in common. They agreed that there was an invisible spiritual realm; that this realm existed in a relationship of what Swedenborg called "correspondence" with the material realm, by which the two realms operated according to parallel laws and spiritual realities had physical expression; that the two realms were so closely connected that distinctions between "natural" and "supernatural" misleadingly obscured the unity of "Nature" (with a capital "N"); that the sources of spirituality and divine wisdom were to be found within each individual soul as a participant in Nature; and that the soul gradually grew in likeness to deity. In emphasizing the close relationship between the material and spiritual worlds, Swedenborg captured the mystical religious imaginations of both Spiritualists and Transcendentalists. But here the similarity ended. If Swedenborg's religious focus on spirits was his most important legacy to Spiritualists, it was a primary point of criticism for the likes of Emerson. His criticism was twofold.

First, Emerson dismissed Swedenborg's claim actually to have spoken with spirits as an unfortunate obscuration of personal spirituality and religious individualism, a misleading depiction of a subjective spiritual experience as an objective one. An "excessive determination to form," he wrote, had led the Seer to describe his religious experiences "not abstractly," as a mystic should, but "in pictures" and "in dialogues." For Emerson, the scientist-turned-mystic remained too much the scientist, too prone to externalize and objectify the sources of religious knowledge. Swedenborg's excessive concreteness had trivialized the spiritual world. Emerson admired Swedenborg not for his "perilous opinion" that he had conversed with spirits but for his "realization that God must be found within" an "introverted mind." This is what he meant when he urged the spread of "subjective religion" in 1854 and said that "this age is Swedenborg's." He understood the mystic's alleged conversations with spirits as symbolic representations of the spiritual freedom and religious authority of the self.[27]

Spiritualists would have agreed with Emerson that the religious age belonged to Swedenborg. But they would have meant that the Seer's experiences had heralded an era of interaction with very real, independently existing spiritual beings who represented a higher order of existence and an external source of religious authority. Far from regarding Swedenborg's spirits as mere figments of the religious imagination or as allegorical symbols of subjective spirituality, Spiritualists emphasized the physical reality of the spirits and the objective dimension of the Seer's experiences. Commenting on a lecture by Emerson, in fact, *New England Spiritualist* editor Alonzo E. Newton took issue with him on precisely this point. And one Spiritualist responded to Emerson's "Swedenborg; or, the Mystic" with a brief essay on Swedenborg "by a mystic" which appeared in *Shekinah* in 1852 and assumed the objective reality of his spirit contacts.[28]

Indeed, proving the objective existence of spirits was the whole point of Spiritualism's scientific dimension. Joseph Rodes Buchanan, an investigator of mesmerism and psychology as well as Spiritualism, called spirits' objective existence "the real question at issue" for investigators of spirit manifestations. To be sure, religious Spiritualists like Transcendentalists emphasized the subjective and experiential bases of religious truth and saw in spirit communication a source of inward mystical illumination and personal spiritual liberation. The title of Andrew Jackson Davis's *The Present Age and Inner Life* (1853) echoes Emerson's declaration that the age was Swedenborg's. But they also shared with most of their contemporaries an enthusiastic respect for the growing cultural authority of science and a belief that the scientific method alone could establish epistemological certainty. They believed that truth was found without as well as within and therefore wanted a religion grounded as much in objective and empirically verifiable fact as in subjective experience. They found reassurance in Swedenborg's insistence on the objective reality of his experiences and pointed with pride to his scientific credentials. They emphasized the matter-of-fact tone in which he described his spirit encounters and tried to imitate it in their own writings. They considered their beliefs well grounded in the Baconian inductivism that guided antebellum American science and solidly supported by the observed factual evidence that converted scientists like Robert Hare claimed to produce. Even Davis, who joined Emerson in emphasizing the importance of inner communion with the divine and came to regret the preoccupation with sensational "spirit manifestations," wanted a scientific basis for Spiritualism. Thus he took a strong and early interest in the Fox sisters' rappings and attempted a scientific explanation of the famous "Stratford manifestations" of 1850.[29]

It is not surprising that Transcendentalists responded to Spiritualists' drive for empirical grounding in much the same way that they responded to Swedenborg. Just as Emerson lamented what he took to be Swedenborg's excessively scientific approach to spiritual knowledge, so he vehemently denounced Spiritualists' fascination with empirical phenomena as trite. Regarding séance phenomena as a vulgarization of the spirituality of humanity and nature, Emerson dismissed Spiritualism as "the Rat-revelation, the gospel that comes by taps in the wall, and thumps in the table-drawer."[30]

Emerson's second criticism of Swedenborg highlights the other major difference between Transcendentalist and Spiritualist notions of religious order. It has so far gone unnoticed because Emerson never mentioned it in his direct attacks on the new religious movement. Postulating a direct and intimate relationship between the free and spontaneous individual and a God that was the source of all order, Emerson repudiated Swedenborg's (and by implication the Spiritualists') vast hierarchy of intermediary spiritual beings. He was repelled by the idea, central to the Swedenborgian and Spiritualist ideologies, that "every thought comes into each mind by influence from a society of spirits that surround it, and these from a higher society, and so on." For Transcendentalists, "relations of the soul to the divine spirit" were "so pure that it is profane to seek to interpose helps."[31] Emerson regarded this "immense chain of intermediation," which he derogatorily compared to a complex system of water pipes, as a threat to "self-reliance." He derived sufficient spiritual comfort and security from his notion of the Oversoul— which like Swedenborg's spirit hierarchy connected the individual with an overarching spiritual community and the fount of divine authority[32]—and felt no need for spirit mediators or a hierarchically ordered cosmos.

Spiritualism and Transcendentalism, then, involved different responses to the anarchic and centrifugal tendencies inherent in individualized and democratized notions of religious authority and experience. They also offered different ways of alleviating the uneasy feeling of aloneness in a universe whose deity seemed so abstract. Adherents of both religious philosophies required the order, certainty, and comfort derived from contact with some spiritual "other." But this need made spirit contact and mediation at once attractive to Spiritualists and irrelevant, even repulsive, to Transcendentalists. The latter interpreted Swedenborg as a model of direct inner communion with a larger divine whole, while the former saw in him the promise of reassuring contact with mediating spirits. In fact, John Shoebridge Williams, a civil engineer, described the "mediatorial system" he deemed essential to a well-engineered cosmic order by using the very water pipe metaphor that for Emerson signified the needless complexity of the Spiritualist cosmos.[33]

The implications of spirit communication for religious freedom and order were similarly a primary point of contention between Spiritualists and Swedenborgians (the name used from here on to refer to members of the New Church), the other major religious group of the period claiming an allegiance to Swedenborg. The two groups did, of course, have much in common. Both embraced Swedenborg's worldview far more completely than did Transcendentalists and were much closer to each other on most questions involving spirit communication and activity than either group was to Emerson. They agreed first and foremost that Swedenborg had actually communicated with spirits, that his experience had been an objective rather than a subjective one. George Bush opened a published reply to Emerson's "Swedenborg" with a discussion of this very issue and defended the Swedish Seer's claims. For him and his peers, the "great and paramount fact" regarding Swedenborg was "*the reality of his intercourse with the spirit world.*" Swedenborgians also shared with Spiritualists the belief in a mediating hierarchy of spiritual beings; Bush replied to Emerson that "it is ordained that man shall be reached by the divine influx conveyed through mediums." For both Swedenborgians and Spiritualists, mortals depended on these spirit agents for spiritual life, insight, and experience. For both, the idea of spirit influence and activity was a source of religious comfort. Asserting the "Dependence of Men Upon Spirits and Angels" in the Swedenborgian *New Jerusalem Magazine* in 1835, Caleb Reed expressed this craving for a warm mediating spiritual presence. Angels and spirits, he assured his readers, are "in real, actual, and most intimate association" with those on earth; the inhabitants of the natural and spiritual worlds are "closely united." Finally, members of the two movements agreed that spirit mediation offered a welcome counterweight to the potential excesses of individual self-reliance. If Emerson regarded Swedenborg's highly structured universe as a threat to individual spontaneity, Bush replied that anarchy and chaos were the frightening alternative. Given the close similarities between the two movements, it is hardly surprising that so many people moved so easily from one to the other.[34]

Despite the similarities between the two groups, however, most Swedenborgians had a very different idea from the Spiritualists of what it meant to follow the Swedish Seer. Unlike Spiritualists, Swedenborgians accepted

Swedenborg's theology. More important, if Swedenborg inspired in most Spiritualists an ideal of democratized spirit contact and a consequent freedom from conventional structures of spiritual authority, he inspired among those who formed and belonged to the New Church a formally organized sect based on what they considered the Seer's exclusive contact with the spirit world and (to some extent) on the resulting authority of his writings.[35] Echoing Swedenborg's warnings rather than imitating his actions, New Church leaders opposed widespread, open, and intentionally sought communication with spirits and denounced the Spiritualist movement as a threat to order. New Church officials were firm believers in spirit influence and communication but had little use for post-Swedenborgian spirit revelations. Indeed, the very intensity and frequency with which New Church officials asserted Swedenborg's caveats in response to Spiritualism suggests that this was the primary ground of dispute between the two groups. John Jewett, a Swedenborgian minister and editor of a New Church newspaper, scolded John Shoebridge Williams that "the danger" of open spirit communication had been "clearly laid down in the writings of Swedenborg." Similarly, New Church minister Chauncey Giles began a discussion of the "fundamental" differences between his religion and Spiritualism in *The New Church and Spiritism* with the Church's position "that conscious intercourse with spirits is not useful or right; that it is fraught with the greatest danger to man's spiritual life, and ought never to be sought by any one." Giles pointed out that Swedenborg's contact with the spirits had been preceded by special preparation, had not been sought, and had been part of a special divine mission. That mission having been "fully accomplished," there was "no necessity for supplementing it." Most of his peers agreed.[36]

Spiritualists objected to this stance because for them spiritual freedom and security required closer and more democratic relations with the spirit world than the New Church allowed. Nathaniel P. Tallmadge, ex-governor of the Wisconsin Territory and a prominent Spiritualist, told the *New Church Herald* that he was "repelled" by the New Church for this reason despite "many prepossessions" in its favor, including the fact that both his parents had belonged to it. In the New Church's restrictive position on spirit communication, its elevation of Swedenborg to a position of special religious authority, and its creation of a formal and rigidified sect based on that authority, Spiritualists saw the very spiritual despotism, monopolization of experience and authority, and threat to independent judgment that they hoped to avoid by contacting the spirits for themselves. They therefore denied that Swedenborg's gift had been exclusive, criticized the Swedenborgian church as "a mere *sect*," and asserted the continuing need for new revelations from the spirit world. They regularly invoked Swedenborg's spirit in support of their contentions that the Seer's writings, neither final nor authoritative, were destined to be supplanted. When New Church pastor B. F. Barrett outspokenly opposed Spiritualism, one Spiritualist denounced as a "bigoted authoritarian" anyone who rejected the opportunity to learn from the spirits as Swedenborg had done. And W. S. Courtney, a Swedenborgian lawyer who converted to Spiritualism, defended the authority of "our own reason and instincts" over that of Swedenborg, whose elevation to "*undue* honors and preeminence" was inimical to spiritual growth and freedom. Too many New Church members, he felt, had compromised their individuality by becoming "mere echoes of their master's voice" and resting religious authority "in history instead of a living experience."[37] Similar convictions, incidentally, led the majority of Spiritualists to close ranks against those few members of the movement who expressed discomfort with democratic mediumship or used their mediumship as a foundation for strong personal authority over others.

A small minority of Swedenborgians anticipated the democratic Spiritualist challenge by launching the New Era movement during the 1840s. New Era Swedenborgians found in Swedenborg an inspiration for direct communication with spirits and looked to spirits, particularly those of Swedenborg himself and deceased New Church members, as religious authority figures. The result was an outburst of spiritualistic activity intended by its practitioners to revitalize the institutional New Church and its leadership.[38] Usually unconnected or loosely connected with the formal New Church organization, New Era advocates challenged its ecclesiastical machinery and urged a greater emphasis on personal experience. Led by Silas Jones, Samuel Worcester, and Henry Weller, the movement continued until the late 1860s. Like Spiritualists, New Era Swedenborgians looked to Swedenborg for their example, imitating his practices rather than heeding his warnings and insisting that his revelations had not been the last. Worcester, for instance, declared that the New Church must accept Swedenborg as a "present as well as past Revelator." Like Spiritualists, they regarded the Seer as the herald of a new dispensation of open spirit communion and claimed to have spoken with spirits for themselves. Henry Weller, whose magazine *The Crisis* was established in 1852 as a mouthpiece for the movement, sounded much like Spiritualists when he declared in the first issue that "continual, direct, open visitations from the Spiritual World" were "an established fact."[39] Like Spiritualists, furthermore, New Era renegades used ideas of spirit communication and authority to validate their own experiences against the authority of Swedenborg's writings and of existing church structures (particularly the New Church clergy).

These similarities were sufficient to generate mutual sympathy between Spiritualists and New Era Swedenborgians in spite of theological differences. The *Spiritual Telegraph,* for example, praised Weller for his open-minded attitude toward Spiritualist claims and his vigilance against New Church sectarianism.[40] Many New Era Swedenborgians, meanwhile, responded favorably to Spiritualism as its popularity increased in the early 1850s. The most prominent example was George Bush's early enthusiasm for Andrew Jackson Davis, whose experiences he believed had precedent in the life of Swedenborg. Although Davis's naturalism and animus toward organized Christianity eventually drove Bush into B. F. Barrett's anti-Spiritualist crusade,[41] his initial openness to Spiritualism led him to publish Swedenborg's *Spiritual Diary*, the account of the Swedish Seer's own experiences in the spirit world, in 1850. The Swedenborgian editor and publisher Otis Clapp, meanwhile, attended Spiritualist circles, usually composed of other readers of Swedenborg, starting in 1850. Perhaps the most well known of those who were involved with both the Swedenborgian Church and the Spiritualist movement was Thomas Lake Harris. Like Bush, he was connected with the harmonial group for a short time before severing his ties with Davis. Unlike Bush, however, he remained involved with Spiritualism. He wrote Spiritualist verse—which he believed was inspired by the spirits of illustrious dead poets—and was co-leader of the Mountain Cove Spiritualist community during the early 1850s. By the late 1850s, Harris had drifted from the Spiritualist movement and become a leading New Era Swedenborgian. More than any other participants in the Swedenborgian subculture, Spiritualists and New Era advocates were alike in their religious practices and conceptions of religious authority. Both were part of the growing tendency to democratize Swedenborg's practice of spirit contact in the interest of realizing a new religious age.

Not surprisingly, New Era Swedenborgians and Spiritualists experienced similarly strained relations with New Church officials, who saw Spiritualism and the New Era movement as mutually reinforcing challenges and therefore fought both. Church leaders became the first religious group in America to attack Andrew Jackson Davis's *The Principles of Nature* when it appeared in 1847. John R. Hibbard, the pastor of the Chicago Society of the New Church, spoke for much of the sect in 1853 when he insisted to both groups that any necessary spirit contact would be initiated by God and that consciously sought spirit intercourse posed a threat to the freedom of human reason. The Massachusetts Association of the New Church issued a report to the same effect in 1858, insisting that spirit communication be orderly (i.e., unsought by mortals) and that it was only rarely permitted because of the potential dangers involved. In the minds of New Church officials, the Spiritualist and New Era movements were twin threats to religious order.[42]

Still, the differences between the two groups were crucial. Unlike Spiritualists, New Era Swedenborgians never pushed spirit communication beyond the confines of Swedenborgian doctrine or the New Church community. They felt that good spirits could relate useful if not essential religious truth, but distinguished and distanced their practices from those of Spiritualism by making compatibility with doctrinal orthodoxy the crucial test for the authenticity of spirit communications. Samuel Worcester, for example, never sought spirits without spirit Swedenborg's permission and limited his contact to New Church deceased. Similarly, Henry Weller consistently supported New Church truth over spirit communications received by those outside the Swedenborgian fold. Swedenborg's warnings were not lost on them, further-more, and they were highly sensitive to the dangers of open spirit contact. A concern with spiritual freedom and with the possibility of immoderate claims made them highly cautious. Many of them eventually retreated from the New Era movement altogether. Another important point of difference is that New Era Swedenborgians were generally uninclined to attach much significance to the rappings and other "scientific" phenomena. They saw the manifestations as remarkable proof of spiritual reality but—like Transcendentalists—empha-sized internal communication with the spirit world over external phenomena. Indeed, the religious "crisis" after which Weller named his newspaper con-sisted in large part in his belief that the phenomenalistic orientation of modern Spiritualism posed a materialistic threat to what he considered true spirit communion.[43] Finally, the spirit-centered practices and beliefs of New Era Swedenborgians remained not only confined within established doctrinal boundaries but also episodic and short-lived, never becoming the basis of a sustained and independent religious movement like Spiritualism.

Transcendentalism, the New Church, and Spiritualism suggest the variety of ways in which antebellum Americans creating new religious ideologies could use Emanuel Swedenborg's legacy to address their needs for religious freedom and order. Their diverging uses of Swedenborg in constructing new bases of spiritual freedom, religious authority, and cosmic order set them apart from both the larger religious culture and each other. New Church Swedenborgians agreed with Spiritualists about the reality of Swedenborg's experience, but most of them feared its anarchic potential and, like many other contemporary denominations and sects, made the charismatic leader-ship of an inspirational individual the basis for a centralized structure of religious authority. Transcendentalists, meanwhile, differed from both of the other groups in allegorizing the Swedish Seer's claim to spirit communication as a symbol of a communion with one's inner spirituality, but joined Spiritu-alists in exalting Swedenborg as the harbinger of an individualistic, demo-cratic, and experiential religion suited to nineteenth-century America.

Of the three groups, the Spiritualists most strongly emphasized the importance of Swedenborg's belief in spirit activity and mediation and his claims to have communicated with spirits. They put their own spin on the Swedish Seer's experiences, fashioning a unique religious ideology and practice and bringing to a focus the tendency among their religious predecessors toward spirit communication. They developed a religion that met their desire for spiritual individualism and liberation on the one hand and religious order and authority on the other. By democratizing Swedenborg's example of spirit communication, Spiritualists participated in the antebellum American democratization of religious authority. At the same time, the comforting concept of spirit mediation and guidance became in their hands a conservative and stabilizing counterweight to the evidently disturbing implications of experiential religion.

Spiritualists helped to establish Swedenborg's place in American religious life. The relatively widespread appeal of the Spiritualist movement helped to spread his influence, and his ideas of spirit communication and mediation in particular, beyond the small elite circles of liberal intellectuals that were attracted to Transcendentalism and the New Church. Even more important, however, Spiritualists used Swedenborg's example to express their deep desire for contact with spiritual beings they considered more advanced than themselves. Through their trialogue about Swedenborg's legacy, they identified and highlighted a popular and persistent theme in American religious culture, one that found expression far beyond the boundaries of the Swedenborgian subculture: namely, the existence and role of advanced but subdivine spiritual beings and their relationship with those on earth. Pondering human nature, LaRoy Sunderland, a mesmerist publicizer who briefly turned his energies to the Spiritualist cause, recognized that Swedenborg had addressed a religious need felt by many people other than Spiritualists. "Multitudes, indeed, who reject the writings of Swedenborg, in respect to the other spheres," he observed, "nevertheless cherish the belief that they are the objects of paternal care on the part of the angels who are good and true."[44] Spiritualists thus underscore Swedenborg's link with the broader currents of American religious life. They used his legacy in their distinctive expression of that search for a cosmic connection that lay at the basis of all religion.

⊷⊹⊶

3
Spiritualist Republicanism

Visions of a Spiritual Republic

In 1851, seventy-five years after the Declaration of Independence asserted human equality and announced American freedom from the perceived oppression of the British monarch and his corrupt government, Andrew Jackson Davis published a new version of that revered document in *The Spirit Messenger.* Modeled on the original, Davis's Declaration was altered in content to emphasize religious concerns rather than political ones. Like the original, it listed grievances against the existing order. Punctuated by frequent references to perceived impediments to the free action of one's "inward Deity" and "innate love of truth, justice, and harmony," this manifesto declared the independence of every individual from the spiritual tyranny imposed by established churches and ministers. This, Davis believed, was the deepest meaning of American independence. He feared that most Americans had lost sight of Independence Day's spiritual meaning; indulging in "thoughtless excitement" every July fourth, they seemed to have forgotten what he considered a national commitment to moral principle. Stephen Albro, editor of the *Age of Progress,* agreed. "Wearied" and "disgusted" with "the hollow-heartedness of mock patriotism," he preferred a "solitary celebration" of Independence Day. He could "not mingle with those who rejoice outwardly, by burning powder, marching with banners, and swallowing alcoholic enthusiasm, in honor of National Liberty, whilst their souls are bound with chains the most galling and tyrannous." Both Davis and Albro sensed that Americans had abused or misinterpreted the legacy of the Revolution.[1]

Six years after the appearance of Davis's Declaration, *Spiritual Telegraph* editor S. B. Brittan offered a similar suggestion that "radical Individualism" was the message of the Declaration of Independence. The doctrines this spiritual patriot celebrated in the July fourth issue of his paper *The Spiritual*

Age were "radical and revolutionary," asserting the "manumission and dis-enthrallment" of the individual "from all restraints and constraints upon his action." Viewing the Declaration through a spiritual lens, he wrote that it set forth the rights of conscience in religious matters and was "radically repug-nant to all sectarianism, to all protestant-popery, to all authority over indi-vidual conscience, to all spiritual rule or dictation, to all bigotry and intoler-ance, and to all prescription and persecution, *in any way* for opinion's sake." The tyrannies of church and priesthood, Spiritualists believed, posed danger-ous threats to the independence and virtue of the spirit. The life of the free spirit, Brittan proclaimed, "*is a declaration of independence.*"[2]

As Davis and Brittan suggest, antebellum Spiritualists shared with many of their contemporaries an aversion to organized religion, including churches, the clergy, and other institutional trappings. They believed that the human spirit was destined to grow in conformity with natural law and derogatorily labeled as "artificial" any perceived unnatural restraint established over it by any person or institution. Their concern to eliminate artificial barriers to what one of them called "the natural man" underlay the intense antiauthoritarian and anti-institutional thrust which pervaded their rhetoric and behavior. This tendency placed them squarely within their culture, in which a number of "insurgent" religious movements challenged existing religious institutions in the name of spiritual democracy and, in the case of the more radical groups, a doctrine of "radical individualism."[3]

Like other "insurgents" on the antebellum religious scene, Spiritualists explained themselves in terms of the American Revolution.[4] The republican ideology that justified the Revolution and the impulse toward disestab-lishment that accompanied it encouraged an increasing role for private judg-ment in religious matters, a reverence for the idea of independent selfhood, and a premium on courageous resistance to perceived tyranny as the mark of manhood. Starting with Davis's *The Principles of Nature,* the Spiritualist literature abounded in references to the eighteenth-century natural rights philosophy that had animated the leaders of the Revolution. In his *Plain Guide to Spiritualism,* ex-Universalist minister and *Spiritual Clarion* editor Uriah Clark invoked "the Jeffersonian Declaration of Independence and Equality" in proclaiming "that 'all men are endowed by their Creator with certain inalienable rights,' not only in a civil, but in a social and spiritual sense." They believed that the citizens of their spiritual republic should have the right to advance without arbitrary external obstruction. Reflecting a con-ception of history common in antebellum America, they tended to single out the Revolution, harbinger of a democratic and individualized conception of authority, as the most important event of modern times. They understood Spiritualism as the culmination of the Revolution, a new religion perfectly suited to the young American republic.[5]

Like the nation's founders, Spiritualists tempered their commitment to freedom and natural rights with the recognition that the individual operated within a larger social whole. If arbitrary encroachment on individual rights constituted tyranny, unbounded individual freedom constituted an equally dangerous anarchy. Thus the republican ideology had urged moral self-restraint, public responsibility, and respect for the rule of law as essential to the health of a political republic. Similarly, Spiritualists believed that the sanctity of the individual soul, its existence in a cosmos governed by natural law, and its ties with all other souls imposed "natural" limits on free action. They and other religious Americans articulated an ideology of "spiritual republicanism" that, like its political counterpart, avoided the extremes of individualism and authoritarianism by emphasizing spiritual freedom, democracy, and equality on the one hand and self-restraint, social obligation, the rule of natural law, and moral order on the other.

In particular, Spiritualists concerned themselves with two kinds of spiritual tyranny and regarded spirit communication as the key to abolishing both. The first was the stifling effect of the religious establishment, whose despotism was over the spirit rather than the body and was therefore considered more insidious than political oppression. New York physician and Spiritualist lecturer Robert T. Hallock suggested this primacy of spiritual over political freedom on July 4, 1856. He observed that the deists "Paine, Jefferson, Franklin, had declared their independence of church creed before they published that other declaration of independence. . . . Without the one we never should have had the other." Andrew Jackson Davis was similarly convinced that political change was merely a vehicle for deeper spiritual progress: "there is a REPUBLIC of SPIRIT embosomed and gestating in the dominant political organism." Religious reform, therefore, was of paramount importance. "Human character is affected so deeply by ecclesiastical institutions," he wrote, "that nothing can require of reformers more investigation." Just as political republicanism involved an attempt to reform political institutions through a democratization of political authority, so spiritual republicans called for democratization and reform in existing religious structures through the spread of spirit communication.[6]

Spiritualists regarded moral corruption within, which they often likened to slavery, as an even greater danger to spiritual freedom and order than despotic religious institutions without. Freedom in their minds meant not thoughtless self-indulgence but something like the "Christian liberty" which John Winthrop had spelled out for the Puritan commonwealth of seventeenth-century Massachusetts: the ability to escape the enslaving grip of sensual behavior and to achieve spiritual self-realization. Adherence to strict moral codes was therefore a standard lesson in most Spiritualist writings. Spiritualists usually supported the social and moral reform movements of the period, opposing slavery, alcohol, restrictions on divorce, the consumption of meat, and anything else they considered discouraging to free spiritual development. As essential to spiritual republicanism as the freedom of the soul from artificial religious institutions was its liberation from this internal tyranny through an internalization of the moral standards imposed by nature and nature's God. Contact with morally purified spirits would help Spiritualists to purify themselves.

It would also counteract what one Spiritualist called "the decadence of public morality." Political competition in a mass democracy seemed to have encouraged politicians in morally dubious practices, and a competitive market economy seemed to have promoted selfishness at the expense of traditional republican values. No wonder that Spiritualists so often sought the spirits of the founding fathers, whose motives they considered more high-minded. In the tradition of the Puritan jeremiad, they imagined Franklin, Jefferson, and especially Washington accusingly pointing their disembodied fingers at the later generations who inherited the nation they had fought to establish. John W. Edmonds, who had enjoyed a distinguished career as a reform-minded judge in New York, invoked the spirit of Washington to blast slavery and greed and to assuage his "feeling of despondency in reference to the future." America, he feared, was looking uncomfortably like Europe, whose perceived moral and political corruption served as a negative reference point for American claims to republican purity and simplicity. From the utopian community of Hopedale, Massachusetts, a hotbed of Spiritualism that had been established by radical reformers dedicated to practical Christian perfectionism, William S. Heywood sneered at the larger society. He considered the majority of Americans "degenerate sons" of the "far more worthy" revolutionary founders. Robert Hallock identified an important source of Spiritualism's appeal when he acknowledged that "the need of such men as . . . Washington, and Franklin" was "perpetual" and that "the patriot, in the hour of doubt and trouble, intuitively invokes the aid of Washington."[7]

Medium Abby T. Hall exemplified Hallock's point on Washington's birthday in 1855 when she claimed that "Freedom Speaks to Earth Again" in the form of a spirit message from the father of his country. Watching the young republic from above, spirit Washington reaffirmed its spiritual mission and called for both freedom and restraint. The nation's founders, he said, had not intended to establish an individualistic free-for-all and had not left their country alone and without moral guidance. Hall helped Spiritualists to cope with and therefore to accept the disturbing changes shaping their nation by assuring them that the founding generation "surround you with our influence . . . and draw you with us" and that the "same fatherly care which has sheltered the infant in its weakness still guides it in its strength."[8] Hall's message was promptly published in the *Sacred Circle* because Spiritualists, worried that economic and political opportunism threatened the innocence of their developing nation, needed symbolic reminders of republican freedom and virtue.

Spiritualists hoped that their spirit guides, by helping them to eliminate both external and internal tyranny and to restore public virtue, would usher in the millennium, that perfect social and moral order predicted in the Christian Scriptures and anticipated by religious Americans. Whether they defended or opposed Christianity, they participated in the broader cultural tendency to identify the American republic as the vanguard of a new and ideal political, social, and spiritual order. Davis expressed certainty (and therefore probably harbored doubts) that the United States, "aided by superintending angel hosts," was destined to become "the new millennial country of peace and abundance," a true "Spiritual Republic."[9] This is why he and other Spiritualists, looking backward to an idealized past and forward to an uncertain future, reached for the ghosts of their grandfathers.[10]

The Yoke of Organized Religion

As religious reformers and spiritual republicans, Spiritualists launched a multifaceted verbal attack on organized religion in the name of spiritual freedom and a new religious order. Their critique began with the concept of religious organization itself, which they considered inherently tyrannical and antirepublican. In this, they participated in what one historian has identified as a wider antebellum American "collapse of faith in the ability of 'external' institutions to express unique points of view." Mary Fenn Davis, a popular speaker on Spiritualism and women's rights and the second wife of Andrew Jackson Davis, warned that "ecclesiastical regulations merge into customs; individualism ceases; and men become automatons, and exist for centuries on a dead level of mental slavery and conservatism." Her husband likewise contrasted a progressive "individualism" with a conservative, stifling, and artificial "institutionalism." "Man-made and essentially arbitrary," he protested, institutions implied "*the innate disqualification of the individual for self-regulation*" and "have ever arrogated to themselves the right to rule the individual." Echoing Ralph Waldo Emerson, whose essay "Self-Reliance" warned that "society everywhere is in conspiracy against the manhood of every one of its members," he argued that institutions "combine and conspire against individual freedom." "American Republicanism will be transformed into Tyranny," he warned, "unless individual man declareth himself independent of all political and ecclesiastical Institutions." Another Spiritualist declared that "the principle of authority and the principle of development are incompatible."[11]

Spiritualists complained that existing religious institutions were rigid and superficial structures—"forms without substance"—that stifled the dynamic inner sources of spirituality. Thus they distinguished the natural inward religiosity of pure Christianity from the artificial denominational and sectarian organizations that constituted "churchianity" and issued primitivist calls for a new religious order based on the former. In an Independence Day address entitled *The Child and the Man,* Robert Hallock called institutional religion a mark of spiritual "childhood" that was destined to be cast aside upon the achievement of spiritual "manhood." Another Spiritualist interpreted Christ as a heroic embodiment of spiritual republicanism whose life and precepts ran counter to the very idea of religious organization. "His life was a beautiful spontaneity, with its governing principle *within,* wholly independent of external authority or organization, with which he lived in daily conflict." Imitators of Christ "become '*disorganizers*'" rather than "authoritarians."[12]

A particularly oppressive feature of organized sects and denominations, according to the Spiritualist critique, was that they espoused fixed doctrines and modes of worship which tyrannically generated rigidity and conformity rather than individualism and development. Religious belief was essential, they felt, but to accord any belief the status of final truth was to set boundaries on knowledge and to require adherence to them as the basis of membership in a religious body was to stifle future growth. Like the early primitivist followers of Alexander Campbell and Elias Smith, then, they referred derisively to "creed" and other artificial religious expressions as anti-republican fetters on the free conscience. Similarly, they dismissed formalized worship as a discouragement to spontaneous spirituality and a routinization of religious feeling. R. P. Ambler, an ex-Universalist minister who bolted the denomination and found a new career as a Spiritualist lecturer, writer, and editor, defended the "infinite unfolding" of the spirit against the "incrustation formed by unnatural habits of thought." He pitied those whose "mental vision remains circumscribed within the precincts of artificial creeds." W. S. Courtney agreed. The power of "natural" over "artificial" religion meant that "no man-made law, creed, or custom" would ever become "legitimated, or so *naturalized,* as to coextend in influence and authority with the 'higher law'— the law written on the heart of the individual himself." In his antiformalist manifesto "Bodies and Souls," S. B. Brittan left no doubt about where true spirituality lay.[13]

Another target of criticism was the clergy, a highly visible and hence obnoxious locus of religious authority. Viewing it through the lens of republicanism (and a broader cultural bias against perceived Catholic authoritarianism), Spiritualists saw in the "priesthood" not leadership and guidance but tyranny and corruption.[14] A large part of the problem was that it had become, in Adin Ballou's words, "merely professional." Ideally a "calling" and a commitment, the clerical role had degenerated in Spiritualists' eyes into little more than a routine. Physician-turned-medium George Dexter felt that ministers performed "a mere mechanical round of ceremonies . . . mainly from the impulse of time-honored custom," producing a "moribund condition of spirituality in the Church." Andrew Jackson Davis agreed that divinity schools taught not inspirational leadership but "the art of whining out prayers" and "echoing the thoughts of leaders." The unfortunate result, said Charles Partridge, was that ministers were "removed . . . from the current expressions of God" and untouched by "his living inspirations."[15]

Worse still, the professional clergy was so financially dependent on the laity that it could not take independent positions on the pressing moral and social reform issues of the day. Concerned above all with being "fed, and clothed, and enriched," lamented R. P. Ambler, ministers echoed the opinions of their parishioners rather than following their consciences and therefore lacked the moral power required to inspire the laity to spiritual growth. In the language of republican political theory, dependence had motivated the clergy to act on the basis of self-interest rather than the public good; "corruption" had undermined "virtue." The result was inertia and conservatism. The minister "cannot easily utter his highest thought," John Murray Spear heard spirits say, since he "feels he must wait" until his followers are prepared. "In this way the truth makes, on your earth, exceedingly slow progress." What the human race needed, said William H. Fish, a reformer and friend of Adin Ballou who cautiously sympathized with Spiritualism, was "a class of teachers, outside of the churches," who would "tell the truths that the pulpit cannot *afford* to tell." A contributor to Ballou's reform paper *The Practical Christian* contrasted the corrupt professional ministry with the "True Preacher," who virtuously and boldly "takes the light of the rising sun of reform first on his own clear forehead." For William S. Heywood, Ballou's Spiritualist son-in-law, a clergy that had to be pushed into reform by virtuous laymen figured prominently among the "Degeneracies of the Church." Neglecting the responsibilities of spiritual leadership, the clergy had ceased to perform their function and therefore lost the support of progressively minded Spiritualists.[16]

Perhaps the most telling charge against the ministry was its hostility to Spiritualism, its denial of the manifestations, and its refusal to investigate the phenomena. To Spiritualists, this behavior smacked of materialism. Ministers, after all, were supposed to believe in the reality of spirit and the afterlife and to monitor the spiritual welfare of their followers. Many Spiritualists explained this lapse in terms not only of materialism but also of corruption and tyranny. Ministers based their livelihood upon an alleged spiritual superiority, observed Spear, and "would fasten fetters upon the people" in order to maintain their power and status. Charles Partridge, another ex-Universalist who became a Spiritualist editor and publisher, agreed that the ministry was a privileged class which had historically stifled lay spirituality to preserve "assumed priestly prerogative." The clergy's selfish concern with power loomed large among the grievances in Davis's "Declaration of Independence." The personal interests of the clergy, like those of lawyers, physicians, and entrepreneurs, conflicted with their responsibilities to the public. The result was a threat to virtue and independence, a perpetuation of ignorance, and an impediment to free religious discussion.[17]

Spiritualists responded to the perceived tyranny, corruption, and ineffectuality of the clergy with threats of rebellion. One said that "we have revered them long enough" and suggested that Spiritualism might "do away with the order of the priesthood." Another, probably early Spiritualist convert William Fishbough, warned that clerical refusal to investigate spirit communication would prompt the laity to "take the matter into their own hands, and dispense with your services."[18] It was clear to Spiritualists that religious vitality, inspiration, and leadership lay not with a spiritually empty clerical profession but with the free and spontaneous spirit. The ministry had become an instrumental part of an oppressive religious superstructure and an obstacle to spirituality. The existence and extent of a religious "crisis of authority" in the early to mid-nineteenth century is a topic of scholarly debate, but there can be little doubt that many Spiritualists felt it acutely.

The career of Adin Ballou provides a good example of a Spiritualist's rebellious opposition to clerical conservatism. Born in 1803, he began a turbulent career as a Universalist minister in 1824. His first position, in Milford, Massachusetts, ended in 1830 when a denominational controversy pitted the majority, who believed in immediate salvation at death, against a schismatic minority called Restorationists, who believed that the nonrepentant experienced a brief punishment after death. Ballou sided with the minority and lost his Milford post. But in 1832 he found a new position at Mendon, where he took a leading role in creating the Massachusetts Association of Universal Restorationists. He soon became alienated from the Association's conservatives, however, as his understanding of Christian duty led him into radical temperance, abolitionist, and nonresistance activity. In frustration, he joined with William Fish and a small group of cohorts in breaking with the Association. Forced to find an outlet for his religious and reform commitments outside of organized religion and the ministry, he and his group published a radical "Standard of Practical Christianity" in 1838, established the *Practical Christian* in 1840 to air their views, and created the Hopedale community in 1841 in an effort to enact their ideals. Spiritualism was readily adopted in the early 1850s by Ballou and the other radical reformers of Hopedale, who looked to him for leadership despite community bylaws discouraging any special status for the clergy.[19]

Spiritualists' distaste for religious formalism and clerical professionalism led them to religious practices (described in chapter 6) that Robert C. Fuller has called "unchurched." Considering existing religious institutions out-moded, spiritually inert, and inherently confining, they were often reluctant to form new ones. Like the antebellum Americans attracted to the "Chris-tian" movement and its claims to have restored early Christianity, they sensed in organization a threat to freedom. They therefore failed to create any permanent large-scale institutions during the antebellum period. The anti-structural impulse within Spiritualism was undeniably powerful.[20]

Many Spiritualists resisted attempts to organize the movement. J. H. Robinson, whose contributions to the *Spiritual Telegraph* dripped with antiauthoritarian rhetoric, clearly identified individualism as the reason for the movement's failure to organize. He responded to A. E. Newton's call for a "central institution" of mediums that would constitute a "nucleus" for the movement with the argument that "spiritual power is so democratically diffused that it will be found extremely difficult to 'concentrate' it." Since "there is a 'nucleus' wherever there is a human spirit," he insisted, authority ought to remain democratized and decentralized. In his autobiography, Warren Chase, a radical reformer who had never forged any formal denomi-national attachments, frowned on an attempt by a group of New York City Spiritualists to centralize, organize, and lead the movement. When they asked for his help, he proudly told them that he "would not aid them to centralize, . . . for he could neither lead nor be led, but paddled his own canoe. His lone and independent mind could never be made to work in a harness." Organiza-tions, he felt, tended to become vehicles of ends more artificial and material than natural and spiritual.[21]

Chase appears to have been referring to plans to establish the Society for the Diffusion of Spiritual Knowledge, Spiritualists' foremost antebellum attempt at large-scale organization. The formation of this institution in June 1854 by Christian Spiritualists fearful of rationalism[22] sparked the appearance of a flurry of antiorganizational articles in the *Telegraph* and other Spiritualist periodicals during the ensuing summer. The remarks of a *Telegraph* corre-spondent who chose the pseudonym "FREE SPEECH" are typical of the whole. "FREE SPEECH" denounced this attempt "to erect . . . stately church edifices" and "to sustain *sectarian* preachers." All such organizations "must eventually become *partial,* one-sided, and sectarian in their natures" since no group of people could reach complete agreement on matters of religious belief. Similar commentaries on the potential tyranny of large-scale organization in general and the new Society in particular appeared in subsequent issues of the

Telegraph. Thomas and Mary Gove Nichols, outspoken radical individualists, opposed "this new Hierarchy, or Spiritual Church Organization, soon to have its Bishops, and perhaps its Cardinals and Popes."[23] "No-organizationism," as this position was sometimes called, was a familiar expression of spiritual republicanism. Although adopted in its more extreme forms by only a relative few, the lack of large Spiritualist organizations during the antebellum period testifies to its decisive influence.

Still, spiritual freedom and individualism were not to generate fragmentation and anarchy. Spiritualists were worried that the sectarian pluralism encouraged by Protestantism and characteristic of American religious life would spawn chaos. As republicans, they desired order as well as freedom and thought a public consensus on basic moral and religious principles vital to the health of society. Like so many other founders of new sects and denominations during the antebellum period, they expressed frustration and bewilderment over the divisive disputation and large variety of sects and denominations that vied for adherents in the cluttered American religious marketplace. Medium Charles Hammond, a Universalist minister and editor who converted to Spiritualism and renounced his denominational affiliation, heard spirit voices express the same frustration that had moved Joseph Smith to establish Mormonism: "Views of God were conflicting and contradictory, and my mind was worn with the wrangling of unsettled controversy. I sought for peace amid the turbulent waters, but found only agitation and discontent." He found his peace after meeting the Fox sisters in 1849. Another exasperated Spiritualist watched a "world of angry disputants . . . indulging in every contrary opinion" about the Bible and wondered, "is *this* my *only* guide?" A confused Joseph Smith had been told in an 1820 vision to avoid the competing sects of the day and claimed to have learned the doctrines of Mormonism from the angel Moroni. Three decades later, Hammond and other Spiritualists sought their religious peace through spirit communication. Spiritualism, John Edmonds believed, would provide "some common platform on which all might congregate and unite." Troubled by Protestantism's centrifugal tendencies, they took up the ancient practice of spirit intercourse in search of a synthesis which would meet the demands of republican individualism without sacrificing republican order and unity. Like the many other primitivist groups of the antebellum period, they "found that the appeal to pure beginnings was the surest way to cut through the confusion of religious pluralism" and "sought legitimacy" in their pluralistic culture by claiming to replicate early Christianity more closely than others. Spiritualist restorationism, like Mormon restorationism, was motivated by a "quest for authority" amidst the "vacuous relativity" of American religious life.[24]

Even the occasional defender of sectarianism in a Spiritualist publication assumed that it was merely an ephemeral result of a free religious system in which liberty of conscience produces a variety of opinions. Like Adam Smith, who convinced Jacksonian Americans that economic individualism and competition would yield order, most Spiritualists believed that religious competition would produce not fragmentation but a broad consensus on fundamental principles. Thus Owen G. Warren advocated sects within Spiritualism as the instruments of free and healthy discussion, confident that the inevitable triumph of truth would produce spiritual unity and harmony. Spiritualists usually agreed with Andrew Jackson Davis and Robert Hallock that existing sects and denominations were the marks of spiritual "childhood," that the exercise of freedom would yield the religious harmony of "adulthood," and that true religion lay in the individual rather than in denominational organizations.[25]

Indeed, it was usually aversion to formalistic rigidity rather than doctrinal disagreement that drove Spiritualists to a rebellious abandonment of their denominations. Uriah Clark left the Universalist fold because he preferred the democratized salvation of "genuine Universalism, in its broadest, truest, eclectic sense" to "the organized sect" with its "enforcement of creeds, authorities, tests, books, and formula that interfere with individual freedom, and would enslave the soul to certain standards of alleged infallible judgment." The author of an article on the relationship between "Spiritualism and Unitarianism" sounded a similar note. Having once placed his religious hopes "in what are called the more rational and liberal denominations—Unitarians, Universalists, Christians, etc.," he regretted that these groups had institutionalized. They had proven to be "only experimental offshoots" that had been "frightened back to the central authority." It was on such grounds that Thomas Wentworth Higginson, a Spiritualist who became increasingly alienated from the Unitarian fold, severely chastised the denomination at a Unitarian convention held in Worcester, Massachusetts, in 1853.[26]

Spiritualists found even the confining liberal Protestant denominations far preferable to the Calvinist orthodoxy that they joined other theological liberals of the nineteenth century in rejecting. Calvinism offended their republican as well as their Romantic sensibilities. They jettisoned the orthodox emphasis on divine sternness in favor of divine love, and adopted the expansive ideas of human goodness, gradual growth into divine perfection, and universal salvation in place of the spiritually limiting doctrines of innate depravity, eternal damnation, and the aristocratic restriction of salvation to an elect few. Furthermore, Calvinist doctrines tended to "cramp the free thoughts and exalted aspirations of the soul" and to rely on fear of eternal punishment to coerce moral behavior. So argued Spiritualist republican R. P. Ambler, who called Calvinists "willing subjects of the fearful despotism of theological tyrants." Medium Charles Hammond invoked the spirit of Revolutionary pamphleteer Thomas Paine to blast "cruel and oppressive" hellfire theologians for controlling "by fear and hope" and ruling "as do tyrants and kings." One Spiritualist claimed the support of the sentimentalized spirit of Calvin himself in urging the orthodox to "let go their long cherished notions."[27] Spiritualists saw little room in their new spiritual republic for outworn traditions.

Declarations of Independence

The perceived spiritual confinement and tyranny of existing religious structures prompted Spiritualists to their rebellious practice of "coming out" of their churches.[28] Many Spiritualists were affiliated with some denomination or sect before joining the movement, but severed those ties either soon before or soon after embracing their new religion. In so doing, they joined members of other new antebellum religious groups, such as "Christians," Mormons, Shakers, and Oneidans. A part of Spiritualism's religious context, "come-outerism" expressed a felt need by those who left their churches or denominations for greater room for conscience, greater commitment to their understanding of truth, and less imposition of formal structure than membership in an institutional church or sect allowed. Experiencing a crisis of religious authority, Spiritualists decided that existing institutions and their leaders had lost their vitality and could no longer command their loyalty. They turned instead to the spirits.

This is not to say that Spiritualists were the only antebellum Americans using contact with the spirit world to underwrite their spiritual republicanism. Indeed, they were only the latest representatives of a long historical link between spirit communication and religious restiveness. Anthropologist I. M. Lewis has discussed this connection in the context of traditional religions, and Clarke Garrett has done the same with regard to radical Protestantism in the seventeenth through early nineteenth centuries.[29] In a specifically antebellum context, Spiritualists joined Joseph Smith, Shaker "spiritists," and New Era challengers to the institutional New Church and its clergy in using contact with the higher authority of the spiritual world for purposes of religious insurgency.[30] If the Spiritualists' strategy of insurgency was derivative, however, they were distinct in making ongoing spirit communication the basis for their new religion. By focusing their attention on the place of spirits in religious life, they took a unique position in the antebellum cultural conversation about how to assert religious liberty and revitalize spirituality. They created their own instrument of spiritual republicanism.

As an expression of spiritual growth and rebellion, the practice of "coming out" was widely encouraged in Spiritualist writings. Spear advised that anyone who "interiorly feels that he has outgrown any institution, religious, ecclesiastical, moral, or political" should "renounce his allegiance thereto." Just as Jefferson had regarded eternal vigilance and occasional political rebellion as healthful to republican liberty, so William Fish believed that the vitality of religion was preserved "only by successive '*come out*' movements" since ecclesiastical organizations tended to become "wholly corrupt and despotic" as they increased in size, power, and wealth. Another writer saw "no limits to the development and the researches of the human mind" and called upon those "thousands in the churches who are ready to adopt a more rational, spiritual and practical religion" to "stand up in their manhood, and 'Act as conscience orders.'"[31]

Many members of the movement had established a history of doing precisely that, often repeatedly. The radical Quaker abolitionists Amy and Isaac Post, for example, joined Amy's cousin Elias Hicks in bolting orthodox Quakerism in 1827 when they felt that formal disciplinary structures threatened their freedom to act on their inner light and speak out against slavery. They then, for essentially the same reason, separated from the Hicksite schismatics to espouse the still more independent position of Congregational Quakerism. As friends of the Fox family and residents of Rochester, they learned of the spirit manifestations at a very early date, approached the girls in search of truth from the spirits, and were among the first converts to Spiritualism. Isaac eventually became a writing medium and published a book of spirit messages. Another come-outer was John Shoebridge Williams of Cincinnati, whose restless spiritual pilgrimage carried him out of Quakerism during the Hicksite schism of 1827, into the extreme anti-clerical wing of the New Church by the late 1830s,[32] and finally to Spiritualism in 1852. Many of the movement's leading figures, including R. P. Ambler, Adin Ballou, S. B. Brittan, Charles Hammond, Thomas Lake Harris, Simon Crosby Hewitt, and John Murray Spear, severed their formal denominational ties with Universalism. Harris established an independent congregation in New York City, a practice which Fish considered "encouraging."[33]

Not all Spiritualists severed ties with their congregations and denominations. Many of them saw no contradiction between their previous beliefs and the idea and practice of spirit communication, remaining in their churches and grafting Spiritualism onto their religious lives. Ernest Isaacs has pointed out that "many believers kept a nominal, and actual, membership in the Methodist or Universalist or other churches." Braude has explored this point at greater length, particularly as it applies to Universalism. Universalists commonly remained active in their churches even after becoming involved with Spiritualism, and ministers in the denomination were able to identify themselves openly as Spiritualists without suffering excommunication. Indeed, Spiritualism often "flourished within Universalist congregations." The same was true, though to a somewhat lesser extent, of Unitarianism.[34]

Still, "coming out" by declaring one's independence of formal congregational or denominational affiliations constituted for many Spiritualists a
heroic act of spiritual republicanism. John S. Adams, for example, consciously
portrayed his 1854 withdrawal from the Chestnut Street Congregational
Church in Chelsea, Massachusetts, in those terms. His *Letter to the Chestnut
Street Congregational Church* resembles the writings of Thomas Paine in its
republican rhetoric, emotional tone, sense of urgency, and even its presentation of Spiritualism as a rationalistic religion of nature. "You charge me with
an exercise of my own freedom," he trumpeted, "with doing as my own
conscience demands that I should do. You charge me with exercising my own
will, in opposition to church authority." Adams insisted that he would
"acknowledge *no* authority but God" and would "not forsake God's truth
. . . no, never!" Having "come out from that church" to "be separate," this
"freed spirit" considered his subsequent excommunication "for conscience'
sake" in May 1854 to be "an *honor,* not a shame."[35]

Perhaps the most conspicuous and certainly the most well publicized
example of "coming out" among the Spiritualists was A. E. and Sarah J.
Newton's departure from the Edwards Congregational Church in Boston. As
Congregationalists, they had been thoroughly exposed to the liberal theological currents of mid-nineteenth-century Boston. They were also interested
in mesmerism by the time they first looked into Spiritualism in 1851. Within
a short time they became convinced, Sarah became a practicing medium,
and the Newtons began to enjoy "almost daily" what they believed to be
"the sweetest and most intimate communion with the spirits of 'just ones
made perfect' above." Their faith had become revitalized—"immeasurably
strengthened, and rendered a *vital principle* instead of a mere speculative
probability"—by personal experience.

Though they continued for some time to attend the Edwards Church, now
convinced that spirits accompanied them and hovered over the congregation,
their understanding of religious authority changed. In May 1853 they
formally announced their desire to be released from the church in a letter
published under the title *The "Ministry of Angels" Realized.* They explained
that since spirit communication had led them to look to more immediate
sources of spiritual truth than the Bible, they could no longer assent to the
church's declared principle that the Scriptures were the chief source of
religious authority. They felt cramped by their membership in the congregation and hoped that their peers would similarly "see the folly of attempting to
confine their expanding natures within the infantile garments of the past, or
to crowd a universe of truth into the meagre limits of a creed." The church
responded to this Spiritualist challenge by attempting to make an example of
the Newtons; it denied their request and moved to release them through
excommunication. Mutual antagonism between the Newtons and the church

set in as an examining committee formally charged them with raising latter-day revelations to equal status with the Bible. They shrugged off this act of "spiritual despotism" and decided to release themselves. Invigorated by contact with the spirit of Preston Pond, the church's recently deceased minister who had addressed the congregation on "the ministry of angels," the couple declared their independence at their December 21 excommunication hearing. In their *Answer to Charges of Belief in Modern Revelations,* they argued that "dread of church discipline or ecclesiastical censure" stifled "the truths . . . of the Dawning Era" and proceeded to make their stand: "*henceforth we acknowledge no allegiance to your body, and shall recognize your authority in no degree.*" The church excommunicated them a few weeks later, on January 6, 1854. Going public again, they wrote a letter to the widely circulated *Spiritual Telegraph. Telegraph* editor S. B. Brittan introduced it with an enthusiastic note of support.[36]

Spiritual republicans like the Newtons who severed old ties and "came out" were not repudiating all authority but rather seeking it in new and more fulfilling forms. John S. Adams turned to the "happy experience" of spirit communion because he felt that church membership had made his spirit "dwarfish," was "dissatisfied with man's theory of God's government," and was "seeking a better and truer one, from a higher and more reliable source." Feeling "weary" of a "pilgrimage in darkness and doubts," he heeded spirit advice to examine the Bible critically and to locate authority in self, reason, and nature rather than in church and popular opinion.[37] Adams's example says much about Spiritualists. Like radical Protestants before them and like many Americans of the early republic, they exalted the individual above all institutions as a locus of authority and a focus of experience. More importantly, however, they looked to the spirits, believing that both disenthrallment from external religious authority and the continuing development of the soul required personal ongoing communication with the spirit world.[38]

This emphasis on personal religious experience put Spiritualists in the company of both contemporary evangelicals, who urged direct contact with the Holy Spirit as a sign of conversion, and the various liberal denominations of the period, which emphasized inner communion with the divine. Direct experience of spiritual reality, Spiritualists said, was a far better foundation for religious authority than the experiences and dicta of others. "We are seeking," wrote Robert Hallock, "to establish *individual observation, personal experience,* and a *living revelation* flowing immediately from heaven into our own souls, as the basis of our religious knowledge and faith, in place of the bare record of such facts and revelations said to have been enjoyed by other men." Thus John Shoebridge Williams, an admirer of Swedenborg's writings, boasted to his son in October 1852 that he had ceased consulting them since his discovery of his own mediumistic powers eight months before.[39]

George Dexter spotlighted Spiritualism's primitivist dimension in the course of arguing that "a present and direct intercourse with the spiritual world" was an essential aspect of a vital religious life. He excoriated the ministry for denying "modern revelations" and suggesting that evidence of the outpouring of God's spirit was confined to Christian antiquity and therefore to be sought only in the New Testament. Like other Spiritualists, he claimed to be restoring a pure Christianity characterized by a close connection between the individual and the spiritual world, direct contact between human beings and spirit messengers, and a lack of artificial institutional embodiment. While Christian and rationalistic Spiritualists quarreled over the relevance of the Bible for progressing spirits, they concurred with each other (and with Mormon restorationists) that it was not the final revelation to the human race and insisted that spiritual freedom required "modern revelations." John S. Adams and other Spiritualists eager to identify their religion with early Christianity agreed that inspiration was "a perpetual fact."[40]

As Spiritualists looked for authority to spirit "revelations," their loyalty to institutional structures of authority and ministerial leadership correspondingly weakened. Sidestepping church and clergy, Spiritualism was potentially and often practically antithetical to human religious institutions in general and to a professional ministry in particular. Isaac Post, whose belief in an inner light easily carried over from Quakerism to Spiritualism, commented that "when a man comes to listen to a Spirit director within his own mind, he will have less need of one without him." One of the most important results of spirit communication, said O. G. Warren, was its *"setting free the minds of men"* not only from the fear of death but also from "the dictation of despotic priests."[41]

The experience of John Shoebridge Williams well illustrates the rebellious substitution of personal spirit communication for "external" and "artificial" forms of religious authority. To be sure, his quest for spiritual independence pushed him to an extreme reclusiveness rarely matched by other Spiritualists and reminiscent of Transcendentalist Henry David Thoreau's withdrawal to Walden Pond. But his exaggerated individualism dramatizes the applicability to Spiritualists of the theory—long a truism among historians, sociologists, and anthropologists of religion—that a pronounced cultivation of inner spirituality tends to weaken the social bonds of organized religious institutions.

Williams's story is in many ways typical of those who became Spiritualists. Born in 1790 and raised a Quaker, he left the Society of Friends in 1827 amid intense infighting between Hicksites and conservatives; his father's spirit later told him that "he had kept me from the sectarianism of Friends." By the late 1830s he had become a devotee of Swedenborgian doctrine, but his relationship with New Church officials was turbulent. He resented "the arrogant claims of the preachers" in the New Church. In particular, Thomas Worcester, long-time leader of the Boston New Jerusalem Society, had been "ruined by wealth, by place, by worldly honors, by the associating with the so called aristocracy." As a Spiritualist, Williams told Worcester in 1853 that he preferred a religious system which "levels all church distinctions, all ordinations, all laying on of hands, . . . and capabilities of being mediums." Because of his independence of spirit, he realized, he was "never . . . able to settle himself in any society of christians, though he is socially inclined."[42]

He first became involved with Spiritualism in October 1851, after attending a circle held by the Fox sisters in Cincinnati. He soon became a convert, consulting mediums and believing himself to be in contact with the spirit of his daughter Eliza, who had died of consumption in 1846. By February 1852 he discovered his own mediumistic powers and began to keep a detailed journal of his dialogues with Eliza, his regular spirit "monitor." What followed was a withdrawal of this "socially inclined" Spiritualist into an individual and outspokenly self-reliant mediumship. Its earliest form was only mildly atomistic, consisting not so much of a total withdrawal as of a reduction of social contact and institutionalized religious practice to small groups. Eliza advised him on April 3, 1852, that he and other Spiritualists should form small and mutually isolated circles which met "secluded to yourselves."[43]

Even at this very early stage of Williams's development as a medium, however, signs of a more thoroughgoing individualism were apparent. Like Emerson, who wrote that society destroys the individuality of its members, Eliza advised that public opposition to Spiritualism threatened "the good influences that your individual states admit of good spirits having upon you." This tendency soon manifested itself more fully. Eliza began to wean Williams away from the *Spirit Messenger,* a Spiritualist periodical which he had read regularly. "We have our peculiar function to perform," she told him on March 30. Therefore he should "be cautious how you let your mind run after what is given through other mediums," for such communications "cannot be so suitable for you, as that which is given to yourself." Eliza warned him again about six weeks later that it was "very dangerous for you to turn to others."[44]

Within a few months, mediumistic self-reliance had led Williams to withdraw even from contact with small groups of Spiritualists and to seek the Spiritualist equivalent of what Emerson had called "voices which we hear in solitude." By August 25, he had retreated from public religious activity and joined other insurgent religious groups of the period in adopting a position of "sola Scriptura." He was "not allowed by my spirit friends to sit in any circle, nor to read any books or papers on [Spiritualism] or any other subject save and except the Bible. . . . I am almost wholly ignorant of what is communicated by or through other mediums. I am kept almost entirely recluse though in the centre of a populous city and for reasons that to myself are satisfactory." Seeking even further seclusion, he wrote on September 30 that he was considering "removing to a room more retired so that we could be more to ourselves" and away from worldly influences. Though Williams balked at such isolation—he hoped that the company of "internal men" might not be detrimental to his spiritual growth—he acted on his monitor's advice that excessive socializing with mortals would distract him from inner contemplation. He even expressed a willingness to "retire from mankind altogether." Spirit communication bound Williams to the authority of spirits as it freed him from "detrimental" social contact and external religious authority. Amid the bustle of antebellum Cincinnati, he found his Walden Pond.[45] Not all Spiritualists sequestered themselves as thoroughly as Williams did, but they were on similar quests.

The Democratization of Spiritual Experience

Williams wrote hopefully of a time when everyone would have a spiritual "monitor" and "know the Lord for himself." He and other Spiritualists recognized that the spirit world would have to be directly accessible to all if spiritual liberation were to be universally realized. Most of them believed that spirit communication did have, or would eventually have, this democratic dimension. Rejecting the exclusivity of special spiritual gifts in the name of republican equality, they (as John Humphrey Noyes put it) "Americanized" Swedenborg on this point. Like Davis and many other Spiritualists, Williams strategically invoked the spirit of the Swedish Seer in arguing that mediumship was not confined "to those called mediums as a separate class of men and women" but was rather "the privalege [sic] of all."[46]

For Spiritualists, the promise of democratized spirit communication made Spiritualism the only suitable religion for a democratic republic. John Edmonds, an ex-Quaker friendly to democratized notions of religious experience, felt offended by the special status accorded such religious mystics as Swedenborg and George Fox. He denied that Fox and Swedenborg were any different from other human beings and bristled at the idea that their spiritual gifts were "peculiar and exclusive." An advocate of equal access to mystical experience, he considered it an unfortunate effect of sectarianism that such experience and the resulting religious authority were confined to "a favored few." O. G. Warren, who co-edited the Spiritualist journal *Sacred Circle* with Edmonds, likewise called for a democratic diffusion of religious authority. He rejected claims by "the priesthood, as well as kings . . . to rule by right divine" and applied the lesson of the American Revolution to Spiritualist mediumship:

> There seems to have been no bad result from this change [the Revolution], and I think it would be as well to democratize religion in the same manner. The host of heaven (for so I style the spirits who are engaged in this cause) seem to be of this way of thinking, for they go about creating priests from the ranks of the laity, sovereigns from the people, until they bid fair to make us all priests and kings unto the Lord. In Spiritualism you see the engine that shall revolutionize and democratize religion.

The few Spiritualists who took antidemocratic positions had to answer to defenders of spiritual republicanism. When J. R. Orton suggested in the New York Spiritualist Conference that "safe" mediumship could be practiced only by those with special training, Robert Hallock asked "*when* and *how* is it that man [is] to become free, if it be *unsafe* for him to look into the spirit-world for himself?" Joel Tiffany, a Cleveland attorney whose concern for independent thinking colored his Spiritualist editing and lecturing, insisted that "every individual who would understand the truths of the Spiritual world must be his or her own medium." The alternative, Uriah Clark pointed out, was that people would become dangerously dependent on others "as though they were under the guidance of an arbitrary priesthood."[47]

American Spiritualists understood their nation as the place where democratic mediumship would first be realized, thus putting their own twist on the cultural premise that the United States had a special religious identity, mission, and destiny. Thomas Lake Harris was certain that the rise of Spiritualism constituted the religious dimension of America's emergent national character. He declared that "whatever tends to render man sternly self-reliant . . . prepares him to be a Spiritual medium" and predicted that "THIS CONTINENT IS DESTINED TO BE INHABITED BY A GRAND CLAIRVOYANT NATION." Andrew Jackson Davis likewise hoped for a "New Era" to be "born through the political and spiritual revolutions of America" and characterized by widespread spirit communication and "perfect faith in the divinity of every man." According to Warren Chase, "democracy in government" and "Spiritualism in religion" were the inevitable and interlinked results of a historical evolution in which the Revolution had been a pivotal event and of which American Spiritualists like himself were the advance guard. Chase, Davis, and Harris understood Spiritualism in much the same way that other American religious primitivists of the period understood their own efforts: as the harbinger of a revolutionary new religious order that would substitute the spirituality of nature for the incrustations of the past, as the consummation of spiritual republicanism, and as the definitive expression of the nation's religious character.[48]

As spiritual republicans, Spiritualists insisted not only on equal access to the spirit world but also on the basic spiritual equality of every individual. All people shared the same inner divine qualities. Andrew Jackson Davis considered it "an incontrovertible proposition" that "every soul is constructed upon identical principles, contains the same elements, and is capable of analogous manifestations. No man," he continued, "is gifted intrinsically above another." The simultaneous belief that the spirit world was hierarchically organized constituted only an apparent contradiction; the hierarchy was merely a temporary result of differing rates and stages of spiritual progress, doomed to disappear when spirits reached their common destiny of spiritual perfection. Robert Hare could therefore consider the hierarchically arranged world of spirits "the *beau ideal* of a republic." Spiritualists here equalized or "Americanized" a conception of the afterlife which in its more purely Swedenborgian form postulated a static and permanent hierarchy of spirits.[49]

Even those Spiritualists who doubted that everybody was equally capable of direct communication with spirits expressed their doubts in a manner compatible with the ideals of spiritual equality and democratic mediumship. This strategy usually involved a distinction between the "phenomenal" mediumship practiced by some and a more universal and important inner communion with the spirit world. Medium Emma Hardinge suggested that true mediumship consisted in participation in a universal "chain of thought" or "inspiration" which like Emerson's Oversoul connects all souls and in which "each creature receives its appropriate share of inspiration." She considered this sort of mediumship, open to all, to be far superior to "mere external phenomena." Addressing the often-asked question "why can not I be a medium?," another Spiritualist acknowledged that not all people were suited to "*externally sensible* communication with spirits" but noted "a kind of orderly mediumship which all may in a sensible degree possess." Attainable through "pure and holy" living, this "most valuable kind of mediumship" involved the manifestation not of any "*particular* Spirit" but of "all good Spirits, . . . and of the Infinite and Eternal Spirit." Uriah Clark's *Plain Guide to Spiritualism* distinguished thirty-one varieties of mediumship, including mediumistic writing and speaking, saving for last a "normal" mediumship that was "without any external signs." Clark assured his readers that this type of mediumship, unlike the others, required no special gifts but simply drew on "the all-pervading atmosphere of the spirit-world" to produce a "calm, deep consciousness of angel guardianship."[50]

The imperatives of spiritual republicanism led most Spiritualists to advocate the "inversion of authority" that Nathan O. Hatch has identified as a crucial element in American religious life during the decades after the Revolution. Like their contemporaries, many Spiritualists questioned the earlier assumption that truth was more likely to be found at the upper than the lower reaches of society. By encouraging independence and resistance to authority, the Revolution had worked to subvert an older social and religious order based on rank, hierarchy, and deference. Increasing numbers of antebellum Americans believed that religious insight and experience were not confined to an aristocratic and learned few, and Spiritualists were quick to point out that mediumship was independent of social class and status. John Shoebridge Williams, who had criticized the elite leadership of Boston's New Church during his Swedenborgian days, was particularly vocal in defending mediumship by the "common" person. "Ministering mediums," spirit voices told him, were best chosen from the ranks of the "simple minded and . . . unlearned ones" who were not excessively mindful of their social standing. They alone could speak freely without fear of how the "fashionable circles" and "best of society" would react. Well aware of his own "lack of a classical education," he lamented that people still seemed to "want some D.D. or LLD or Prof. to teach them." He felt confident, however, that the religious future lay in "those beloved little communications from departed loved one[s] coming in their unlearned fisherman, publican simplicity."[51]

Similarly, the Society for the Diffusion of Spiritual Knowledge (SDSK), established in June 1854 by a group of prominent New York Spiritualists, was criticized for its socially top-heavy membership. Eliab W. Capron, who promoted the Fox sisters in New York City and became one of the movement's earliest publicists and historians, was quite disappointed with it. A Congregational Quaker who had been involved with Spiritualism from its socially humble inception in rural New York and attended séances with the Fox family and Amy and Isaac Post, he was saddened by the "strange absence of old and tried friends" in the SDSK. It seemed more interested in a "display of learned professions and great names" than in recruiting "the earliest and most experienced in the investigation." Another critic, mindful of Christianity's unpretentious beginnings, pointedly noted that the SDSK included "governors, senators, lawyers, merchants, and manufacturers" but "not so much as *one carpenter* or *fisherman*." Such critics sensed in the Society an aristocratic threat to Christian humility and republican values.[52]

A commitment to spiritual egalitarianism led Spiritualists to join Quakers in rejecting the idea of special ministerial status. The fact of spiritual equality, said R. P. Ambler, "effectually forbids the institution of any oracular authority" over others. Ex-Quaker J. H. Robinson insisted that neither a "special priesthood" nor any other ecclesiastical structure of authority was necessary since all people were "responsive to the great invisible Heart" and "recipients of a common inspiration." Wanting "no man between God and our souls," he thanked Christ for "thy leveling, republican gospel!" Another Spiritualist saw Christ not as a "monopolizer" of religious experience but as "the great Apostle of Democracy."[53] At Adin Ballou's Hopedale community, the principles of spiritual republicanism were built into the regulations and put into practice. Community bylaws stipulated that the community "shall never assume to commission, appoint or forbid any person to preach the gospel or to act as a public religious and moral teacher, but shall always leave that matter to the conscience and judgment of individuals." Those who did act as ministers were to be placed "on a level of temporal subsistence with the generality of their fellow members." To be sure, these laws were adopted before the rise of the Spiritualist movement. Still, they indicated the democratic mood that proved conducive to Spiritualism in the nation at large and at Hopedale in particular. Ballou and other Spiritualists not only spiritualized republicanism but republicanized spirituality.[54]

Spiritualism's opposition to a special clerical caste, both a cause and an effect of its appeal to such ex-Quakers as Amy and Isaac Post, John W. Edmonds, J. H. Robinson, and John Shoebridge Williams, was highlighted in Charles Partridge's editorial sketch of an ideal "Church of the Future." Convinced that worship in most churches was too often dominated by a single person whose religious training had not encouraged living inspiration and faith, he called for a "new Church service" in which "all will be invited to take part." Religious meetings, he argued, should be "edified by the spontaneity of thoughts rather than by a hired priesthood set apart for that purpose." This style of worship, which assumed spiritual equality and lacked a special ministry, resembled the Quaker meeting and would probably have appealed to the radical Quakers who were among Spiritualism's first converts.[55]

Spiritualists' aversion to clerical authority and exaltation of the laity led a number of them to approve the "laymen's revival" of 1857–1858 in spite of their distaste for the evangelical-led revivals of earlier decades. At a session of the New York Spiritualist Conference devoted to this revival, J. R. Orton observed that it was "more of a spontaneity" and "less under clerical management" than earlier ones. "The masses take the lead" while the clergy "seem to hang on, or to be carried along with it, rather than, as heretofore, to be its motive power." Andrew Jackson Davis, too, was encouraged that the revival "was commenced, and has been carried on, chiefly by the people, and not the priests." The result, he said, was a more genuine religious experience since participants in earlier revivals had been converted psychologically and artificially to "the *man*" rather than spiritually and naturally to a true love of God. Furthermore, the current revival lacked the strongly sectarian flavor and purposes of earlier revivals. The 1857–1858 meetings, then, unlike those of previous years, served the cause of spiritual freedom rather than clerical despotism by transferring religious authority and leadership from a professional and privileged clergy to the laity.[56]

Spiritual democratization could lead to claims not only that no one had a right to wield special ministerial authority over another, but also to the very different idea (with very different implications, as we shall see later) that anybody could exercise such authority. Many Spiritualists urged that quasi-clerical functions and status ought to be as open as access to the spirit world and staked their claims accordingly.[57] Anyone who felt so inspired by the spirits, the argument went, should be permitted to preach freely regardless of professional status and training. This stance, hostile to a formal clergy and to the notion that ministerial authority could derive from a merely artificial institution, had deep roots in American religious culture and figured prominently in the antebellum democratization of religious authority.

Self-styled inspirational leaders therefore populated Spiritualism much as they did the other "insurgent" religions of the period. Thomas Lake Harris used the ideas of spiritual equality and inner divinity to assert the superfluity of a formalized church and his "right to the pulpit" on the basis of spirit inspiration. "I must utter the thoughts that burn within me," he told an audience of Spiritualists in May 1854, "if not in the pulpit as recognized by external men, then in my own hired room, in the woods, or wherever two or three are gathered together." He understood himself as a harbinger of the new "Ministry of the Spirit" that was "at hand" and disapproved of Swedenborgian and Catholic ordination practices which assumed that the power to confer priestly authority was lodged in the hands of mere mortals. Reformer Warren Chase, a deist and rationalist before converting to Spiritualism, "turned preacher" when he began lecturing on behalf of his new faith and was proud that in the autumn of 1852 "the dispensation of the new gospel absorbed his time." He took comfort from his belief that "the voices of his [spirit] guardians were ever urging him on" in his self-appointed ministry. Trance speaker Charlotte Beebe Wilbour joined Harris and Chase in contrasting the open Spiritualist lecture platform, which she called a "democratic pulpit," with the "dictatorial and authoritative" pulpit of the institutional church.[58]

As a woman who would have been barred from religious authority and public speaking by all but a few denominations and sects, Wilbour had even more to gain from spiritual republicanism than did men like Harris and Chase. Since the spirits, like the Holy Spirit to which Quakers looked for inspiration, were no respecter of gender, Spiritualism joined Quakerism among the few religions of the antebellum period that encouraged women to speak publicly (though Spiritualist women usually claimed to speak in a trance condition) and to assume positions of religious authority as inspirational lecturers. As Ann Braude has pointed out, the individualistic element of the Spiritualist ideology formed the basis of a close historical relationship between Spiritualism and the emergent women's rights movement.[59]

Like the Spiritualist podium, the Spiritualist press served as a democratic platform for the expression of opinions and ideas. Braude has noted that Spiritualist newspapers continued a tradition of democratic journalism exemplified by the radical abolitionist paper the *Liberator,* whose editor, William

Lloyd Garrison, became a Spiritualist sympathizer in the 1850s. The connection here is more than coincidence. A belief that free inquiry and expression was the best route to truth was important to both Spiritualism, in which séance investigators were supposed to explore the manifestations and become convinced for themselves, and the ideal of democratic journalism. Like Garrison's *Liberator,* many if not all Spiritualist newspapers claimed to be champions of freedom of opinion and independent judgment. The *Spiritual Telegraph,* for instance, ran an editorial defending "Freedom of Conscience" in an early issue. Brittan, the editor, denounced any attempt to deny an individual the right to hold and articulate his or her views as "*a flagrant outrage against the just prerogatives of the human mind, an open violation of the precepts and spirit of the Christian Religion, and utterly subversive of the essential principles of Republican Liberty.*" Papers like the *Telegraph* claimed to provide the movement's members with "a Free Platform" for their inspirations. Like the lectern, the Spiritualist periodical was to be a vehicle of spiritual republicanism. The *Sacred Circle* symbolized this commitment when it published an extract from a 1776 defense of the rights of conscience and private judgment by Revolutionary patriot Samuel Adams.[60]

While both spiritual republicanism and claims of spirit communication pervaded the religious life of antebellum America, Spiritualists carved out a distinctive cultural niche by bringing them together. As we saw in the previous chapter, the New Church declared that divine revelations had ceased with Swedenborg, tried to discourage communication with spirits, reacted sharply against episodes of widespread spiritualistic activity within Swedenborgian ranks, and centralized religious authority in its ministry. Other religious movements of the period involving spirit communication in some form, such as Shakerism and Mormonism, likewise avoided intertwining it with a democratized notion of religious authority. Joseph Smith's claim to exclusive contact with the spirit world and his ongoing function as revelator resulted in an arrogation of all religious authority to himself and a tightly organized and centralized sect. Shaker leaders similarly channeled their movement's spiritualistic episode of the 1830s and 1840s toward a revitalization of existing institutions and a strengthening of their authority. Spiritualist J. R. Buchanan, in fact, singled out these two groups for criticism on the grounds that they used spirit communication for authoritarian purposes. He and other Spiritualists outspokenly opposed any religious movement, even those that assumed the reality of spirit communication, that appeared to violate the tenets of spiritual republicanism.[61]

But their aversion to authority had its limits. These spiritual revolutionaries exhibited a conservative uneasiness about the excesses to which liberty, individualism, and decentralization might be carried. As noted at the outset of this chapter, Spiritualists understood republican freedom to mean not anarchy but a proper balance between liberty and order. Spiritual rebellion, Uriah Clark warned, should not foster "anarchy and licentiousness" or encourage a dangerous rejection of "all authority, all restraint . . . all laws and institutions . . . all beliefs and religious order." Like other spiritual republicans, Spiritualists reconstituted rather than repudiated authority. Their calls for self-reliance were grounded in a belief that they had found a higher authority in the framework of a cosmic spiritual community. Indeed, their strident antistructural manifestoes betrayed an inability to conceive of the spiritual universe in any but ecclesiastical terms, an irony of which more thoroughly anti-institutional Transcendentalists like Emerson were well aware. The result, we shall see, was a body of ideas and practices reminiscent of the tightly organized religions of the period and at odds with the rhetoric of spiritual individualism. Spiritualists' declarations of independence hardly involved an entire abandonment of religious order.[62]

◆┼◆

4

The Structure of the Spirit World

The Cosmic Institution

When the imperatives of spiritual republicanism led John S. Adams to declare his independence of the Chestnut Street Church, he was not simply "coming out" of a religious institution. The rhetoric of republican freedom and individualism which suffused his published manifesto was interspersed with language of a very different kind. Explaining his withdrawal, he expressed his preference for God's own "church," which was "as broad as his limitless universe" and had "foundations lying deeper than human plummet ever reached." His reference to the universe as a church with structural "foundations" suggests that this free spirit was in fact "weary of its pilgrimage," seeking haven from "darkness and doubts." Adams wanted not just to "come out" of his church but also to "come in" to some substitute for it.[1]

This need for spiritual shelter and structure was central to Spiritualist religion. Medium Charles Hammond heard spirit voices say that their object was "not . . . to destroy, but to establish," not "to lay waste" but "to build up." A convention of Spiritualists in Massachusetts resolved that their movement's "*constructive* element . . . teaches us that while it may be necessary to *tear down the old,* our great work is, after all, to *build up*—to construct a new world of thought, of feeling, and of life." Emma Hardinge offered a distinctly Spiritualist articulation of the constructive processes that always accompany the destructive impulses of religious "antistructure":

> it is for the purpose of initiating the great church of the universe, for building up the great altar of the human heart, for installing the high priest, God himself, and bringing into your visible presence the ministering acolytes, that beings who are in the experience of immortality, who

> know spirituality as a reality, have manifested their presence to you. . . .
> modern Spiritualism has come, not to break down your religions, but to
> build them on the Rock of Ages—not to subvert your churches, but to
> build one large enough to contain the great, round, rushing world—not
> to take away aught that is good, but to give you that truth that shall
> make you free.

Despite their discomfort with institutionalized religion, Spiritualists understood their preferred alternative in institutional and ecclesiastical terms. Like
other antebellum primitivist groups, they showed as intense a concern with
ecclesiastical order as with spiritual liberty and embarked on a "quest for pure
forms." Abandoning "artificial" religious structures, they believed—much
like other contemporary practitioners of what Catherine L. Albanese has
called "nature religion"—that they were entering a "natural" religious institution less constricting but no less structured. A lack of institutional affiliation
evidently created a void which their theological imaginations filled through
spirit communication and the feeling of belonging to a larger and more real,
if also invisible, religious community.[2]

Metaphorical comparisons of the spirit world to human institutions are as
old as the idea of a spirit world itself. In this respect, the Spiritualist vision was
simply a variation on an ancient theme. But that vision was shaped and
enhanced by two features of antebellum American culture. One was a
commitment to the ideals of spiritual republicanism. Those who subscribed to
the ideology of republicanism were convinced that individual freedom had to
be limited in the interest of social order, that democracy had its dangers. In
spiritual terms, republicanism meant containing the spontaneity of a free soul,
whose natural growth required a minimization of external restraints, within a
framework of discipline for the sake of its orderly development. The second
was the related conviction, common in antebellum reform thought, that the
proper development of the individual required a morally wholesome, strictly
controlled, and thoroughly institutionalized social environment.

The importance attached to institutional environments by antebellum
Spiritualists was best expressed by Andrew Jackson Davis as he considered the
relationship between "individualism" and "institutionalism." Although he
warned against artificial institutions as impediments to development, he
acknowledged "a degree of Institutionalism which is natural to man, in all
stages of growth, and absolutely necessary to that growth—viz., the Institution of THE GREAT HARMONIUM." The "great harmonium" or spiritual universe
constructed by Spiritualists offered the comforts of a "natural" church and
"natural" religious authority. It was on this conceptual foundation that they
based their often antiformalistic behavior. As spiritual republicans, they
understood order and freedom as facets of a single ideal; individual liberty

meant self-realization within an overarching social, spiritual, and moral construct. Individualism and institutionalism, then, went hand in hand. As anxious to avoid anarchy as despotism, they sought an ordered freedom and found it in an institutional cosmos.[3]

The Spiritualist universe was above all a structured and ordered place. Its central architectural feature, and a metaphor crucial to their visions of the spirit world and the physical world alike, was the circle or sphere. Spiritualists conceived of the spirit world as a series of concentric "spheres," thus imagining themselves within a highly organized and centralized construct (see illustration 1). In this, they drew on an ancient tradition of scientific, philosophical, and religious thought appropriated by early Christian thinkers (particularly Neoplatonists) and transmitted through Swedenborg. The circle and sphere served in Spiritualist religion as what Clifford Geertz has called "sacred symbols." That is, they functioned "to synthesize a people's ethos—the tone, character, and quality of their life, its moral and aesthetic mood—and their world view—the picture they have of the way things in sheer actuality are, their most comprehensive ideas of order."[4]

Following Swedenborg, Spiritualists divided their spiritual universe into seven hierarchically arranged and concentric "spheres." At the center of these spheres or the top of the hierarchy was God. The source of all life and force, God emanated "influences" which radiated outward from the metaphysical center of the universe, passed through the hierarchy of spheres, and finally reached the lowest corporeal and terrestrial beings. Occupying the seven spheres, that vast spiritual and moral space between the deity and the outermost reaches of the universe, were finite spiritual beings who embraced a virtually infinite number of degrees of development. These spirits passed on the influences they received from those above them in the hierarchy to those below. Souls initially assumed a position in the spheres corresponding to the level of development attained on earth—a position which was not pleasant for those whose terrestrial behavior warranted some period of contrition—and then progressively and inevitably advanced toward perfection as they grew spiritually under the influences (or, to use Swedenborg's term, "influxes") of higher spirits. But while the progressing spirit's ultimate destiny was, in Edmonds's words, "return toward the source whence it sprang," a commitment to individualism led Spiritualists to resist final and total union with God. As spirit Swedenborg explained to Edmonds's circle, the return of the soul to its source "does not suppose it necessary that the Godhead should absorb it within itself." Rather, "each germ possesses specialty," has a "separate existence," and "stands in its own individuality free."[5]

The Spiritualist emphasis on gradual spiritual growth was part of a "kinetic revolution" in nineteenth-century Western culture and thought in which the world was conceived in developmental terms and motion became increas-

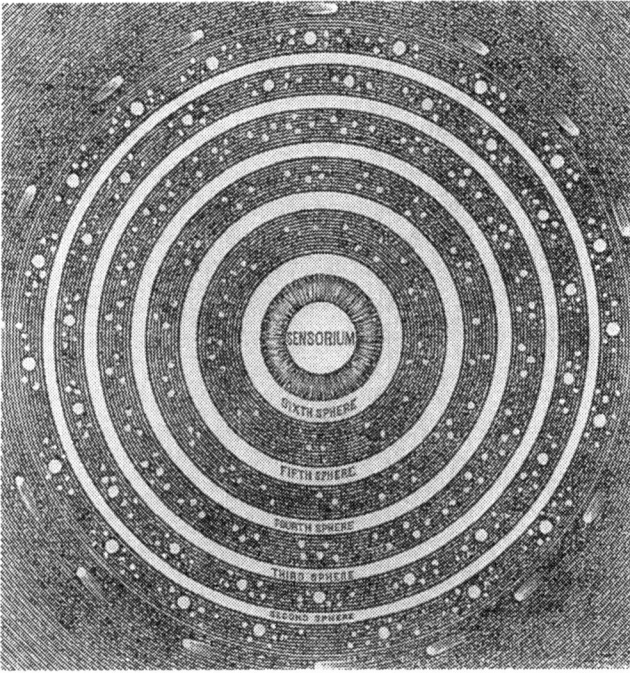

Illustration 1: Andrew Jackson Davis's "Diagram of the Spiritual Spheres." This image suggests the importance of the concepts of the circle, hierarchy, and centralized authority in Spiritualist ideology, as well as the idea of correspondence between the physical and spiritual realms.

ingly accentuated at the expense of stasis. Conceptions of the next world as well as this one were affected by this trend; heaven became less a place of static bliss and more a place of activity and progressive improvement.[6] More particularly, Spiritualist developmentalism resonated with the trend in American religious liberalism away from the concept of a single and sudden life-altering conversion experience and toward progressive notions of the soul's destiny. Echoing Horace Bushnell, a Congregationalist theologian whose *Views of Christian Nurture* (1847) emphasized gradual spiritual growth and urged parents to cultivate their childrens' souls, Spiritualists virtually ignored the idea of conversion and understood spiritual life as an ongoing process of nurture and orderly development under the tutelage of parentlike spirits.

Spiritualists considered advanced spirits superior to the mortals of earth and to any spirits below them in the cosmic hierarchy. There were many dimensions to this superiority. Most fundamentally, higher spirits occupied a higher position in a universal system of cause and effect in which relative proximity to deity involved causal priority and a powerful influence over those below. But the spiritual hierarchy also involved spiritual, moral, and even social status. Like other antebellum Americans who feared the potentially unsettling and atomizing effects of a society that seemed uncomfortably unstructured, Spiritualists trying to imagine the structure of the spirit world hearkened back to the older notions of social order and hierarchy which had shaped the republican model of society and the notion of a "great chain of being" that pervaded nineteenth-century Western biological discourse.[7] They combined these with Swedenborg's vision of the afterlife to produce an elaborately structured, thoroughly stratified, and precisely arranged cosmos well suited to their need for order. Andrew Jackson Davis summed up the idea of a hierarchical and mediatorial order binding the universe into a harmonious socio-spiritual whole:

> In truth, there is a *great* sphere of spiritual existences, which, touching it, girdle the material sphere, a part of which we are at present existing in; and again, encircling that sphere, are a galaxy of greater spheres, more refined and more magnificent; which are inhabited by spirits, drawn onward by the eternal magnet of Supreme Goodness. Thus there is a chain extending from man to Deity!

John Murray Spear called it "a connected channel of influx,—one general principle of giving and receiving from highest to lowest."[8]

In this conception of the universe as a hierarchically arranged mediatorial order lay the most comprehensive meaning of mediumship in the Spiritualist ideology. Each spirit was a channel of spiritual influence and divine activity, a "medium" between those that affected it and those that it affected. To be sure, the narrower definition of mediumship, namely the process by which spirits were believed to communicate with mortals through the instrumentality of some specially suited person, has received more attention from scholars. But the broader sense, referring to the modus operandi of the spiritual universe, was at least as important to Spiritualist religion. It constituted the mechanism of divine influence, the spiritual and social glue of the cosmos. Adin Ballou expressed this broader understanding when he described the universe as "one vast complication of mediumship" in which the "higher and lower . . . are linked together by intervening grades." Popular medium and trance speaker Cora Hatch, too, understood mediumship to be the very life force of the universe. She regarded her career as a medium, which began in Wisconsin in 1851 when she was eleven and soon developed into a national speaking tour, as a high calling which connected mortals with the fundamental spiritual forces of the cosmos. The central point of her "philosophical investigation of the nature of mediumship," published when she was seventeen, was that "nature itself is mediatorial."[9]

Spiritualist theorists, most of whom were male, imposed order on their spirit world not only by looking to earlier ideals of social hierarchy but also by applying to their conception of cosmic mediumship the notions of gender hierarchy which structured social relationships in antebellum America.

They took an important cue from Swedenborg, whose sharply gendered spiritual universe operated through a combination of what he considered the feminine principle of love and the masculine principle of wisdom. The ideology of gender hierarchy pervaded their descriptions of the functioning of the cosmic institution. Higher spirits were understood as "masculine" relative to lower ones, whose role in the mediatorial exchange was identified with the "feminine" traits of receptivity, passivity, and submission. By means of this system, spirit was thought by virtually all proponents of Spiritualist religion to pervade (or, to use their terms, "penetrate" or "impregnate") the natural world and, as mentioned above, to exercise causal control over it. In the words of John Murray Spear, "the spirit-world being impregnative,—the world of causes,—it affects or controls the negative or receptive world." "Throughout all nature," he believed, "the *female and male principles* are exhibited." Some Spiritualists joined the Shakers in suggesting not only an androgynous universe but a bisexual God; "the Mind of all minds," said Spear, is "both feminine and masculine."[10]

To be sure, this notion of a male-female deity suggested gender equality and hence the leveling potential of the Spiritualist ideology. Indeed, status and power in the Spiritualist universe were a function of spiritual elevation rather than of sex, Spiritualists often advocated women's rights, and Spiritualists like Shakers placed women in positions of religious authority. Still, they did not question the identification of dominance with masculinity and submission with femininity by which antebellum Americans justified less equitable gender relationships. Moreover, many of them continued to apply the masculine label to the first cause, stopping short of declaring a father-mother deity. Andrew Jackson Davis, among others, distinguished "Father-God," the final source of causation, from "Mother-Nature," the body of the universe and the object of divine causation. While the Spiritualist universe was considered both masculine and feminine in its operations, the male component was clearly envisioned in a dominant role in keeping with Victorian notions of social order. Thus Spiritualists combined liberal and conservative notions of the gender of deity, notions of cosmic androgyny and of masculine dominance, in their search for cosmic order.[11]

Spirit and the Natural Order

Spiritualists constructing an ordered spirit world also looked to science, which antebellum Americans believed had reduced the physical world to a comprehensible system of law and order. Not all Spiritualists had flirted with deism—a religious outlook that was grounded in natural law and human reason and enjoyed considerable popularity in America during the decades after 1820—but a deistic religious sensibility pervaded Andrew Jackson Davis's *Principles of Nature* and became an important element in Spiritualist religion.[12] Spiritualists were convinced that science, which enjoyed a growing cultural authority during the nineteenth century and seemed capable of wondrous advances, could not only prove the existence of spirit but also provide clues about its nature. Their almost worshipful attitude toward science, virtually unlimited estimate of its capabilities, belief in the underlying harmony and order of the universe, Swedenborgian concept of "correspondence" or parallelism between the material and spiritual worlds, and belief with most antebellum scientists that analogical reasoning could guide them reliably from the seen to the unseen fueled their expectation that the lawful natural order revealed by science could be extended from the physical realm to the spiritual realm. They therefore applied the ideas and vocabulary of the physical sciences to their understanding of spirit, tapping the epistemological authority of empirically based knowledge to suit their religious ideology to the demands of a scientific age.[13]

Indeed, their attempt to extend their conceptions of scientific order to the realm of spirit led them to blur the line between the physical and the spiritual. As suggested in chapter 2, they like Transcendentalists followed Swedenborg in substituting a "correspondential" worldview, in which the realms of sacred and profane were ultimately merged and causality was understood to operate along a spectrum, for the more traditional and sharply dualistic "causal" one in which sacred and profane realities were sharply separated and a simple cause-and-effect relationship was assumed to exist between them.[14] Anxious to bring spirit within the domain of science and convinced with orthodox scientists that matter alone was amenable to empirical methods, they merged spirit with matter by insisting on its materiality. Following Swedenborg, they replaced a spirit/matter dichotomy with a hierarchical spectrum in which the ordinary matter detectable by the senses shaded off into higher and more elusive forms and higher spirits were composed of a finer matter than lower ones. As one Spiritualist explained, "the whole universal creation . . . is entirely, and without exception, composed of matter in thousands and tens of thousands of different shapes, figures, and forms, more or less refined, rarefied, and elevated."[15] Far from feeling uncomfortable with the notion of material spirit, Spiritualists took comfort in its implication that the spirit world was within the reach of science, was subject to natural law, and was therefore an orderly and comprehensible place. As believers in correspondence, they were conversely reassured that the orderly harmony of the invisible world was operating to shape the visible world around them.[16]

It was also mentioned in chapter 2 that Spiritualists joined Transcendentalists in entirely obliterating the category of supernatural. They argued that nothing lay outside of the realm of divine order and conceived only of a single Nature whose spiritual and physical dimensions intermingled and operated according to the same principles of natural law. Driven by antebellum cultural currents to fashion a religion they considered scientific and rational, they departed from Mircea Eliade's model of religious experience as a fundamentally suprarational "encounter with the sacred," which "always manifests itself as a reality of a wholly different order from 'natural' realities." Some Spiritualists went as far as to adopt the pantheistic identification of God with nature. Andrew Jackson Davis, for example, could conceive of "nothing outside of, or superior to, that stupendous organization of matter and mind which I am impressed to term, NATURE."[17]

Fired by a sense of mission at once religious and scientistic, Spiritualists moved from this expanded idea of Nature and their belief in material spirit to a broadened understanding of science's scope. They argued in protest against scientific orthodoxy that science, as the study of nature and matter, should free itself from a sense-based epistemology and a narrow concern with the ordinary physical world to include the invisible spiritual sources of causation and inner sources of illumination. Like other antebellum Americans, including orthodox scientists, they thought that scientific and religious concerns were harmonious, converging on the same ultimate truth. But in claiming that science could study the spiritual realm directly, they moved with a wide range of religious theorists of the mid-to-late nineteenth century beyond the traditional notion that the study of the physical world constituted a sufficient contribution by science to religious truth. Most scientists, separating matter from spirit and confining the domain of science to the former, were not nearly so sanguine about their work as the Spiritualist who rhapsodized that a science "freed from all shackles" could pierce "the mystic penetralia of the *Omniscient" and* "determine the nature of that holy and wondrous Essence." S. B. Brittan, who outlined the "Elements of Spiritual Science" in the *Shekinah,* considered the advance of science into these empyrean realms to be part of Spiritualism's "nature and mission." He was convinced that there was more to reality than was dreamed of in conventional sense-based philosophy.[18]

Spiritualists similarly hoped that a "spiritual science" would illuminate the nature of the soul. Davis complained that "materialistic intelligence only seeks for knowledge in the *outer* world," thus "divert[ing] attention from the *inner*-life." R. P. Ambler too anticipated the development of a "science of the soul." The "exploring eye of Science," he lamented, "could not penetrate . . . the sanctuary of the soul" as long as philosophical materialism confined it to "the narrow sphere of sense" and the "realm of physical being." But the "revelation of the spirit-life" had finally "disclosed the true science of the soul as a bright and substantial reality." The empirically minded spirits of Francis

Bacon and, more frequently, Benjamin Franklin, appeared to Spiritualist circles as symbols of this union of science with spirit. It is ironic that Spiritualists, concerned that the rising prestige of science would encourage a neglect of higher spiritual things, battled materialism by suggesting that spirit was matter. But they willingly paid this metaphysical price for incorporating scientific notions of order into their religious ideology, for reconciling science with spirituality, and for achieving a knowledge of "the real cause of all effects" that they believed "makes us free."[19]

Essential to Spiritualists in imagining their scientifically ordered cosmos was their belief in a universally pervasive but invisible fluid called ether. Too attenuated to be detected by scientific instruments, this fluid had been postulated by Isaac Newton early in the eighteenth century to explain electrical and magnetic phenomena. It was accepted by most scientists of the early nineteenth century and assumed by theorists of mesmerism to be the mechanism of universal magnetic activity and the integrating agent of the cosmos. Sharing antebellum Americans' fascination with electricity and magnetism, Spiritualists appropriated the concept from mesmerism and incorporated it into their religious cosmology. Some of them understood it to operate in both the physical and spiritual realms, while others spoke of separate but parallel spiritual and physical ethers. In either case, they followed Newton and their own scientific contemporaries in supposing that this matter was the medium of the divine will and of all spiritual activity. As such, it ordered the cosmos by binding deity, spirit mediators, and mortals in a single system of spiritual influence.

Electricity in particular became for Spiritualists a crucial metaphorical concept in comprehending the operation of the spiritual universe. Indeed, Benjamin Franklin, who symbolized electricity in the minds of many antebellum Americans, was the only non-Spiritualist pictured in Emma Hardinge's history of the movement; he appeared in front of a bolt of lightning. Andrew Jackson Davis called electricity "the vehicle or medium of divine vitality," used by the deity "as a medium of communication to all parts and particles of the universe." Adin Ballou coined the term "spiricity" to denote the medium of spirit activity and influence. He imagined that spirits could "impregnate" this "subtle element" with "their peculiarities of *thought, affection,* and *will*" and "transmit influences to inconceivable distances." Scientist Robert Hare likewise understood electricity as the mechanism of cosmic mediumship and advanced spirits as "electrical conductors, whose attracting points bend downward as well as upward, dispensing, equally, thought and strength to their less harmonious fellows."[20]

Medium John Murray Spear offered an extended discussion of electricity's integrative function in the Spiritualist cosmos. His God was a "GRAND CENTRAL ELECTRICAL FOCUS" from which "ALL ELECTRICITY EMANATES," and he considered electricity to be "the grand instrumentality, the native element, by which all things move." The *élan vital* of the spirit world, it was the mechanism by which higher beings influenced lower ones.

> Between the Grand Central Mind and all inferior minds there subsists a connection, a telegraphic communication, by means of what may be termed an Electric chain, composed of a greater or less number of intermediate links. The greater mind, being always positive to the lesser, can affect, impress, or *inspire* it.

Spear employed the circle metaphor to compare this system to a wheel in which influence passed outward from God, the hub, along the spokes, through the higher spirits nearer the center to the less advanced ones further from it. Awestruck by the recently invented electromagnetic telegraph, which seemed almost miraculously to transmit messages instantaneously over long distances, he termed this mechanism of divine government and spiritual communication the "spirit-telegraph."[21]

Other Spiritualists understood spirit communication in the same way and displayed a similar propensity to attach religious significance to the advance of technology. They saw in the "spirit telegraph" or "celestial telegraph" of which they spoke so often an extension of technology just as they understood Spiritualism itself as an extension of science. They usually credited spirit Franklin for the discovery of this new invention—"Franklin's Discovery of the Rapping Telegraph" was revealed to Andrew Jackson Davis on the day of the epiphany, January 6, 1851—and made him what one scholar has called their "patron saint." *The Spiritual Telegraph* became the title of the movement's premier periodical of the 1850s, which served its readers as a major vehicle of communication within the movement and a purveyor of the truths which they believed were being transmitted from the spirit world. The paper's title, like Spear's discussion, illustrates how Spiritualists used concepts of electrical interconnectedness and telegraphic communication to make their universe into a strong and tightly knit community.[22]

The "electric cosmology" created by Spiritualists in their search for order was virtually identical with the "magnetic cosmology" described by Catherine L. Albanese with reference to mesmerism, its impact on the alternative religious scene of the mid-nineteenth century, and its status as a "nature religion." In their physical reading of the spirit world and their use of physical science to shape their ideology, Spiritualists were fashioning their own unique variety of nature religion. In fact, during the mid-nineteenth century Spiritualism became for many Americans "a leading cultural conduit for nature religion."[23]

Scientist Robert Hare provides an instructive example of Spiritualist attempts to develop a "spiritual science" and a cosmology at once religious and scientific. Before converting to Spiritualism in 1854, he had been for thirty years a professor of chemistry at the University of Pennsylvania, a prolific contributor to the *American Journal of Science,* and, during the 1830s and 1840s, an enthusiastic investigator of electricity and magnetism. Although strongly rationalistic and deistic, he had been influenced by his mother's "sincere" Episcopalianism. He acknowledged the powerful influence of his early education as "an orthodox Christian" and commented late in life that "theology and religion were subjects always near to my heart."[24] His interest in questions of spirit and the afterlife long preceded his first direct consideration of spirit manifestations in 1853. As early as 1842 he had speculated that heaven was located at the center of the universe, and in 1848 he had suggested to the American Association for the Advancement of Science (AAAS) that spirit was a form of matter amenable to scientific analysis. His first response to Spiritualism was to dismiss it as a fraud, but a plea from an old acquaintance, telescope maker Amasa Holcombe, moved him to begin a serious investigation late in 1853. When his experiments convinced him that the phenomena had an intelligent source and that the medium could not possibly have produced them, he felt compelled to conclude that spirits were responsible. Certain that his experiments had left no room for fraud, he became a convert early in 1854.[25]

With the zeal of a new convert, a conviction that Spiritualism would reconcile religion with a "positive science" based on observation and experiment, and the encouragement of Spiritualist promoter S. B. Brittan, Hare became a publicist for the movement. He embarked on a lecture and demonstration tour in 1855, published a letter to the Episcopal clergy, and made an unsuccessful and embittering attempt to put an investigation of spirit manifestations on the agenda of the AAAS. The capstone of his campaign was the publication in 1855 of his *Experimental Investigation of the Spirit Manifestations.* This thick volume opened with a description of his experiments and an argument that Spiritualism was a legitimate concern of empirical science. Hare appended several essays on the nature of matter and his ether-based theory of electromagnetism, previously published in the *American Journal of Science,* since he assumed that "a correspondence" between the physical and spiritual realms allowed an extension of his theories to the spirit world "by analogy." He also proposed an all-pervasive "spiritual ether" as the conductor of the divine will and spirit influence and suggested that manipulations of this ether by spirits was the cause of mediumistic phenomena. But Spiritualist leaders, hoping that he might bring the authority of science into the service of spirituality, were disappointed by the fact that Hare devoted the bulk of his book to issues strictly religious and theological. Partridge and Brittan, who published the book with the intention of enhancing the movement's scientific credentials, were particularly irritated, the latter wishing that Hare had considered Spiritualism "in its relations to science and natural law—instead of mainly regarding its theological bearings." Hare's agenda was evidently different. "I am now more than ever a theologian," he commented, and the content of his *Experimental Investigation* indeed suggests that Spiritualism was more a religion than a science for him. The aging scientist joined other Spiritualists in looking to science for support of a religious worldview in which the spirit world could be understood as a lawful and orderly system.[26]

The Government of the Spirit World

At the heart of the Spiritualists' distinctive worldview, and essential to their notions of cosmic law and order, were the spirit mediators they borrowed from Swedenborg. The spirits, they believed, acted on mortals from above, integrating the universe into a hierarchically organized spiritual whole by serving as the point of contact between humanity and deity. Contact with spirits, then, did much more for religious Spiritualists than provide consolation or proof of immortality. It reinforced their sense of cosmic belonging. It was crucial to their expression of an "esthetic spirituality"—that is, their "consciousness of the beauty of living in harmony with divine things—in a word, being at home in the universe"—which has been a perduring element in American religion.[27]

Spiritualists looked to spirit mediators for cosmic comfort because of alienation not only from the earth at the bottom of the spiritual universe but from the deity at the top. God remained uncomfortably remote to them. Like many other liberal Protestants of the mid-nineteenth century, they harbored serious doubts about the extent of direct divine interaction with the world. Although Andrew Jackson Davis spoke only for rationalistic Spiritualists when he told a New York audience in 1854 that the abstract terms "Deity" and "Divine Mind" were preferable to the more personal term "God," his distressing sense of divine distance was shared even by the more strongly Christian of them. At the same time, however, they were reluctant to bring God into intimate involvement with the universe by embracing the pantheistic notion—which had increasing appeal among theological liberals and was implied by their own blending of natural with supernatural—that God operated on the universe from within rather than from without. The solution to their theological dilemma was to call on the spirits to bridge this perceived gap between God and the universe. Postulating a world of mediating spirits through which God acted on the world, they could have a deity both transcendent and immanent, exalted and involved. But if their universe was unmistakably theocentric, their worldview, focused far more on spirits than on God, was decidedly not.[28]

Spiritualists understood spirits to be the instruments by which a remote deity carried out the divine will and enforced the divine government. According to most of them, and indeed to most antebellum religious liberals, God operated by means of general laws and did not deviate from this "universal providence" to perform particular actions or "special providences." The problem of "special providence" had considerable currency among thinkers concerned with the relationship between God and the universe and with the implications of that relationship for religious faith. For Spiritualists, spirit agency was a ready solution. Andrew Jackson Davis explained in his *Philosophy of Special Providences* (1850) that "the embracing nearness of the Spiritual World, with its accessibleness, furnishes the spirit with every advantage and gratification it should desire, through the mediums of providential dispensations or Divine interposition." John Shoebridge Williams defended a strongly Christian and biblically based Spiritualism and was an outspoken opponent of Davis's anti-Christian position, but he agreed with Davis that God "in His infinity is universal, not special nor finite," and that "by finite angels, spirits, men, &c., it is that the Lord works His special or finite providences."[29]

As agents of day to day divine governance, spirits were responsible for the maintenance of the physical, spiritual, and moral order of the cosmos. This role was vividly portrayed by John W. Edmonds in one of the many detailed allegorical visions which he experienced as a medium. He used metaphors from physical science to describe a group of spirits struggling to prevent a "wayward world" (presumably earth) from flying apart and "to . . . reduce its matter to an orderly obeisance to the laws which were developing it." The function of spirits in this "disturbed and deranged" world was clearly redemptive:

> I saw each spirit acting in his sphere, having a portion of the task to perform, some daringly penetrating even to that burning center, seeking there, at the very seat of the disorder, to overcome its destructive action; others at the extremity of the nebulous matter seeking there to prevent its being thrown beyond the redeeming power of the central attraction; and others, in great numbers, essaying to enforce the law which aimed at the final amalgamation of this vast mass into a well-organized world.

Spirit voices explained to Edmonds that the law graphically illustrated in his vision "when applied to matter you call attraction, and when applied to man you call love," and that "its action is sometimes disturbed in man as well as matter. Then the power of His ministering spirits is employed to restore the due operation of the law." Edmonds provided a particularly clear example of how Spiritualists used the idea of spirit activity to express their aversion to disorder and centrifugal tendencies.[30]

Spirits' special responsibilities in the Spiritualist universe brought with them a special status which Spiritualists described with awed respect. Indeed, authoritarian and centralist imagery pervaded their descriptions of spirit administration as it did their descriptions of cosmic order more generally. The graphic theological imagination of John Edmonds again provides a particularly vivid image. Regarding spirits as "instruments of the Great Creator, charged with the duty and clothed with the power of executing [divine] laws," he envisioned a "bright and majestic spirit sitting in a sort of throne" and giving orders to a number of subordinate spirits. This spirit, "guide and director" of a host of worlds, was "evidently of a higher command, in the execution of God's laws, than any I had yet seen." Behind it Edmonds saw "a very bright light, most gorgeous, like a blazing sun, approaching him from behind, and forming a background to him." This spirit's quasi-monarchical authority was established by divine right.[31]

Even more striking, because linked to a Spiritualist's thoughts about the American system of government, was Robert Hare's conception of the "government of the spheres." A conservative who took a nostalgic and even reactionary pride in being "a Washington Federalist," he favored strong central government in the United States and was therefore inclined to emphasize it in his vision of heaven. This preference explains why there were many more Whigs than Democrats among the deceased political figures in the "convocation of worthies" which he contacted for information about the spirit world. Although the government of Hare's heaven was "republican, exercising legislative, judicial, and executive powers," his description of the flow of authority among spirits emphasized the centripetal rather than the centrifugal dimension of spiritual republicanism.

> As order is a primary object in the spheres, there are of course laws for its preservation. Fundamentally, these proceed through his ministering angels, from the Divine Lawgiver, who . . . employs myriads of ministering angels as the means of intercommunication between their Supreme Master and his creatures throughout the universe. . . . The results of these functions are realized in simultaneous and homogeneous opinions awakened in the minds of the ruling spirits. . . . The conclusions in which the chief spirits thus unanimously concur, are by them impressed upon their constituents, who, thus impressed, are constitutionally unable to resist the sentiment which, like a magic spell, operates upon their sense of right, and overrules any rebellious passion.

Not that rebellion ever could or would occur in Hare's spirit world, for its "atmospheres of peculiar vital air" had "soft and balmy undulating currents" which produced "a most pleasurable and invigorating effect." Since any "rebellious passion" among the spirit masses was counteracted by this opiate, "the decisions of those whose authority is intuitively evident in moral or legal questions, meet with acquiescence." Only in the lowest sphere of Hare's afterlife did "disorder and confusion reign supreme, each spirit vieing with the other," but even these "undeveloped" beings were destined for the order of the higher spheres. One can only wonder what Hare thought of Thomas Jefferson's belief that an occasional rebellion is the sign of a healthy republic, although Jefferson's absence from Hare's "convocation of worthies" is conspicuous.[32]

One did not, of course, have to identify with the Federalist or Whig party to believe that the government of the spirit world was centralized, for Judeo-Christian thought traditionally depicted divine government in such terms. John W. Edmonds, whose descriptions of divine government have been described, was a Democrat (if also a conservative) during his political career as a judge. Even Spiritualists who idolized Jefferson and Paine imagined a strong and highly centralist divine government. Indeed, Spear, who claimed to have received his *Twelve Discourses of Government* from Jefferson's spirit, suggested authoritarianism when he used images of concentric circles, radiating spokes, and powerful emanations to describe his electrical cosmos. To underscore the tangibility of his system of divine governance through spirit mediators, he called it "a material government, as truly so as any statutory system ever engrossed on parchment." For Hare, Edmonds, Spear, and other Spiritualists, obedience to institutionalized structures of law and authority was essential to spiritual freedom in the republic of heaven.[33]

The Social Structure of the Spirit World

Spiritualists constructing their republic of heaven on the antebellum American model understood the spirits' enhanced cosmic status as the result of their successful conformity to the values of an emerging market economy. That American economic life colored the Spiritualist cosmos was made clear enough when John Shoebridge Williams likened it to a business establishment. He called a spirit mediator "one who transacts business between parties" and compared the relationship between his spirit contact and himself to that between a boss and a clerk.[34] Although few Spiritualists were so explicit, they did understand advancement through the spirit hierarchy as a kind of upward mobility that brought with it not only personal growth but increasing stature in the socio-spiritual order. One author has called this the authority of success.[35]

The relatively fluid and democratic social, cultural, and economic conditions of antebellum America led Spiritualists to introduce significant modifications into older conceptions of the afterlife. Because they accepted the cultural premium on being "self-made," they joined a growing number of their contemporaries in rejecting the orthodox Calvinist notions of predestination and divine election. In its place, they envisioned a cosmos much like their understanding of how Jacksonian society functioned; hard work and free action resulted in spiritual ascent, status and authority were achieved rather than ascribed, and success (salvation) was within the grasp of all.

They also departed from the orthodox Swedenborgian model of the spirit world. To be sure, Swedenborg, too, had emphasized achieved over ascribed spiritual status and made position in the spheres a function of one's free actions on earth. But his spirit world was socially static, involving fixed status rather than upward mobility. Furthermore, because Swedenborg had denied the possibility of communication between spirits of different levels, lower beings in his cosmos were not able to learn from relatively advanced ones or to experience the resulting growth. Spiritualists, by contrast, added fluidity and open communication to their socio-spiritual order, making growth and upward mobility possible. Indeed, they denied that the soul was ever settled in a permanent status and considered improvement after death not only possible but inevitable. Though subject to influences from higher levels of the spiritual hierarchy, the rising spirit would defer to a decreasing number of spirits above and thus become progressively liberated as it became subject to the increasingly unmediated authority of God. This understanding of the afterlife reflected both the entrepreneurial ethos of a commercial economy and the democratization of religious authority in the early republic. Spiritualists imagined an Americanized spirit world, remarkably like the fluid society in which they lived.[36]

Still, republican notions of social hierarchy commonly accepted during the eighteenth century tempered the fluidity of Spiritualist visions of the afterlife. Rather than translating their belief in spiritual equality into an enthusiasm for social leveling, they imagined a heavenly social system based on hierarchy and rank, deferential relations between lower and higher spirits, and Jeffersonian notions of meritocracy and natural aristocracy. Most Spiritualists readily admitted that while all souls were spiritually equal and shared the same final destiny, there was wide variation in abilities, qualities, and rates of advancement. Like most other Jacksonian Americans, they were more committed to equality of opportunity than to equality of condition. Perfect equality would be realized only in the indefinite future. In the meantime, in the Spiritualist model of heaven as in the Swedenborgian model of the spirit world and in the republican model of society, differing levels of merit would produce inequalities of status and authority. Robert Hare was not alone in considering the spirit world as "the *beau ideal* of a republic" because "virtue and mind give respect" and "ascendancy is founded on real merit." He and other Spiritualists evidently found comfort in traditional structures of social authority even as they challenged those structures in the name of individual-ism. Their conception of the afterlife pointed up the tension between their ideal of the free individual and their need for social certainty anchored in a structured hierarchy. By resolving that tension in their fluid hierarchy, they both resisted and accepted a social order they feared was excessively individu-alistic. Their cosmos supports anthropologist Mary Douglas's suggestion that cosmological theories are rooted in social experience.[37]

Robert Hare, a wealthy, well educated, and status-conscious urban profes-sional, was especially attentive to the niceties of rank and status in the spiritual hierarchy. In his spirit world, where "we take a rank proportioned to our merit," knowing one's place was evidently important. Spirits were kept at their proper level by a "moral specific gravity," status was "intuitively suscep-tible of estimation," and there were many "means of distinction." Among the badges of status was "a circumambient halo by which every spirit is accompa-nied, which passes from darkness to effulgency as the spirit belongs to a higher plane." Spirits in the upper spheres, of course, possessed an especially strong "distinguishing effulgence." Although traditional modes of deference were being challenged in antebellum America, they were very much alive in Hare's heaven. As a scientist and emeritus professor, he expected that there would be a "deference shown to spirits on the same plane commensurate with their superiority in learning, science, and wisdom." One can assume that a similar "deference" was shown to those of a higher sphere, who often visited those below for the purpose of teaching and moral uplift. George Dexter, a medical doctor, also envisioned a spirit world in which lower spirits look to those above with "deference and respect." If notions of deference among spirits were explicitly articulated only by such well-heeled social conserva-tives as Hare and Dexter, it was nevertheless built in to the spirit hierarchy in which all Spiritualists believed.[38]

Spiritualist cosmology clearly suggests a conservative and defensive re-sponse to the democratizing tendencies at work in antebellum America. Spiritualists invented a neatly ordered invisible world to cope with an uneasy sense of disorder and with the "crisis of authority" that according to Hatch accompanied religious democratization. Conservative English essayist Mat-thew Arnold once wrote that a democratic society faces a problem of main-taining high ideals since a repudiation of aristocracy and deference leaves it without the models of virtue that an aristocracy had once provided. Spiritu-alists, leaving behind traditional social arrangements and patterns of social thought, and lacking confidence in their ministers as moral models, looked to the spirit world for a moral aristocracy and the behavioral trappings of a disappearing social order. They used their religious imaginations to allay their fear that egalitarianism and individualism were plummeting their society into chaos.[39]

The Limits of Spiritual Freedom

Spiritualists so firmly grounded the spirit in an overarching socio-spiritual and institutional order that they were forced to acknowledge sharp limits on the independence, spontaneity, and freedom of the will that had become important values in the larger culture. Their universe was an interactive social network in which individual existence could not be understood apart from the social whole, nor selfhood separated from the influence of others. One Spiritualist writer considered it a basic principle of nature that "there is no such thing as absolute individual independence in the Universe." John Murray Spear agreed that "independence does not exist" since "mind flows into mind" through a "grand, universal sea of magnetism." Indeed, his belief that this "sea of magnetism" broadcast inner thoughts implied a complete lack of individual privacy in his intensely social cosmos. "There may be no spot," he imagined, "where the knowledge of our most secret thoughts and purposes, as well as our most trivial outward act, may not be transmitted on the lightning's wing." Other Spiritualists made similar statements, but Spear's example is especially interesting because he was quoting Congregationalist minister and prominent geologist Edward Hitchcock and thus underscoring the theological connections between the Spiritualist imagination and the larger religious culture.[40] Made uneasy with the idea of an independent and unattached self by the social and economic forces shaping Jacksonian America, Spiritualists denied its existence in the name of order by emphasizing the powerful cosmic influences that bound the individual to a socio-spiritual community.[41]

They considered these influences essential to spiritual growth and therefore liberating, but the concepts they borrowed from physical science to describe them conjured up images of inviolable natural law and overpowering force. Progressive growth and development, for example, was "the great, eternal, all-powerful law of the Universe and of the Soul" from which "there is no escape." John Edmonds compared spiritual growth under influences from above with an object accelerating in free fall. The influence of God and the spirits on the soul was most commonly compared to the irresistible attractive force of the magnet. References to God as a "Spiritual Magnet" or "Supreme Attraction" whose force binds the spiritual universe together dot the Spiritualist literature. Andrew Jackson Davis's deity was the "HOLY MAGNET of the universe" and the "irresistible Magnet which attracts upward the human soul," and Asaph Bemis Child imagined spirit intermediaries as "celestial magnets" whose "immortal currents force me on." Spiritualists found security and order in the belief that they and their society were subject to benevolent spiritual forces beyond their control.[42]

Such images suggest a thoroughly deterministic universe, and the imperatives of cosmic order indeed led Spiritualists to limit the freedom of the will and sometimes to deny it outright. Universal and inevitable salvation through progressive growth implied that all spirits were gradually liberated from enslavement to evil and rendered incapable of wrongdoing by what one Spiritualist called "divine pressure." John S. Adams could "not conceive of any such idea as retrogression in God's works." A. B. Child agreed that the soul "can neither go backward, nor be retarded" in its advance. "Hell is ever shut beneath us, and heaven is ever open above us." In her *Discourse on the Immutable Decrees of God*, medium Cora Hatch frankly avowed that while the soul was "free to do good . . . and free to soar to realms of light above," it was "not free to sin, for sin is slavery's chain." Some Spiritualists even spoke of predestination. One writer, defending "The Doctrine of Necessity" and denying "The Moral Freedom of Man," said that all spirits are "predestined to eternal progress" and appealed to Puritan theologian Jonathan Edwards to support his case.[43]

Swedenborgians such as George Bush regarded Spiritualists' denial of hell as tantamount to a denial of free will and were quick to criticize Spiritualist theology on this point. Joining a broader cultural conversation on moral agency, he and ex-Universalist Adin Ballou argued the issue in 1855. Ballou's attempt to reconcile universalism with freedom suggests that his spiritual republican commitment to personal experience, individualism, and freedom made him uncomfortable with determinism. But because he respected the logic of inevitable salvation as much as he did his culture's exaltation of the self-made person, he grounded his defense of free will in personal experience rather than theological rigor. He admitted that nobody could escape God's "moral control" or "the reach of wholesome discipline," but cringed at the thought of a "universe of puppets" and insisted on the feeling of freedom experienced in "normal consciousness." J. R. Orton agreed that "man's consciousness affirms his freedom." Spiritualists also suggested that the gradual nature of spiritual development indicated God's regard for human freedom. The *Spiritual Telegraph* reprinted an article from the *Universalist Quarterly* in which minister Thomas Starr King expressed his preference for the idea of salvation through "slow and patient spiritual training, which respects the freedom of man" over the orthodox notion of salvation by the "coarse power" of divine grace. An editorial in the *Spiritual Age* acknowledged that many Spiritualists accepted the "radical and mischievous error" of progression "*per* force" but argued, as did many other members of the movement, that spiritual growth is actually driven internally rather than externally.[44]

The difficult Spiritualist effort to reconcile universalism with the Swedenborgian contention that freedom implied sin and hell was perhaps best expressed in a series of articles aptly entitled "Swedenborgian Restorationism." Writing for Ballou's *Practical Christian*, "G." explained that the spirit enjoyed "the fullest possession of *infernal* freedom" until its "inverted" will destroyed itself, leaving only the "remains of good and truth" inherent in every individual. With "the sinner . . . destroyed," the approach toward perfection could begin. As "G." and other Spiritualists understood the process of development, the soul in the afterlife underwent a gradual moral lobotomy, progressively losing the will to do wrong and then conforming voluntarily to divine moral law. But although "G." argued that this process allowed "the fullest exercise of . . . freedom" as "the very means by which a final Universal Restoration from evil is secured," he also understood it to be "the known Law of order, from which there is no escape or appeal."[45]

Despite their outspoken defenses of free will, then, Spiritualists bound the individual in a moral universe whose architecture included no discernible ceiling but an emphatically impenetrable floor. Davis compared the freedom of all beings except the deity to that of goldfish in a globe of water. "All liberty," he said, "is comparative—all freedom is unqualifiedly relative and partial." Even Ballou had to acknowledge that human freedom existed only within a "limited sphere." Spiritualists like S. B. Brittan advocated an ordered freedom, distinguishing the unbridled "liberty" which they feared from the "Christian liberty" which they approved. They believed that true freedom consisted in voluntary conformity with the natural spiritual order and that divine restrictions on the will limited freedom without destroying it. Thus John Shoebridge Williams could say that all spirits are "led in freedom" and John S. Adams could call a soul progressing in obedience to natural law "free." A *Spiritual Age* editorial declared, under the title "None But the Just Are Free," that the free spirit "makes the Divine Order his order and God's freedom his freedom." Liberty for the Spiritualist did not mean the complete autonomy which was the bugbear of the antebellum middle class.[46]

A Catholic Cosmos

The limitation of individualism in the Spiritualist cosmology was a reaction against the patterns not only of Jacksonian society but also of the Protestantism that dominated antebellum American cultural and religious life. Indeed, its quasi-ecclesiastical hierarchy of spirit intermediaries resembles the structure of the Catholic church. To be sure, most Spiritualists themselves tended to share the American cultural bias against Catholicism. As spiritual republicans, they criticized it for being too rigidly institutionalized, too centralized under the rule of a single human being, too opposed in spirit and practice to American institutions, and in sum too antidemocratic and "authoritarian." Still, an understanding of the Spiritualist ideology makes it easy to understand how Spiritualists like John Shoebridge Williams and Spiritualist sympathizers like Mary G. and Thomas L. Nichols could become attracted to it despite beginning their religious lives in the highly decentralized and individualistic Quaker denomination.[47]

Williams provides a particularly illuminating example. His spiritual pilgrimage carried him from the Society of Friends through the New Church, whose aristocratic nature he opposed, to Spiritualism. From this last religious perspective, he found Catholicism appealing and even compatible with his Spiritualist views and practices. Even as he practiced self-reliant mediumship, he professed his "love of the Catholic church" and noted his 1852 attendance at a Catholic mass on (of all days!) July fourth.[48] Some of his interest in Catholicism stemmed from an anti-sectarian desire for Christian unity, which many Spiritualists shared and which fueled a simultaneous interest in Catholicism among the group of Protestants that created the Mercersburg theology.[49] But he was also strongly attracted by its institutionalized hierarchical structure and emphasis on intermediary spiritual authorities. It is no coincidence that he began an "investigation of the principles and practices of the Catholic church, so as to be myself satisfied respecting her nature and functions" just as he was becoming seriously involved with Spiritualism. Describing the investigation to Archbishop John B. Purcell, a group of Catholic priests, and the clergy at St. Peter's Church in Cincinnati, he made special reference to his laudatory pamphlet whose very title—*Truth Its Own Witness for the Church; Or Scientific Demonstration by Analogy, Simillitudes [sic] Centers and Intermediates*—suggests his strong attraction for centralized authority, hierarchy, and religious mediation. In particular, he understood the mediatorial function of the Catholic clergy in much the same manner that he and other Spiritualists understood that of the spirits:

> The control which that clergy have kept of the minds of laymen have been salutary in the condition in which the laity is and have been, and it will now by the divine Power of the Lord operating on and through the clergy of that church produce more good than could be produced by three times the number of protestant clergy of equal standing and abilities.

In Williams's Catholicism as in his Spiritualism, a strong class of intermediate spiritual authorities was important to spiritual order. Within a few months of becoming a Spiritualist, he reported having been "impressed" by the spirit of his daughter Eliza to attend a Catholic service. During the service, "Eliza manifested herself joyfully" and commented that Protestants ought to think better of the Church.[50]

Clearly, then, Spiritualism and Catholicism had more in common than most Spiritualists would have been willing to admit. Indeed, George Lawton has interpreted Spiritualism as "a partial return to Catholicism." While Protestantism represents a trend toward liberalization, he explained, "some persons cannot stand this liberty, this vagueness and austerity and try to work their way back to the fixity and warmth . . . of Catholicism."[51] In this, Spiritualists were hardly alone among antebellum Americans. The emergence of their religion parallels the attraction of the antebellum Transcendentalists Orestes Brownson and Isaac Hecker for Catholicism, the rise of High-Church Episcopalianism, and, later in the century, the fascination among many American Protestants with medieval Catholicism. But Spiritualists took a unique route, responding to Protestantism's troubling features with quasi-Catholic notions of spirit communication and mediation. The "Catholic" features of Spiritualism suggest one of its basic ironies: it constituted both an expression of and a reaction against Protestant individualism. They underscore the distance between Spiritualism and the larger Protestant religious culture even as the atypicality of Williams's behavior and the general Spiritualist aversion to Catholicism remind us of the smallness of that distance.

The structural similarity between the Spiritualist cosmos and the Catholic church illuminates its status as an "excursus religion" of the type that Robert S. Ellwood considers particularly appealing to Americans uncomfortable with the unstructured character of Jacksonian society.[52] The Spiritualist worldview emphasized an ideal of strong group ties that could find its fullest expression "only symbolically" amid the atomizing tendencies of the period. Excursus religions postulate "invisible but very real" networks and groups which give the initiate a sense of belonging to a cosmic community. The excursus ideal, according to Ellwood, is expressed in an absolute nonpersonal God and a "vast but ordered hierarchy of intermediate masters, spirits, polytheistic gods, or kabbalistic spheres" between the Absolute and the world below." Spiritualists required this invisible religious community to justify their desire for the spontaneous, unstructured, and personal religiosity called "communitas" by anthropologist Victor Turner. They could not have the latter without the former, for in excursus religion "lack of structure implies a chaos in which no real transcendent (or interhuman) communication or relationship is possible." Imagining themselves in a cosmic church staffed by a mediating spirit hierarchy, these unchurched religionists found their home in the universe.[53]

A School, an Asylum, a Home

Spiritualists craving order amid the unrelenting transformations of Jacksonian society conceived of the cosmos in terms not only of the church but also of the other institutions they considered most important in preparing growing and potentially disorderly Americans for a disciplined life in a free society. The antebellum school, which fostered orderly growth in an often hierarchically structured environment, provided as recurrent a metaphor as that of the church. In the spirit world, called by Emma Hardinge "a glorious school-house for the soul," students were educated to assume the obligations of spiritual freedom by acquiescing to properly constituted authorities in an institutional regime. Robert Hare compared the concentric spheres surrounding the earth to a "great normal school" in which spirits received the wisdom required to teach those below them. Here, spirits advanced from one level to the next, eventually graduating beyond the seventh sphere and entering the boundless and relatively unstructured space of the "supernal heaven." There they would join the higher spirits in spiritual and spatial freedom under the more direct government and authority of God.[54]

Spiritualists' social and cultural surroundings supplied another institutional metaphor, though it was rarely made explicit. Their universe closely resembled the rigidly structured and tightly controlled prisons and asylums that had begun to dot the American landscape during the 1830s and 1840s.[55] The designers of these corrective institutions assumed that a strictly regimented lifestyle would foster in inmates the self-discipline needed to cope with the relatively free and unstructured social and economic environment of Jacksonian America. Spiritualists like Robert Hare, who imagined spirits confined by a "moral specific gravity" to a narrow band of spheres surrounding the earth before their release into the "supernal heaven" beyond, concurred. In fact, a number of Spiritualists, including John Edmonds and John Murray Spear, had promoted prison reform. Just as "the essence" of antebellum corrective institutions "was obedience to its rules," spirits experienced sharp limits on their freedom and obeyed the rule of natural law under the voluntary internal restraints of conscience and the external pressure of spirits. As Hare noted, there was "no possible escape from the natural results of crime." All spirits, then, were essentially inmates in a cosmic asylum. They were being prepared, through an intensive program of discipline and education that amounted to a moral lobotomy, for the rights of freedom and citizenship in a cosmic republic.[56]

Like prison and asylum designers, Spiritualists imagining the spirit world as an institution with well defined structures of authority, regimentation, discipline, command, and obedience drew on military models and used military imagery.[57] A. B. Child envisioned the spirits "standing in ranks," an army of "soldiers marching to the great battle field of life." Spiritual militarism, patriotism, and republicanism mixed well, as medium Abby T. Hall illustrated through a message from the often contacted spirit of George Washington. Spirit Washington, whose heroic generalship on earth was only the beginning of his eternal fight for spiritual freedom, portrayed spirits as leaders over their mortal followers: "girding on the armor of faith and hope, we come to you, surround you with our influence, . . . and draw you with us." According to Charles Hammond, Thomas Paine was also called to battle upon reaching the spirit world. Hammond's Paine received a helmet and spear in order to "fight the good fight of wisdom" under the direction of his "commander." He also received a crown to wear during his campaign, symbolizing his spiritual authority and leadership over those below him. Laura Edmonds, whose religious experiences as a medium were much like those of her father, John, received a succession of orders from her spirit commander in one of her visions. Wielding a banner which itself read like a series of commands ("God is Truth. Onward! still onward! for Truth shall prevail. Hope on! Hope ever!"), a spirit shouted in sergeant-like tones:

> Arise from your darkness. Behold the light of heaven which is for one and all! See the armies of God's messengers hastening to the rescue. Arise! Gird on the armor of courage! Behold that banner! Ponder on its words, and forward!

Like antebellum reformers, Spiritualists and the spirit voices they heard considered a military style effective in meeting their need for an ordered society.[58]

But they wanted a heaven that provided comfort as well as stern discipline, and found in the metaphor of the home a counteractive to the rigidity of the military and prison models. Spiritualists imagined a sentimentalized heaven well in accordance with the Romantic mood, referring explicitly and often to the spirit world as a Victorian home.[59] One ode written for use in séance meetings suggested their desire for contact with a "higher home." According to the ideology of domesticity which pervaded middle-class culture in Victorian America, the home was a warm, nurturing, pious, and friendly environment that served as a refuge from the impersonal, amoral, and competitive commercial world outside of it. Spiritualists similarly understood the spirit world as the moral reverse of earthly society, a utopian place of cooperative living and a permanent refuge from the tribulations of an ephemeral terrestrial existence. Spirit communication represented for Spiritualists a much-needed escape from the perceived disorder of their own society, a reassurance that the alienating chaos of earth was an aberration in a welcoming and orderly universe. Warren Chase, whose autobiographical *The Life-Line of the Lone One* recounts a life plagued by orphanhood, anomie, and alienation, believed that "the soul of man is not at home here" on earth but rather "finds his home in the skies." Contact with spirits was his "life-line" to that home.[60]

Spiritualists underscored the homelike qualities of their universe and the cultural identification of the home with women by using female spirits as symbols of cosmic belonging. After a turbulent childhood wracked by his father's chronic drunkenness and financial troubles, the resulting frequency of relocation from one town to another, and the death of his mother, Andrew Jackson Davis looked to the spirit world for a home and a mother. He wrote in his autobiography that his first vision of heaven was of his deceased mother beckoning to him to see her "new house." John S. Adams told the potential come-outer to heed the call of the "spirit-mother whom you loved" and departed sister who "comes to tell you of the glorious home she has found beyond the skies." Domestic metaphors made the Spiritualist cosmos not only rigidly structured but warmly intimate, not only institutional but cozy and familial.[61]

Visions of the spiritual universe as a cosmic institution were not original with the Spiritualists. Nor was the notion of spirit communion. But Spiritualists combined these into a unique belief system well suited to the needs of the early Victorian middle class. They found comfort in their belief that their spirit world, like their churches, schools, asylums, and homes, was working to ensure discipline, provide education, control potentially unruly individuals, and maintain social order. The importance of spirits in their ideology was made especially clear when Spiritualists extended their metaphors of the spirit world as a church, a school, a corrective institution, and a home to the relationship between the spirits and themselves. The vacuum in Spiritualists' religious lives was created not only by the absence of institutional affiliation but also by a felt lack of ministerial guidance. The result, explored in the following chapter, was an inclination to assign to spirits the functions of the clergy. In the excursus cosmos, "an assemblage of masters, spirits, buddhas, gods, or archetypes" are postulated to "give texture and color to the One" and to "reach down to guide pilgrims along the way."[62] Feeling like lost and wandering spiritual children, the architects of the Spiritualist universe not only constructed a secure church, school, prison, and home, but also peopled them with warm, wise, and loving ministers, teachers, wardens, and parents.

─✦─

5

The Ministry of Spirits

The Ministry of Spirits Realized

Alonzo and Sarah Newton chose the title *The "Ministry of Angels" Realized* for the published letter announcing their conversion to Spiritualism and their desire to withdraw from their church. Their choice was appropriate, for it expressed the central, most distinctive, and most attractive feature of their new religion. They made it clear that they sought not only independence but also a new way to structure their religious lives. Their church had "forfeited all right . . . to exercise any authority over us," and they sought "instruction from sources more congenial with our present convictions of truth and duty." They found in the spirits "ministers of His . . . appointed to be the channels of communication between our spirits and the Infinite Fountain." If the universe was an invisible "church" community, spirit mediators were its invisible "ministers," divinely authorized guides who would meet their spiritual needs more effectively than could the mortal clergy. As the Newtons abandoned their traditional institutional moorings, they contacted unseen ministers to anchor their free and "unchurched" spirits in an ecclesiastical cosmos.[1]

An ideology based on spirit ministry, as opposed to belief in the fact of past or present spirit communication, made Spiritualist religion a distinctive expression of antebellum American religious culture. The notion of spirit communication was hardly new, but Spiritualists were unique in their emphasis on the religious functions of the spirit world. They were more apt than other religious Americans to play down the role of God and to look to spirits as a surrogate spiritual presence. They were also more consistent in connecting their belief in spirit communication and spirit activity to dissatisfaction with the conventional clergy, and in suggesting that spirits behaved like ministers in their interaction with those on earth. Only Spiritualists made spirit intercourse, considered episodic at best by other Christians, into a fully developed conception of ongoing spirit mediation and ministry.[2]

This feature of the Spiritualist ideology has usually been underappreciated. The focus has been, rather, on the individuals with whom and through whom the spirits were said to communicate. One recent study's interpretive focus on radical individualism led its author to declare that Spiritualists sought truth "directly" and "without mediation by minister, Bible, or church," and sought "a form of religious practice in which truth revealed itself to individuals without recourse to external authority." Another scholar has said that Spiritualists sought "direct revelation (via spirit messenger)." But while spirit communication effectively transferred religious authority to mediums who claimed to channel spirit voices or to individuals who claimed to hear them, ignoring spirits or noticing them only parenthetically slights the importance that Spiritualists themselves attached to them. Spiritualists not only *believed* that spirits existed independently but located them in a cosmic order in which spirit mediators and not they themselves were the central actors and authority figures.[3]

Two developments in antebellum American religion nourished Spiritualists' desire for regular spirit contact and encouraged their notion of spirit ministry. One, discussed in chapter 3, was a crisis of religious authority in which they doubted the effectiveness of established ministers as spiritual leaders. This problem was exacerbated by a broader loss of faith in humanity as the antebellum reform impulse weakened by the 1850s, reformers resorted to more forceful means of achieving their ends, and the social and economic environment of Jacksonian America undermined traditional mechanisms of ensuring self-restraint. The other, alluded to in chapter 4, was a crisis of faith among liberal Protestants, a troubling feeling of divine abstractness, remoteness, and inaccessibility. A spirit-centered religion helped Spiritualists to cope with both of these religious dilemmas. Indeed, it was not only fitting but logical that Americans feeling alienated from both God and humanity should focus on the partly divine and partly human spirits that mediated between the two.

A Spiritual Presence

Spiritualists adopted their new belief system in part because they found it difficult to believe that an infinite God could be involved in their personal lives. Most Spiritualist publications, R. Laurence Moore has pointed out, deemphasized or flatly denied any idea of a personal God and embraced pantheism.[4] Spiritualists participated in broader developments in which the idea of a personal God, like the belief in miracles or the divine authorship of the Bible, was being increasingly questioned in liberal Protestant circles. They joined other liberals in rejecting the concept of the "supernatural," identifying God with nature and natural law and reducing deity to an impersonal principle. When the New York Conference of Spiritualists addressed the nature of deity at one of its weekly meetings, physician Robert Hallock claimed to find God in an "underlying law of all the diverse phenomena of nature . . . by which they are reduced to order." Most of the other participants, including Andrew Jackson Davis and S. B. Brittan, held similar views.[5]

Spiritualists far less rationalistic and pantheistic, too, questioned and compromised the idea of a personal God. A. E. Newton argued in *The "Ministry of Angels" Realized* that even the Old Testament prophets had communicated with spirits and angels rather than with God, and indeed that no one had ever had direct contact with God. Although Isaac Post had believed as a Quaker in direct divine inspiration, he now doubted that God could be "personally present with every intelligence in bodily existence." He concluded that what he had once "considered God's impressions on my mind" had actually been "made by angel Spirits." John Shoebridge Williams, another ex-Quaker who had "felt impressions all my life," agreed. The Friends had made the "great error" of "not allowing for the interposition of other mediums, between the Lord and them, so that the truths that come down from the Lord to them could be moulded to suit the forms of all." Nor did his belief that "the Infinite communicates with the finites by immutable laws or principles" suggest a direct and personal relationship with God. He defended Christian Spiritualism against rationalists like Davis, but no more than Davis's God was his a comforting and accessible spiritual presence.[6]

Many Spiritualists resisted these troubling implications of Protestant liberalism, asserting their need for a personal and even sentimentalized God. W. S. Courtney complained that "The New Theology" had sacrificed religious feeling for rationalism and had led some Spiritualists to conceive of God as an abstract principle. But "an abstract principle, or set of principles, however divine, is no God for the human heart to love and worship." A. E. Newton likewise wanted his cosmos guided by an "affectionate Being (as distinguished from a lifeless principle or impersonal force), capable of loving and of being loved, and who thus sustains to all the tender relation of Universal Parent."[7]

In short, Spiritualists were caught on the horns of a dilemma. The logic of liberal theology and the Enlightenment dictated an impersonal, remote, and abstract deity of natural law, but spiritual security and Romantic sentimentality required a warm and personal cosmic presence; both facets of deity were essential to the order of their universe. The result was ambivalence as Spiritualists struggled to make their deity both a principle and a person. A confused John Edmonds, for instance, asserted that God was "a principle . . . represented by his law" but also "must be a person" with an identity and attributes. John Murray Spear's God was a "GRAND CONCENTRIC POWER" that could be called "what you please,—God, Parent, or Father" for "names do not alter principles." But he longed for a "divine, all-controlling Parent" so that "the child feels that he is never alone—that a loving parent is interested in his welfare."[8]

Spiritualism emerged just as divine remoteness was becoming a serious religious problem and atheism and agnosticism were becoming plausible options in Western (and particularly American) culture. According to James Turner, the idea of a natural law deity and the declining belief in special divine providence meant that "the intimacy, security, and immediacy of God's presence" was "compromised, psychologically if not logically." Perceiving a gap "between ordinary human life and an increasingly remote God," religious Americans had to "restore immediacy" in their spiritual lives. Mary Farrell Bednarowski applied this insight to Spiritualism, interpreting it as an expression of a mid-nineteenth century "malaise of doubt." Many religious Americans, she said, experienced a "fear of nothingness and of an indifferent or nonexistent God" and a "horrible suspicion that man was abandoned in an indifferent universe." They felt "spiritually alone." George Lawton too recognized the appeal of spirits to a group of religious Americans who had pushed God "into the remote center of the cosmos" and needed "personality in the universe of an intimate and approachable kind."[9]

In typically Victorian fashion, Spiritualists addressed this need by postulating finite mediating spirits as a personal and tender presence in what would otherwise have seemed a coldly impersonal universe. Like participants in other excursus religions, they emphasized "the reality of numinous but anthropomorphic beings with whom one can have a warmer relation than to the impersonal Absolute." In doing so, they contributed to the ongoing process in American religion, described by Perry Miller, in which a transcendent God had to be made "understandable in human terms." Contact with spirit mediators, medium Abby T. Hall's spirit voices assured her, was "breaking down the partition walls that have so long separated . . . man . . . from God." Even in what he knew was "God's universe," A. B. Child looked to spirits for comfort and security. Convinced that "we're not in solitude" since "guardian spirits are ever hovering, spreading around their wings of protection," he made his universe a warm and friendly place. Spirit ministry allowed Spiritualists to have both the distant deity that their Enlightenment theological intellects required and the intimate spiritual companionship that their Romantic religious feelings demanded.[10]

A Humanized Cosmos

Spiritualists adjusted to the "new theology" by adopting what Colleen McDannell and Bernhard Lang have called Swedenborg's "modern" conception of heaven. That is, they understood the spirit world as a humanized place inhabited by humanized spirits. But their conception of spirit ministry constituted a significant leap beyond Swedenborg. They not only humanized the spirits but made them familiar and accessible, emphasizing interpersonal relationships between spirits and mortals (as well as among spirits themselves) in a new and distinctive way that Swedenborg had positively discouraged. The spirit ministers with whom Spiritualists enjoyed "intercourse" were usually known to them by name, had been specifically chosen by them for consultation, and could be contacted virtually at the will of the medium. The result was easy sociability between mortals and "a class of beings in the other world interested primarily in their humble personal concerns." The spirits they sought out, having once (and usually very recently) been mortal themselves, were intensely human beings, sharing the cares, concerns, and emotions of those on earth. The spirits of close friends and relatives could be especially comforting companions. These aspects of Spiritualist belief and practice made possible a realistic, living, and full-blooded spirit "ministry."[11]

They also suggest an important difference, brought on by antebellum cultural and intellectual conditions, between Spiritualist experience and the "encounters with the sacred" described by Rudolf Otto. What Otto called "the holy" exhibited "absolute unapproachability" and evoked "shuddering," but Spiritualists felt alienated from a transcendent deity and sought contact with something more human and less "wholly other." While the sacred was a "mysterium tremendum" that was "beyond the sphere of the usual, the intelligible, and the familiar," Spiritualists consulted familiar human spirits and probed the nature of their existence in an effort to demystify the other world. Far from "shrinking before the presence" of spirits, they generally felt comfortable with their contacts from beyond. They undoubtedly considered communication with spirits to be an encounter with an "other"—spirits were symbols of the sacred, occupying an entirely different order of existence and eliciting by their presence a measure of awe—but this was an "other" of a friendly and approachable kind. As anxious to humanize as to sacralize their universe, Spiritualists humanized the sacred.[12]

This humanizing thrust located them within a broader strain of Victorian religiosity that Richard Rabinowitz has termed "devotionalism" or "sentimentalism." "Devotionalists" felt distant from their impersonal God and sought an intimate and emotional relationship with the divine. They humanized the object of their devotion by focusing less on God and more on the "companionable qualities" of Christ, his human incarnation. Spiritualists did something comparable. They and "devotionalists" alike emphasized the likeness and reduced the distance between the human and the divine, even to the point of blurring the distinction between them. As mediators between humanity and deity that shared qualities of both, the spirits were perfect symbols of this sentimental religious mood.[13]

The importance of this facet of Spiritualist religion is indicated by the prominent treatment it received in Uriah Clark's *Plain Guide to Spiritualism*. In imitation of Martin Luther's religious rebellion, Clark offered ninety-five questions designed to explain the new religion. One of them suggested the need for spirit mediators to link deity and humanity: "How can God, the Infinite, reveal to man, the finite, a knowledge of the infinite and eternal, unless through the intermediate agency of angels or spirits occupying a plane between the Infinite and finite, and adapted to the appreciation of man?" Another pinpointed the specific need for *human* spirits: "In communicating with man, would God select messengers from some foreign realm, or the spirits of departed human beings in sympathy with man, and best capable of interpreting between God and man?" A. E. Newton agreed that a "ministry of love" should be carried on by "those who have been here united to us by the ties of affinity, relationship, and affection" and had "sympathies in common with us."[14]

The intimacy and emotional comfort of spirit companionship was articulated with particular clarity by sentimental novelist Harriet Beecher Stowe. Describing the "Ministration of Departed Spirits," this careful observer of human emotion wrote that spirits were well suited to their purpose because they had once been mortal themselves and could therefore understand those on earth. The spirits of those that the Spiritualist knew and loved on earth were especially well qualified to "minister" to those they had left behind because the communicating mortals had "unfolded [their] soul in its most secret recesses" to them. "If we are to have a ministering spirit," she asked, "who better adapted?" To Harriet N. Greene, a follower of radical reformer Adin Ballou, a participant in his communitarian experiment at Hopedale, and co-editor of the *Radical Spiritualist,* spirits were tender, intimate, and affectionate friends. "There are no cold and chilling voices coming from the spheres above, chiding us when we weep, but rather gentle whispers fall upon our ears, while angel hands smooth back the damp hair from our brows, press their angel-lips to ours, and sing to us of heaven."[15]

It was fitting that these descriptions were offered by women. Not only were women particularly inclined to seek intimate relations with the divine,[16] but Spiritualists seeking cosmic companionship emphasized spirit qualities—such as warmth and love—that the ideology of domesticity identified with women. This feature of spirit ministry reflected the broader association of the ministry with the feminine among liberal Protestants of the American middle class. As Spiritualists sought the security and comfort of home in God's universe, they often thought of their spirit guides as cosmic mothers and sisters and gave them distinctly feminine voices. A. B. Child, whose mawkish *Lily-Wreath of Spirit Communications* (1855) and *The Bouquet of Spiritual Flowers* (1856) occupied the intersection between Spiritualist and sentimental literature, looked to "Flora" for spiritual security and intimacy. Flora soothed him with images of "angel tears shed," of spirits that "whisper comfort" and offer a "beckoning hand" to the "lonely" and the "wanderers" of earth, and of "pleading, earnest, throbbing" spirit hearts that "swell for thee." The mast-head of the Spiritualist periodical *Journal of Progress,* featuring winged females clasping their hands over the prostrate figures (infant and adult alike) in their laps, gave visual expression to a sentimental cosmos that seemed as warm as Spiritualists' own firesides (see illustration 2).[17]

Other "feminine" qualities, such as piety and moral purity, were equally important to spirit ministry. Like the mothers of middle-class Victorian America, spirits were moral teachers, symbols of the conscience who served as models of virtue and looked after the spiritual welfare of mortals on a wayward earth. Indeed, Spiritualists reflected the larger "feminization" of clerical authority in Protestant liberalism, in which a method of gentle and nurturing "influence" supplanted the stern, harsh, and fear-based "power" of the orthodox male ministry, by accentuating the motherlike tenderness and love with which spirits leavened their moral discipline and authority.[18] The spirits who would "minister unto us," said A. B. Child, employ "gentle chidings." Medium Abby T. Hall's spirit contacts would reform the soul "with a strong but gentle hand."[19]

The experience of John Shoebridge Williams offers an especially well developed example of how the feminization of religious authority was incorporated into this central Spiritualist concept. An intimidating patriarch in his family life, he believed as a medium that he was in regular contact with the spirit of his deceased daughter Eliza and transferred moral authority and governance over his soul to her. Like a model Victorian woman, spirit Eliza became his self-effacing moral teacher and made his salvation her mission. He heard her spirit sermonize about the gentleness of authority in the spirit world and chastise him for "severe" disciplinary methods that had evoked fear rather than love. She, by contrast, clothed her discipline in "shrouds of love" and gently led Williams to "quite different views of many of the acts and habits of my life." The result was tearful repentance and a softening of his patriarchy. Warren Chase reported precisely the same change in his behavior. In these cases of personal reform, as in liberal Protestantism more generally, the loving and mild influence of a domesticated spirit ministry triumphed over stern patriarchal power.[20]

The triumph, however, was incomplete. Since cosmic order required "masculine" as well as "feminine" elements, the feminine "influence" of spirit ministry often involved an unmistakable exercise of masculine "power" over the passive recipient.[21] John Shoebridge Williams, for example, understood Eliza's occupation of his body and control over his conscience as an aggressive act: "you might think it a kind of encroachment for me to enter and take

Illustrations 2 and 3: Mastheads of The Journal of Progress, *published in New York City, and the* New Era, *published in Boston. Viewed together, these mastheads illustrate both the maternal/"feminine" and patriarchal/"masculine" aspects of Spiritualist ideology. The* Journal of Progress *masthead (Courtesy New-York Historical Society, New York City) emphasizes the gentle and maternal nature of spirit authority as well as themes of sentimentalism and spiritual childhood. The* New Era *masthead (Courtesy American Antiquarian Society) suggests not only patriarchal authority but also the theme of spiritual pilgrimage and the importance of military imagery.*

possession of your body," Eliza told him. He described the operation of spirit influence, moreover, in terms as suggestive of the severe disciplinary methods of Calvinist fathers as of the milder methods of Victorian mothers. Although "gentle titillations and mild influences" worked "to soften the distorted form" and mold it "into forms entirely different," spirits would also "lay hold of" their objects and "twist and turn" them in order "to restrain soften and bend them into manageable forms."[22]

Forceful spirit power was especially apparent in a visiting spirit's earliest manifestations, which witnesses often perceived as aggressive and even violent. William T. Coggeshall, an early investigator of Spiritualism in Cincinnati, watched at a séance as "the left arm of one of the ladies at the table, was drawn back with great force" as if a spirit had "grasped" it. In Rochester, meanwhile, Charles Hammond gaped as "a lounge behind me was shaken violently" and a tremendous vibration of the door "caused everything in the room to shake most violently for several minutes." But such disorderly displays were part of the process by which spirit ministry would achieve order. Uriah Clark assured his readers that if the spirits "at first, permit anything of a seemingly violent nature, it is for the purpose of developing a mediumship at last resulting in good."[23]

Furthermore, as we have seen, Spiritualists (particularly male ones) frequently used military imagery in describing spirit ministers' efforts to reform human society. Williams believed that he was among the "spiritual soldiers" doing "service" in the name of the Lord, and Spear, who was called to his religious mission by a group of male spirits that included revolutionary leaders Franklin, Jefferson, Benjamin Rush, and Roger Sherman, prominently featured men in military garb on the masthead of his periodical *New Era* (see illustration 3). "By waging Christian warfare," E. Anthony Rotundo has argued, "a minister could act with manly aggression while pursuing the sacred goals of love and goodness that his culture linked to women." Williams also, we have seen, used the strategy of depicting spirit ministry in terms of the business world identified by antebellum Americans with men. Male Spiritualists in particular, living amid a "feminization of American culture" by Protestant liberals and immersing themselves in a religious world dominated by female mediums, needed the reassurance of gender identity and male power that such masculinizing strategies could provide.[24]

Finally, Spiritualists never questioned Swedenborg's identification of wisdom as a "male" principle and love as a "female" one. Indeed, contemporary gender definitions reinforced these notions. Even John Murray Spear, a radical reformer who strongly supported women's rights, assumed that "the female" is an "especial embodiment of the love element" and "the male . . . of the wisdom element" and was confident that this notion would be "conceded by all." Philosophical spirit messages therefore came generally from male spirit ministers like Swedenborg, Washington, and Franklin, and expressions of love and the domestic features of the cosmos from such female ones as Flora and Eliza. John Shoebridge Williams explained that Eliza's profound messages originated in a group of higher male spirits called "Swedenborg" since "her feminine form could not so clearly receive and communicate scientific truths as if the impressions were made from a male form in which the understanding predominates." Robert Hare claimed to learn about the "physical economy," "moral economy," "political economy," and "social constitutions" of the spirit world from his father's spirit and a "Convocation of Worthies" that included Washington, Franklin, Newton, William Ellery Channing, and Henry Clay. A "truly angelic creature" named Maria, meanwhile, described to him the spirit world's beautiful music and breathtaking scenery as well as the charms of a spirit poet's home. Spiritualists gave a human dimension and a homey quality to their androgynous cosmic order—and fashioned a religion of both scientific law and sentimental feeling—when they heard the voices of both spirit fathers and spirit mothers.[25]

Spiritualists naturally compared their spirit ministers to parents since the retreat of God from their personal lives left them feeling like spiritual orphans. Meanwhile, the concept of cosmic mediumship postulated a relationship of parental nurture and discipline between higher spirits and lower ones and discontent with the clergy left Spiritualists looking to parents as crucial figures of spiritual authority and discipline over the children of the young republic. John Shoebridge Williams advised mortals to look up to their spirit guardians "as children look up to parents." A. E. Newton used the same metaphor in advising that the duty of both advanced spirits and parents was "to minister to their [children's] wants, and to aid and guide the unfoldings of their being." Perceiving themselves as disorderly spiritual children at the outset of an immortal existence, Spiritualists craved stern fatherly voices of wisdom and Christian soldiery and gentle motherly ones that touched the conscience by exuding love and nurture. They looked to an androgynous spirit ministry for warmth, security, nurture, and discipline because their "Father" God, like many fathers in a changing antebellum American economy, seemed increasingly absent from home.[26]

The Invisible Pastorate

In the most remarkable passage of The "Ministry of Angels" Realized, the Newtons suggested that they consulted spirits precisely when their less heterodox contemporaries might have consulted a minister or priest.

> When care and perplexity, as regards the affairs of this life, have borne
> upon us, they have been ever ready with words of counsel and of cheer.
> . . . in the quiet hours of retirement and contemplation, when we have
> sought to know more of ourselves and our relations to the universe
> around us, to solve the great problems of life, and to comprehend more
> of His ways, . . . then also we have found ourselves under the guidance
> and teaching of instructors whose knowledge extends beyond our high-
> est previous conceptions.

Nor were these spirit ministers' duties confined to life's larger problems and
issues. The Newtons' unseen pastors were concerned to watch and order their
personal lives down to such details as the food they ate.

> They are by our side, sensibly and often visibly, at morning, noon, and
> evening, and encamp around us and our little ones through the silent
> hours of the night. When we bow in worship around the family altar, they
> join their worship with ours, 'helping our infirmities' and 'making
> intercessions for us,' in words full of wondrous meaning and sublime
> adoration. When we approach the table to partake of God's bounties,
> they are ever nigh to remind us of the great Giver of all good, to inspire
> our hearts with thankfulness, and to instruct us in the nature and qualities
> of the different kinds of food . . . in all the common walks, trials, and
> vicissitudes of life, whenever we feel the need of assistance, strength and
> light from above, we find them at hand, bringing to us, from the great
> Source of Good, those supplies of grace and wisdom which we require.

Their rebellion against the clergy certainly was not produced by a diminished
need for intimate and watchful pastoral care.[27]

Spiritualists consistently linked spirit communication not only to their
sense of divine distance but also to their loss of confidence in the clergy. They
contrasted the natural and therefore legitimate authority of spirits, grounded
in cosmic law, with the illegitimate authority that earthbound ministers based
on such artificial credentials as education and ordination. R. P. Ambler was
convinced that the spiritual authority which "sits in the sanctuary and reads
lectures from the pulpit" was "corrupted." "Sighing and thirsting" for
something more than the "thoughts of the religionist and theologian," he
considered spirits far better "prepared, authorized, and commissioned to act
as teachers" than ordinary ministers. Spirits, he explained, were "entirely
freed from religious bigotry, released from the chains of creed and sect,
delivered from the bondage of sectarian dogmas, and introduced into a
sphere of light where the soul may expand." Another Spiritualist agreed that
spirit ministry was "more absolute, more freed from secular considerations"
than mere "earthly ministration." Unlike the ministers of earth, moreover,
spirit clerics were "in the experience of immortality" and "know spirituality as

a reality." Shorn of their mortal bodies, they were more fully spiritual and divine, closer to pure truth, and more suitable models of spiritual freedom and spiritual order than the relatively unworthy ministers of the American religious establishment. They were not simply "preaching as a business" on matters beyond their knowledge as were the "mere pulpit expounders of the day." For Isaac Post, spirit communication meant "having an unselfish counsellor always at hand."[28]

Not every instance of spirit communication brought Spiritualists into contact with such beings—undeveloped spirits sometimes visited séances seeking instruction from their mortal superiors—but religious Spiritualists usually sought contact with spirits they considered more advanced than themselves. John Murray Spear was certain that his invisible companions enjoyed a state "just above" him, and George Dexter thought most spirit communications "a *little above* the moral and intellectual *status* of the *particular persons* who receive them." As surrogate ministers and administrators of divine order, these advanced spirits were believed to wield representative religious authority. Cora Hatch and S. B. Brittan explained that spirits were "armed" with "mediatorial influences" which made them "His ministers, sent forth in His name," displaying "functions, powers and manifestations which represent His mind, His soul, His power." In short, Spiritualists invested their spirit contacts with what Newton frankly called "superhuman authority."[29]

This is not to say that they considered spirits infallible or omniscient. Spiritual republicanism required a vigilant wariness of external authority and therefore warnings against placing too great a trust in spirits. Moreover, Spiritualists believed with Swedenborg that mortals attracted spirits with whom they had a natural "affinity" or likeness of spiritual and moral inclination. Many of them were well aware, therefore, that their experiences did little more than confirm their own previously held opinions. Still, their tendency to seek such confirmation underscores their perception of spirits as authority figures. And those who "feel [their] opinions changed or swayed" when conversing with spirits, a possibility noted by O. G. Warren, were similarly seeking cosmic confirmation. However imperfect their spirit ministers, Spiritualists considered themselves more imperfect still and therefore believed they could profitably look to the spirit world in their search for knowledge and certainty. Indeed, John Edmonds argued that communication with spirits would hardly be worthwhile if they had no instruction to offer.[30]

Operating under this view of spirits, Spiritualists envisioned them in a variety of practical ministerial roles. The most important of these was the teaching of spiritual truth. Religious Spiritualists like Edmonds regarded this function as the major reason for establishing communication with a spirit ministry. Regarding the earth as a "rudimental sphere" in which only the most basic spiritual truths could find expression, they were hopeful that instruction by advanced spirits would open the door to a higher order of existence and thus set their souls free from terrestrial limitations. This hope led R. P. Ambler to title his 1852 volume of spirit messages *The Spiritual Teacher.*

Much of that teaching came in spirit communications that had obvious sermonesque and prayerlike qualities and treated the same moral and religious themes that conventional homilies did. Spirit minister Swedenborg greeted one of the regular Sunday meetings held by John Edmonds and his circle of Spiritualists with words that might just as easily have come from any minister addressing any congregation. "I am glad to meet you all my friends," he began, and continued his opening benediction by urging the gathering to "love one another, and be true, be holy." At another meeting, spirit Francis Bacon led the group in prayer, supplicating "Our Father" to "teach us thy law."[31]

The invisible clergy also represented a religious unity and certainty which Spiritualists, fatigued by the doctrinal disputes of antebellum sectarian religion, felt the ministers of the establishment were failing to provide. Newton was certain that people seeking the meaning of the Bible and experiencing "increasing doubt and perplexity" amidst the "conflicting opinions of men" would welcome the spirits as bearers of an attractive religious alternative. To be sure, Spiritualism did not always deliver on its promise; the content of spirit messages tended to reflect the beliefs of the medium or the audience. But Spiritualists' alienation from organized religious partisanship was clear enough in their frequent contentions that the spirits, unlike too many professional clergy, had progressed beyond narrow sectarian considerations and disputes. Free of what a disgusted Edmonds called the "conflicting sophistries of church and priest," their presumed agreement on the essentials of religion made them symbols of religious harmony and order.[32]

The case of Adin Ballou is illustrative. His experience of bitter infighting as a minister in the Universalist denomination and then in its Restorationist offshoot led him to regard clerical professionalism and partisanship as serious obstacles to reform and spiritual growth. By the time he turned to Spiritualism, he had abandoned the ministry, "come out" of his denomination, and declared himself above sectarian bias. He saw in the "doctrine of the spirits" an antidote to sectarianism and a promise of Christian unity around essential truths. He acknowledged minor "discrepancies and contradictions" in spirit messages but was satisfied that "ninety-nine one hundredths of these testimonies harmonize in every essential particular." It was especially satisfying to him that this broad agreement characterized "spirits who, in the life of the flesh, were connected with the most hostile sects, whose communications have been made through Media educated in these opposing sects."[33]

Spiritualists' distaste for yet another feature of the terrestrial ministry inspired the most striking way that they credited the spirits with taking over and improving clerical functions. Most of them had dismissed the revivals of earlier decades as artificially induced and ephemeral outbursts of religious emotion that had been engineered to increase church membership rolls but had not produced substantial and lasting religious conviction among the laity. But they tended to smile on the "laymen's revival" of 1857–1858 and to attribute it to spirit ministry. As believers in a remote deity and in the genuinely cosmic dimension of human spirituality, they considered older theocentric explanations of revivalism unlikely and emergent human-centered explanations focusing on psychological manipulation unpalatable. Their spirit-centered theory of revivalism provided a suitable compromise. They were convinced that their invisible clergy had sparked authentic religious experiences through natural spirit prompting.

To be sure, skepticism and antipathy toward revivalism ran strong enough among them to prevent an uncritical approval of this latest event. Indeed, disparaging comments about revival methods punctuated an April 1858 debate in the New York Spiritualist Conference, indicating that the participants were by no means agreed on either its spirit sources or its difference from its dubious predecessors. But their shared concern with revivalists to promote personal religious experience combined with the absence of clerical exhorters to prompt among them a generally less negative view of this episode than of previous ones. Led by a pious laity acting under spirit influence, it was "less of man's work" and "less under clerical management," noted one of them. Another considered it "more of a spontaneity . . . it is a spiritual manifestation."[34]

Approving Spiritualists commented that the spirits had produced an episode far more subdued and "feminized" than previous ones. The evangelical ministers who had prompted the earlier meetings, said Andrew Jackson Davis, were "large, loud-spoken, physically-vigorous men" who relied on raw "psychological power" and therefore failed to produce any real change in the soul. The meetings of 1857–1858, on the other hand, were caused by a gentle "spiritual influence exerted through the nearness of the spirits to mortals at this time." Davis's comments were not entirely positive—he felt that the revivals paid insufficient attention to moral edification and reform—but he happily reported that its spirit sources had produced genuine and orderly religious feeling without "that vulgar excitement which has been so disgustingly prevalent in previous revivals."[35]

Dr. John F. Gray saw in spirit-inspired revivalism an effective escape from the hellfire theology of the evangelicals, which he felt had mistakenly grounded piety in fear rather than love. Likewise, he and other Spiritualists joined other liberal Protestants in rejecting evangelicals' emphasis on a sudden conversion experience, which seemed unpleasantly suggestive of coercive power, in favor of the softer notion of gradual growth and nurture through spirit influence. They thought they were witnessing a gentler and safer kind of religious expression than those fanned by irresponsible or overzealous ministers. Spirit ministers, they were glad to say, produced not emotional excess but tamed expressions of spirituality that kept spontaneous experience within the confines of order.[36]

Spiritualists looked to their invisible ministry not only for higher wisdom, homiletic inspiration, and religious awakening but also for assistance in personal regeneration and redemption. Lacking faith in the moral power of the mortal clergy, they looked to the purifying influence of what they called spirit "redeemers," "saviors," and "evangels" in much the same way that evangelical Protestants assigned ministers an important role in the conversion process. The author of "The Angels' Care of Mortals" rhapsodized about the spirits' intense pastoral concern for the moral welfare of their mortal flock and their aid in the "great work . . . of human regeneration." Emma Hardinge's history of the movement recounted several instances in which "kind spirit friends, either through clairvoyant prescriptions or magnetic passes, have succeeded in entirely destroying the taste for intoxicating liquors and to-bacco." In a typical story, called "Spirits at a Gaming Table," she described a card player who was taken over by a spirit and proceeded to deliver "a homily against gambling." This speech was followed by "a most touching address, purporting to come from a deceased sister of one of the company, couched in such a tender and affecting tone that the whole company were irresistibly moved to tears." Needless to say, "there was no more card-playing that night."[37]

In social regeneration, too, Spiritualists looked to the spirit world for the agency they could not expect from themselves and for the help and leader-ship they could not expect from the terrestrial ministry. Since corruption and dependence on often conservative parishioners prevented the clergy from taking independent stands on controversial social issues, Adin Ballou ex-pected the far freer spirits to be "everywhere Reformers, Regenerators of the world, individually and socially." Frustrated by repeated conflict with clerical conservatism, he agreed with S. B. Brittan that spirits were social activists and that the "true reformer" would be "always moving, and would not be still even in Heaven."[38]

Spiritualists were, of course, too thoroughly imbued with the values of spiritual republicanism, human capability, and free will to rest the burden of regeneration entirely on spirits. Edmonds insisted with most of them that spiritual progress, while inevitable, required their own "toil," "earnest labor," and "unceasing efforts." Their anxious concern to preserve a role for deity in the regenerative process similarly militated against too strong an emphasis on the role of spirits. John Shoebridge Williams was often reminded by the voice of Eliza that she had been merely "the Lord's medium." But Spiritualists were sufficiently unsure of human capability and the immediacy of God's presence to postulate spirits as an intermediate level of regenerative activity between humanity and deity. Even while acknowledging God, Williams credited spirit Eliza "for having saved as they call it, her father." Emma Hardinge summed up the Spiritualist view when she urged that "each spirit, in or out of the body, *must work*" while recognizing the "aid, light, counsel, strength and blessing God vouchsafes to pour upon the soul through the ministry of angels."[39]

The concept of an invisible pastorate was sometimes pushed to authoritarian extremes. If the conception of the cosmos as church, home, and school invited comparisons of spirits to ministers, parents, and teachers, the image of the universe as a corrective institution implied that mortals were inmates under the watchful eyes of spirit guards. Uncertain that the limited eyes of a corrupt clergy or the sweeping eyes of an impersonal God could ensure moral order, they turned to their invisible ministry, whose combination of superhuman powers of perception and concern with events on earth ideally suited them to the task. Thus one Spiritualist expected belief in spirits to "produce a universal reformation and a purer state of Christianity, than all the external appliances of church and state." Thomas Wentworth Higginson's liberal Unitarian beliefs, meanwhile, left him hoping that the eyes of the spirit world would be a more effective restraint than a "vague belief that God sees." John Edmonds, who inspected prisons for New York state during the 1840s, portrayed this aspect of spirit guardianship in particularly ominous terms. Like many authoritarian regimes, he defended the necessity of "placing you under guard and watch" as essential to the achievement of a "great and noble object."[40]

This strategy of preserving order was not unusual in the context of antebellum social development. Many Americans feared that economic growth and urbanization had eroded traditional communal restraints on the individual and raised the possibility of social chaos. They urged self-control, but uncertainty led them to devise various ways of applying external moral pressure. Some retreated into utopian communities, where they could rely on mutual watchfulness among a small group of people. Others established reform organizations as communities that would set and enforce moral standards. Others piqued the male conscience by appealing to the example of women. Spiritualists applied similar methods of social control when they postulated spirits as the invisible chaperones of Jacksonian society. They imagined a community of watchful spirits who, like Victorian mothers or wives, could touch the conscience dulled by life in a competitive and impersonal society even when they were not physically present. Extending from the "home" above into the harsh "world" below, the moral influence of spirits like that of mothers and wives would be, in the words of one historian, "discreetly omnipresent and omnipotent."[41]

The Ministry of Hope

Spiritualists looking to spirit ministry for assistance in transforming their souls and their society—particularly those who understood spirits as guards over a cosmic asylum—evidently harbored a considerable mistrust of human moral capability. They blended an optimistic Arminianism, which emphasized human capability and dominated antebellum American religious culture, with a pessimistic view of human nature not often associated either with Spiritualism, antebellum religion and reform, or antebellum American culture generally. Indeed, they sometimes sounded almost Calvinistic in suggesting that the people of earth were incapable of improving themselves and required help. Abby T. Hall thought that unaided mortals were trapped by their "helplessness" in "a retrograde life, that the cycle of an eternity can scarce redeem." R. P. Ambler, too, believed that "the labors of men would be hopeless and comparatively fruitless, without a direct and special interposition of spiritual power." They regarded humanity as spiritually ill and in desperate need of spirit doctors (though they never explicitly compared their spirit ministers to doctors or the cosmos to a hospital), and certainly did not trust the individual to exercise self-control amid the manifold temptations of Jacksonian society.[42]

This lack of confidence made them decidedly uneasy with the antebellum cultural emphasis on individual responsibility. They echoed that emphasis but also hoped that spirits would lead them. "Does the soul shrink," Abby T. Hall asked, "from the responsibility involved in its very nature and construction, and disclosed by its own spirituality? Let it take courage. No law of nature, spiritual or moral, will be required of man without its attendant aids to assist and teach its fulfillment." By locating the individual in a socio-spiritual order, Spiritualists shifted moral responsibility away from the individual in accordance with the belief among many antebellum reformers that personal immorality could be attributed to environmental sources and eradicated through the creation of proper social and institutional conditions. The reassuring ministers, teachers, parents, and guards of the cosmic institution lightened the burdens of individualism through their aid. They prepared these uncertain Americans for the responsibilities of freedom by teaching them about law and order.[43]

Spiritualists' suggestion that spirit and mortal reformers were working together to perfect human society constituted a combination of two religious moods often postulated as opposing and mutually exclusive categories in analyses of antebellum culture. The first, often identified with reformers of the period, was an optimistic "postmillennialism" which assumed human beings to be capable of contributing through their efforts to the gradual achievement of the perfect society or millennium prophesied in the Bible. The other, usually considered a recessive trait among antebellum reformers, was the impatient and pessimistic "premillennialism" characteristic of such groups as the Millerites. This outlook assumed that a human race incapable of substantially improving the world required a sudden and imminent infusion of supramundane aid to reach the millennial state. Spiritualists at once emphasized the importance of human effort and hopefully summoned the superhuman help of spirit ministry to sustain their millennial expectancy (the latter helps explain the appeal of Spiritualism for ex-Millerites). This fusion suggests that postmillennial optimism and premillennial pessimism were two facets of a complex historical reality.[44]

Spiritualist cosmology was well calculated to soothe idealistic reformers who experienced disappointment during the 1850s as the antebellum reform thrust entered its twilight. Andrew Jackson Davis complained at the outset of the movement that social critics and reformers were generally opposed and hindered by the world at large and suggested that discouragement had led them to look to the spirit world in search of a future. A similar sense of despair led Adin Ballou's son-in-law William S. Heywood to give a Spiritualist pep talk to the residents of Hopedale in 1853. He assured his audience of unhappy reformers that "pure and good" spirits were "co-workers" who would help them overcome their "repeated stumblings." Heywood's remarks were published in the community's periodical under the title "Be Not Disheartened." S. B. Brittan launched the *Spiritual Telegraph* in 1852 certain that his new religion would appeal to those who like himself "weep over the grave of their buried hopes."[45]

Americans like Brittan worried that they were unable to prevent their rapidly changing society from descending into moral chaos. According to Michael Barkun, the increasing complexity of an antebellum society being transformed by industrialization, urbanization, and immigration eroded their sense of mastery and control. Their response was to postulate the invisible forces and unseen realities of electricity, mesmerism, and Spiritualism in an attempt to comprehend their society and to come to grips with human limitations. "Mastery had given way to incomprehension, and incomprehension to anxiety," but the belief that spirits were pushing what Edmonds called a "wayward world" in a proper direction assuaged Spiritualists' uneasiness. John Shoebridge Williams felt that he and his contemporaries were "powerless amid the cross occurrences and discordant elements with which society is perplexed." He therefore saw "the necessity of a better power to be given to man for his guidance than his own intelligence, perplexed and confused as it now is." He and other Spiritualists sustained their faltering faith in Jacksonian America through the hope that spirit ministers, symbols and embodiments of a redeemed humanity, were better able than human reformers to impose divine order on an intractable society.[46]

Indeed, a number of studies have suggested that Spiritualist ideology served as a failure mechanism for its adherents. Feeling impotent in their own reform efforts and lacking confidence in the efforts of others, they found solace and a salve for feelings of disappointment and personal guilt in their spirit ministers' assurances that higher powers were working with humanity to realize its goals. Moreover, they believed that the changes they desired had already been realized in the spirit world. According to Sandra S. Frankiel, Spiritualists transposed their elusive utopian and millennial visions onto an imagined spiritual realm whose conditions were far more malleable than those of earth. Like the disappointed Millerites, who responded to the failure of William Miller's prophecies of Christ's return by insisting that the expected event had actually occurred on schedule in the world of spirit, Spiritualists "spiritualized" their expectations as a defense against guilt and despair.[47]

Their commingled hope and despair were succinctly allegorized by Brittan in the inaugural issue of his *Shekinah*. "The Ministry of Hope" told the story of a reformer caught in the crosswinds of resilient optimism and bitter disappointment. It opened with a "Youth" in futile pursuit of frustratingly elusive "palaces and castles of the most ethereal and delicious splendor." Failure left the youth "weary of his fruitless toil," and he sighed as "the castle walls dissolved away." He lost faith, cursed "cruel Hope," resolved to "listen and believe no more," and fell victim to "Despair." Spiritualism and hope entered the story at this point in the form of a sentimental female spirit. "Hope from her bright abodes witnessed the distress of the poor Youth" and, "taking an aerial form, invisible to mortal eyes, she approached and whispered a sweet prophecy in his soul." Despair promptly vanished as a resurgent Hope endowed the youth with "the strength of Manhood." The allegory closed as the youth, now an "Old Man," died and realized his dreams in the "supernal magnificence" of the spirit world. Spiritualism literally allowed hope to spring eternal.[48]

The case of Warren Chase illustrates more concretely the way in which belief in a supramundane ministry of hope fit into Spiritualists' life patterns and fed on their disappointing experiences as reformers.[49] The very title of his 1857 autobiography, *The Life-Line of the Lone One*, suggests his feelings of anomie and isolation and his turn to spirits for guidance, support, and strength. Born an illegitimate child in 1813, he was orphaned at age four and, as he later said, left with "no voice in kindness to direct me." He moved as a young man to Wisconsin, where he experienced an unpleasant marriage, poverty during the hard times of the late 1830s, and the death of two children. Finally, he gained success and recognition in the 1840s through participation in the Wisconsin constitutional convention and a term in the Wisconsin state Senate. He devoted his political activity to the abolition of capital punishment, women's and black suffrage, women's property rights, the liberalization of divorce laws, and land reforms. He also became drawn to phrenology and mesmerism by the denunciations of a conservative clergy that he felt "abus[ed] the world's best reforms and reformers." His opposition to competitive capitalism and economic injustice moved him to embrace communitarianism and to lead the establishment of the Fourierist Wisconsin Phalanx, also called Ceresco. He reformed his personal lifestyle as well, renouncing the use of alcohol, tobacco, coffee, tea, and pork, and ceasing sexual relations with his wife.[50]

His life as a reformer was frustrated by his unsupportive wife and what he considered the unreadiness of a conservative citizenry for his proposals. His alienation climaxed with the failure of Ceresco in 1851. Bitterly disappointed but "yearning still for a millennial dawn," he and his cohorts wailed a pathetic song of profound despair: "My heart is sick, my soul is pained within," it began. "Talk not of brotherhood; / Man lives for self, not for the common good. / . . . Talk not of heaven, or of a golden age, / While social ills in ceaseless battle rage." The group also wrote what Chase called an "epitaph" for the "dead Phalanx," convincing themselves that it had been "prematurely born" and therefore "must die and be born again." Looking back in 1888 at the 1853 collapse of the North American Phalanx, he again employed imagery of death and rebirth in spiritualizing its success. This Phalanx, the last of its kind in the United States, had "succumbed" and now awaited "a renewal in the other world, as society here was not ready for that state of social life." Chase was mourning not simply two defunct phalanxes but his destroyed faith in humanity.[51]

He turned hopefully to the world of spirits as a source of order over the chaos of both American society and his personal life as a reformer. He sensed in the advent of Spiritualism "the dawn of millennial day" and "a new religious phase of society." He enthusiastically embraced Davis's *Revelations*, became a writer and agent for the *Univercoelum*, and, after the demise of Ceresco, devoted himself fully to his new religion. Through it, he found a new sense of missionary zeal and an assurance that his mother's spirit had always been guiding him. He also found an explanation and rationalization for his lack of financial and political success. Spirit influence was "the cause of his abandoning every field of labor where worldly honor and distinction was before him . . . and the reason why he had let every opportunity to acquire wealth escape him." Most importantly, he found sorely needed confidence that his work in behalf of "all odious or unpopular truths and rights" was appreciated and encouraged by forces in the spirit world if not on earth, where "he had been clubbed and pelted all his life." He now knew, he said, that he had been "chosen by a society of spirit-teachers" whose "discipline and influence" had resulted in his change in lifestyle and "the true development of the affections and loves."[52]

By the autumn of 1852 he had "dispensed with all other business" and "was getting out of politics" while "the dispensation of the new gospel absorbed his time." Amid this bustle of activity, the "voices of his guardians were ever urging him on in his mission." Chase summed up the importance of Spiritualism to him when he wrote that "this has been to me an unfriendly world; only the light and life of, and in, Spiritualism had given me comfort and hope." "Were it not for the single hope which spiritualism holds out of a better future for us," he said, again employing the language of bereavement, "we might . . . go mourning the rest of our lives." A loss of faith and a need for psychological healing could be as potent as the death of a friend or relative in sending Spiritualists in search of psychic renewal through a belief in the spirits. Chase continued to find solace in Spiritualism when, in 1888, he recounted his *Forty Years on the Spiritual Rostrum*.[53]

Even more than Chase, John Murray Spear exemplified the pathetic extremes to which a frustrated and alienated idealist desiring to restore a lost sense of control could carry a faith in spirit ministry.[54] Born in Boston in 1804 and raised by a widowed mother, he overcame financial difficulty and a poor education to become a Universalist minister. An outspoken commitment to radical abolitionism led him into conflict with his congregations, and his impatience with clerical silence on the issue created tensions between him and his denomination. An 1844 beating at the hands of an anti-abolition mob finally drove him from the ministry into full-time reform activity and feelings of social isolation and martyrdom. He coupled his abolitionism with work for prison reform, opposing capital punishment and identifying with social outcasts through personal visits with prisoners during the late 1840s and early 1850s. He refused various offers of official appointments, choosing instead the lone reform efforts he deemed essential to effective work and to his sense of Christian duty and mission. This often ungratifying work heightened his feelings of alienation.

He discovered Davis's *Revelations* in the late 1840s and by early 1851 was convinced that "a Hand unseen has guided me" and that "I have often communed with higher intelligences." This belief was "to my soul a source of inexpressible comfort. As I go from town to town . . . laboring for the destitute prisoner, they comfort, soothe, and strengthen me." His spirit-driven mission soon broadened to include traveling trance healing.[55]

However comforting the spirits may have been to him, he did more to intensify than to alleviate his sense of martyrdom and isolation as he followed his belief in "reform through the aid of spiritual interposition" to excessive lengths. Inspired as he believed by an organization of technologically minded spirits called the "Association of Electricizers," he attempted in 1854 his grandest reform project yet: the construction of a perpetual motion machine and the technological salvation of the human race.[56] He received support from Simon Crosby Hewitt (another ex–Universalist minister who edited his *Messages from the Superior State* and the Spiritualist periodical *New Era*), the Newtons, Samuel G. Love (the first husband of Davis's wife, Mary), and other radical reformers who shared his high hopes for what might be achieved on earth with help from the spirit world.[57]

The machine was modeled on the human body and designed to harness "the *electric life-currents of the universe.*" It was to be "a thing of life," tapping the "outflow of Deific energy from the 'Grand Electrical Focus,' vitalizing and quickening all things." Spear's construction site was a cottage on a hill called High Rock near Lynn, Massachusetts, a place which he thought had enhanced electrical properties and therefore special spiritual significance (see illustration 4). To set the motor in motion, Spear invited his supporters to sit around the table on which it was built and place their hands on it. The purpose of these séance-like rituals, which expressed the group's religious reverence for technology, was to use their "personal magnetisms" to connect the motor with "that very fine quality of invisible fluid which it was designed should act upon and in it."[58]

Finally, Spear allowed himself to be entranced and encased in an elaborate apparatus "from a rational confidence in the wisdom and good faith of the invisible directors." He and a Boston medium who was to serve as the "mother of the 'new motor'" and "the Mary of the New Dispensation" brought their "higher degree of celestial magnetism" to bear on the machine. Although "Mary" claimed to experience labor pains and a clairvoyant present claimed to see "a stream of light, a sort of *umbilicum,* emanating to and enveloping the mechanism," the climactic birth of the New Motive Power amounted to little more than "a slight pulsatory action" which "became perceptible in the extremities." Still, Spear and his followers sensed that the application of spirit wisdom had brought the human race to the threshold of a technological millennium. Spear thought he had witnessed "the action of a *heart,* beating, possibly, in sympathy or connection with 'the Grand Central Magnetic Heart of the Universes.'"[59]

Beaming over the blessed event, Hewitt announced in the *New Era* that "THE THING MOVES" and that "Unto your earth a child is born. Its name shall be called the ELECTRICAL MOTOR." He thought the machine would be "the physical Saviour of the race" and "lead the way in the great speedily-coming salvation." S. B. Brittan cautioned readers of the *Spiritual Telegraph* that only "some little balls connected with the machine" and not "the grand revolver" itself had moved, but Spear like Chase refused to admit failure even after a

Illustration 4: Andrew Jackson Davis's vision of a "Spiritual Congress" at High Rock tower near Lynn, Massachusetts, August 1852. Davis's vision inspired many of the activities of medium John Murray Spear. The nearby cottage was the construction site of Spear's "New Motor" in 1854. The illustration suggests High Rock's importance as a sacred spot, a point of contact between earth and the spirit world.

hostile mob destroyed the machine. He remained convinced that spirits had demonstrated the possibility of harnessing electrical energy and concluded that his New Motor had been introduced to the world before its time. He also noted with satisfaction the parallel between the martyrdom of his machine and that of the early Christians. Retaining his faith, he went on to follow other spirit directives that included an attempt to establish a utopian community and a search for buried treasure. In 1873 he reviewed his long and comforting interaction with spirits in *Twenty Years on the Wing*.[60]

The Sources of the Self

The concept of spirit ministry entailed the difficult problem of separating the subjective self and personal agency from the objective spiritual forces that were assumed to shape them. After over ten months of carefully recorded mediumistic dialogue with Eliza, a spirit "monitor" who was "always there, watching and influencing your will," John Shoebridge Williams was still unable to distinguish his own impulses, thoughts, and words as a medium from hers. "What you prefix the word '*medium*' to," Eliza's spirit superiors tried to explain to him, "is from our world through Eliza more directly into yourself and moulded more especially by your form than that to which you prefix the word '*monitor*.'" Williams seemed satisfied of his autonomy, but it was clear that he traced his own thoughts and words to the spirit world.[61] He believed that "presentiments, internal monitions, conscience, perceptions, and the like" were often spirit "impressions." John F. Coles similarly saw the word "conscience" spelled out after he asked his "guardian spirit" to identify itself. Uriah Clark noted that since human beings are "constantly receiving more or less from the celestial hosts," mediums are "frequently troubled to know what manifestations are their own, and what may be ascribed to the sole and direct agency of spirits." He frankly confessed that "we may never know where to draw the line of discrimination."[62]

The classic metaphysical dilemma of reconciling personal autonomy and independent selfhood with divine activity and cosmic order characterizes most religious ideologies. But a concern with the nature of selfhood was intensified by a variety of factors specific to the changing social, economic, cultural, intellectual, and religious circumstances of antebellum America. Motivated to examine selfhood by the same factors that moved their con-temporaries, Spiritualists seeking to understand it resonated in many ways with broader cultural trends. But their unique understanding, based on the concept of spirit ministry, also jarred in crucial respects with widely accepted American ideologies of selfhood.

Spiritualists derived their version of the problem of selfhood in part from mesmerism, which emphasized the close connection between the self and the cosmic magnetic influences which acted on and shaped it. They were espe-cially intrigued by the trance (which they often called the "superior state"), a state of heightened consciousness induced in mesmerist practice when one's personal portion of the universal magnetic fluid was manipulated by an "operator" or "magnetizer." Mesmerists believed that through a scientifically demonstrable clairvoyant mental faculty, the entranced mind could become "freed . . . from the obstructing influence of the material organization," transcending the physical senses and the self to establish an enlightening mystical and magnetic contact with a higher spiritual reality.[63]

Attempts to communicate with spirits through the trance had become part of mesmeric practice as well; indeed, George Bush had suggested in *Mesmer and Swedenborg* (1847) that the Swedish Seer himself had communicated with spirits in this way. Therefore, although Spiritualists believed with most antebellum Americans that sensory experience was an essential source of knowledge, even of a religious kind, they eagerly appropriated the trance as a scientifically verified vehicle of spirit ministry and looked beyond the physical phenomena of Spiritualism to what John Edmonds called a scientific "inves-tigation of spirituality." They shared Bush's expectation that mesmerism would "open a new chapter in the philosophy of mind and in man's relations to a higher sphere" when "taken in conjunction with the developments of Swedenborg."[64]

These "developments" referred to Swedenborg's belief that every person acted under an unconscious influence proceeding from God through mediating spirits.[65] To Spiritualists like A. E. Newton, it was a logical step from mesmerist notions of magnetic influence to Spiritualist notions of spirit influence. If mesmerism had shown that "minds *in the body* can and often do exercise the . . . power of control over the organisms of impressible persons," it seemed reasonable to suppose that "minds *out of the body,* and possessed of a more intimate knowledge of the relations of body and spirit" possessed "at least equal abilities." Placing greater emphasis on spirit agency than Swedenborg had, Spiritualists made this assumption one of the "essential truths" of their religion.[66]

Sacred Circle co-editor George Dexter devoted an entire article to "Spirit-Influence," which to him was a logical consequence of the basic ontological assumption that the whole of existence was "the divine manifestation of spirit through matter." This influence, he explained, operated on the mind, conscience, and will as much through "invisible association" as through "positive communication." John Murray Spear explained that "influxes from above" were continually "agitating, acting upon, forming, shaping, and controlling the actions of each individual" after "enter[ing] the cranium through countless minute pores." As a result, "the individual becomes spiritualized," and the self "assimilated to, and harmonized with, the Divine Mind."[67]

Spirit influence meant that feelings, thoughts, and ideas were not spontaneous products of the self but derived from higher spiritual beings. Spear attributed "that *inner light* which so safely guides the pure in heart" immediately to spirit prompting and ultimately to *"impregnation"* from a deity he called the "Source of all selfs." John S. Adams agreed that "every pure and holy thought, every new idea, all wise impressions" reached mortals through "myriad grades of intelligences." All knowledge, he believed, "is from above and not of ourselves. . . . Man cannot *create* anything." A. E. Newton and other Spiritualists also included the phenomena of religious ecstasy—"exhibitions of the gift of tongues and the interpretations of tongues, of prophecy, of discerning of spirits, or working miracles, and of healing the sick"— among the "manifestations of spiritual influence or inspiration." (Conspicuously absent from their lists were such revival phenomena as shouting and writhing on the ground; acts of religious insanity were not permitted in their cosmic asylum and church, nor unruly children permitted in their cosmic school and home.) Like most religious ideologies, Spiritualist cosmology thoroughly minimized the ego. John Shoebridge Williams saw "no such thing as the I-myself-big-man-me in true mediumship."[68]

Spiritualists also, we have seen, traced personal moral growth and regeneration to spirit influence. They drew from Christian thought a dualistic conception of selfhood that juxtaposed a lower sensual nature with a higher spiritual one, considering it the duty and destiny of every person to liberate the latter from the corrupting and enslaving influences of the former in a process called by R. P. Ambler "the spiritualization of the human system." The spirits, they believed, had made this process of spiritual liberation (or "salvation") their mission on earth. Indeed, medium Abby T. Hall considered this a primary reason for spirit visitation. Spiritualists believed that their invisible ministry contributed as decisively as they themselves did to self-control and self-discipline.[69]

The belief that spirit influence and in particular the trance might enlighten and purify the individual suggests a close similarity between mediumship and the mystical illumination that shapes spiritual selfhood in many religious traditions. R. Laurence Moore drew a theoretical distinction between them—"the entranced Spiritualist medium receives unreliable information from nondivine sources and undergoes no inward transformation as a result of the experience"—but correctly acknowledged that the distinction breaks down in practice. According to religious Spiritualists, both personal mediumship and vicarious spirit communion (both kinds of experience were common in Spiritualist religion) were introspective experiences bringing inner religious illumination, contact with at least semidivine beings, and spiritually transformative effects. The mesmeric trance (and by extension the mediumistic trance), according to Robert C. Fuller, "prepared the patient for an almost sacramental encounter with a transmundane spiritual agent" which "momentarily transformed and elevated the patient's very being." Indeed, Spiritualists democratized mystical enlightenment when they democratized mediumship, for they believed all individuals to be mystics of a sort, in continual if unconscious contact with higher spiritual powers.[70]

Spiritualists like Andrew Jackson Davis had no doubt about the identification of mediumship with mystic experience: "when an individual human mind . . . reaches nigh unto the spirit-world, then spiritual enlightenment and direction flow into the soul's affections and understanding." Another Spiritualist agreed that "communings with the Spirit-world . . . must purify and elevate all who receive them." It is not entirely true that Spiritualist religion, unlike Transcendentalism, slighted matters of religious selfhood by appealing "not to the inward illumination of mystic experience, but to the observable and verifiable objects of empirical science." Nor did religious Spiritualists simply trivialize the sacred by "transforming a concern for man's inward spiritual nature into an empirical inquiry into the nature of spirits." They wanted a spiritually uplifting religion grounded as much in personal experience as in empirical evidence. Giles Stebbins, whose belief system combined

Spiritualism, Transcendentalism, and Swedenborgianism, summed up this dualistic religious epistemology: "the transcendentalist would say immortality is a truth of the soul; the spiritualist would grant that, but would verify that truth by the testimony of the senses."[71]

Spiritualists postulating spirit ministry as a source of mystical experience and religious selfhood participated with Swedenborgians, mesmerists, and religious groups ranging from Transcendentalists to evangelical Protestants in the exploration of consciousness and spirituality that was taking place in mid-nineteenth-century America. According to Robert C. Fuller, mesmerism and phrenology (the belief that the brain was divided into "organs" whose size and structure determined the nature of the mind and personality), which became faddish during the antebellum period, contributed to the process by which religious theories of consciousness, which traced selfhood to a divine source, gradually gave way to the science of psychology, whose search for the wellsprings of personality focused on humanity and natural causation. Spiritualists opted for an intermediate approach that hinged on the influence of spirit mediators between humanity and God. Like the devotees of mesmerism, they rejected older theological notions of selfhood. But "a purely subjective psychological reality was beyond their conceptual horizons" and they believed that "personal wholeness" derived from "some transpersonal source."[72]

The Spiritualist concept of selfhood appealed to many inquirers into the nature of mind, personality, and spirituality, especially those whose investigations had already led to mesmerism. The career of Joseph Rodes Buchanan exemplifies the path from mesmeric to Spiritualist notions of selfhood followed by many antebellum Americans who stood on the threshold of modern psychology and psychiatry. A professor at the Eclectic Medical College of Cincinnati, Buchanan experimented with phrenology and mesmerism in his search for a science of mind. Mesmerism suggested to him that the mind is as susceptible to nonphysical or spiritual influences as to physical sensations, both of which he considered essential to a complete theory of mental phenomena and human nature. Purely physicalist theories, he felt, ignored human spirituality and led to materialism, pessimism, and atheism, while purely theological ones undermined the inductive scientific spirit. In mesmerism, and then Spiritualism, he saw ideologies that would synthesize the physicalist and theological approaches and extend the reach of science into the soul.

Convinced of the extrapersonal sources of selfhood, he established the *Journal of Man* in 1849—featuring on its cover a brain surrounded by bolts of electricity—and argued in it that the individual cannot be understood apart from the surrounding universe. In a series of articles entitled "Impressibility," he suggested that the self was "affected by surrounding influences."

An invisible mesmeric fluid, he said, "binds man to the universe, and establishes active relations between every element of his constitution and every element of the surrounding world." He noted that this fluid can be used to entrance and control a susceptible mind, influencing it to perform actions which appear to be its own spontaneous volitions.

When Spiritualism emerged, Buchanan welcomed it as an important new perspective, and his scientific investigations of its claims were instrumental in introducing it to Cincinnati. Long convinced that the mind could be "impressed" and behavior affected by external agents, he now speculated that "electricity, magnetism and galvanism are not the only forms of imponderable and invisible agency that affect the constitution of man." He suspected that "other imponderable fluids . . . exert a powerful influence upon man" and hinted that "the spirit world may have more to do with human development than has heretofore been supposed." In a piece on "Spirituality" published in the *Journal of Man* shortly after his acceptance of Spiritualism, he further argued that belief in guardian spirits was "sanctioned by the results of many experiments upon subjects in whom the Spiritual faculties have been excited." He and other Spiritualists believed that spirit ministers shaped and ordered selfhood from both without and within.[73]

LaRoy Sunderland embarked on a similar quest for the origins of spiritual selfhood. His search for a psychology of religious experience and a scientific approach to mystical illumination, like Buchanan's, led along a path that led through mesmerism to Spiritualism. But because he began his study of religiosity as an evangelical Methodist preacher, he brought revivalism into the cultural interaction between mesmerism and Spiritualism in the investigation of spirituality.[74] He began preaching in 1823 and, like his more famous contemporary Charles Grandison Finney, had a powerful effect on his listeners. He attributed his success to human rather than divine agency and experimented with revival techniques in an effort to understand the source of his power. His curiosity led him to mesmerism, whose effects seemed to him to resemble those of religious ecstasy.

He concluded by 1835 that the effects of revival preaching were induced by magnetic manipulation of the spiritual "organs" of the brain and that revivalism was therefore akin to mesmerism. By 1842, phrenology and mesmerism entirely supplanted Protestant orthodoxy in his thinking as the key to understanding the mind and soul and he left the Methodist denomination. He established the *Magnet,* one of the first mesmerist papers in the country, and devoted himself to what he called "phrenomagnetism," or the notion that behavior may be modified by the mesmeric manipulation of the "organs" of the brain. Mesmerism promised him both scientific proof that the individual is subject to higher influences than physical sensation and a means by which to experiment with religious ecstasy and mysticism. He developed a phrenological and mesmeric system of mental manipulation and healing called "pathetism," which he saw as a vehicle of moral reform and a way to achieve harmony between people and their environment.

For Sunderland as for Buchanan, Spiritualism revealed the cosmic main-springs of spirituality and the phenomenology of religion by identifying spirit influence as the source of pathetism. He became an ardent if circumspect champion of the new doctrine, introducing it to New England, establishing the *Spiritual Philosopher* in Boston in 1850 to spread the word, and lecturing three nights per week on "The Realities and Laws of the Spirit World." He held high hopes that advanced spirits, like revival preachers, would inwardly "influence" mortals toward harmony with each other and the universe. Indeed, he drew parallels between Spiritualist and revivalistic experiences. In his *Book of Psychology* (1852), he suggested the "identity of results" brought about by revivalism, pathetism, and spirit activity, including the "strange phenomena" of religious ecstasy: muscular rigidity, "loss of strength," trances, visions, and clairvoyance. Similarly, a chapter on "Psychology" in his *Book of Human Nature* (1853) compared the spirits and the Holy Spirit as "invisibles" whose influence shaped personal spirituality. But despite the similarities, Sunderland like other Spiritualists regarded Spiritualism as a decided improvement on revivalism, the latter being merely a crude way of producing "machine-made converts" and a "stepping stone to something above."[75]

Sunderland's pilgrimage from revivalism through mesmerism to Spiritual-ism reflected a broader process in which psychological conceptions of self-hood and religious experience began to replace theological ones. Like Buchanan, he found in Spiritualism a compromise between theocentrism and anthropocentrism, one that allowed for both transpersonal and intrapersonal dimensions of human spirituality. Both investigators pursued the mission of Spiritualism: to avoid the unacceptable poles of orthodoxy and a materialistic denial of spirit by applying science to a cosmically grounded spirituality. Like mesmerism, Spiritualism "responded to a growing concern to unite the forms of both ecstatic experience and 'scientific' thinking in a single religious system." George Bush identified this source of its appeal when he explained that it offered a scientific analysis of mind and spirituality "just at that point where anthropology welds itself to Theology."[76]

The concept of spirit ministry reflected not only a broader search for the nature of consciousness but also a wider cultural anxiety among middle-class Americans of the mid-nineteenth century over what was called "character." Rooted in the religious introspection of seventeenth-century Puritanism and reinforced by the republican ideology of the eighteenth century, this concept referred to "self-reliant virtue based on fixed inner principle." Many Ameri-cans feared that an emerging market economy and the growing anonymity of life in large cities would destroy character by undermining traditional moral and spiritual restraints on the individual. They were worried, according to Karen Halttunen, that these developments encouraged the neglect of the inner "soul" in favor of a subjectively wrought "personality" that was socially acceptable but shallow, hypocritical, and deceptive. As changing social and economic conditions freed the individual to formulate and reformulate a public image to meet the requirements of self-interest, character seemed more superficial and malleable, true identity more elusive, selfhood more fluid and less certain. The result was a threat to social trust. Americans operating in the new social and economic conditions of Jacksonian America needed reassurance that people still harbored morally reliable cores of selfhood beneath the layers of social convention.[77]

Uncertain about people's reliability, they created a "cult of sincerity" which emphasized the importance of linking outer personality to inner character as the foundation of trust and hence of social order in the new republic. In doing so, Halttunen has written, they betrayed their fear of "a threatening modern world" and "their nostalgia for a static, hierarchical social order and a fixed reference point for personal conduct." Spiritualists, with whose decidedly pessimistic and nostalgic tendencies we are already familiar, were at least as anxious as other antebellum Americans about the state of the self.[78]

That they shared this concern with sincerity and reliability is suggested by Andrew Jackson Davis's definition of character as "'the medium' through which the soul expresses itself openly." Their concerns were reflected even more powerfully in their persistent anxiety about spirits' moral reliability. Swedenborg had urged that spirits, being essentially human, retained the personalities they had formed on earth, were just as likely as mortals to be of dubious moral character, and were therefore to be approached with caution if at all. Spiritualists agreed, revering only those they believed superior. Thus John Shoebridge Williams, convinced by life in the bustling city of Cincinnati that people could only "*conjecture* in relation to . . . intentions or motives," needed the assurance of his spirit voices that good spirits, like good mortals, were worthy of confidence and trust. Robert Hare was comforted by his belief that in the spirit world, if not in his earthly home of Philadelphia, cosmic community and enhanced insight into character rendered hypocrisy and duplicity impossible. Among the spirits, who lived in circles analogous to the "circles of society, in a city," one's character "may be read by all. The hypocrite can remain hypocrite no longer, as he will inevitably appear in his true colors." Character in Hare's heaven was "intuitively susceptible of estimation" by "the grossness being greater as the character is more imperfect." Hare's interest in this feature of spirit society betrays his uneasy sense that sincerity was too rare in his own.[79]

Spiritualists found reassurance not only in their conviction that the spheres were free of earthly hypocrisy but also, and more to the point, in their belief that spirit ministry sustained genuine moral character in those under its influence. They could rest assured that the unbound and malleable self was in fact cosmically grounded, subject to and shaped by powerful spiritual forces that instilled moral principle as the foundation of character. If the ideal of being self-made had considerable cultural power, Spiritualists nonetheless took comfort in their belief that the self was made at least in part by others, that character was as much externally imposed as internally wrought. Their religion reconciled them to massive social and economic change by convincing them that the apparent social and moral chaos fostered by their uncomfortably unstructured environment was contained within an orderly cosmic structure.[80]

Spiritualists' interest in consciousness and character suggests that their exploration of selfhood reflected wider currents in antebellum American culture. At the same time, however, the concept of spirit ministry sufficiently conflicted with American ideas of selfhood to generate considerable tension between Spiritualists and other Americans, among Spiritualists themselves, and within the minds of individual Spiritualists. One source of tension was the implication of an androgynous cosmos and a bisexual spirit ministry that androgyny was the ideal spiritual state at a time when Americans were constructing sharp gender boundaries to accompany their new social and economic order. Men were expected to be assertive, rational, independent, while women were defined as submissive, passive, emotional, and dependent. Spiritualists aspired to be all of these, but the power of reigning gender definitions prevented them from squarely addressing the androgynizing implications of their ideology. Those that did were decidedly uncomfortable.

John Shoebridge Williams, for instance, believed that the spiritual perfection toward which he was progressing involved an increasing likeness to a deity in whom the "male" and "female" principles were "exactly one." But his attitude toward this goal was mixed. As the spirit of his deceased daughter Eliza took up residency in his soul to exert her feminizing influence, he submitted to her divinely derived authority in acknowledgment of Christian duty and the moral power of Victorian womanhood. But he also resisted it in defense of what he considered his threatened masculinity. His understanding of his sixty-one-year-old body reflected his ambiguous feelings about the androgynizing effects of Eliza's spirit ministry. On the one hand he welcomed his loss of pectoral definition as the development of breasts "like a females [*sic*]" under Eliza's influence; on the other he began to advocate the wearing of a beard as an emblem of manhood. His evident discomfort highlights the Spiritualist challenge to regnant American ideologies of sharply gendered selfhood.[81]

For male mediums, the trance through which spirit ministry was often exercised underscored this problem, for it required that "masculine" independence and self-control be temporarily suspended in favor of "feminine" submissiveness and passivity. LaRoy Sunderland therefore repudiated trance mediumship since its "*possessed* and *controlled*" practitioners were "unfitted for the duties of Manhood." John Edmonds likewise distinguished his spirit-inspired visions from trances. He masculinized his mediumship by insisting on his "full possession of my senses through it all" and "full exercise of my reason as to every thing that occurred." Andrew Jackson Davis, on the other hand, masculinized the trance by identifying it with independence. In his autobiography, he recounted with manly pride the day he discovered his ability to enter the trance independently of a mesmerizer. On this "day of my unconditional emancipation," he commenced "an independent life" and an "individual pilgrimage." His clearly identified this religious style with masculinity when he blended phrenological vocabulary and phallic symbolism to boast of his "large and projective organ of individuality." More or less consciously, these three men sensed an inconsistency between their practices and the values of their contemporaries.[82]

Even apart from the trance, spirit ministry conflicted with dominant American strategies of defining selfhood by suggesting that the self was not entirely of one's own making and was reliant on others. American notions of selfhood, designed to support the political, economic, and religious democratization unleashed by the American Revolution and the market revolution, valued independent agency, rational judgment, self-control, and resistance to arbitrary external authority as essential to the functioning of a democratic republic and to success in a competitive capitalist economy. Antebellum Americans admired the self-made person and reformers urged the importance of human effort in remaking their society. The idea of spirit-driven selfhood and social reform therefore left Spiritualists vulnerable to charges of violating these cultural imperatives. The problem was not that they encouraged submission to a higher power, which after all they had in common with other religious groups, but that that higher power was subdivine. Most religious Americans considered the individual subject only to the authority of God and the divinely inspired conscience, but Spiritualists looked to spirit mediators as an important point of reliance between their untrustworthy selves and their distant deity.

To be sure, Spiritualists themselves were troubled by this feature of their ideology. Isaac Post worried that spirits' involvement in mortals' wills would "take from them, their self-dependence." Andrew Jackson Davis strained to convince himself and his readers that they were not "insensate automatons under incessant inspirations of spirits" but "self-existent and responsible

beings." Most Spiritualists, moreover, urged a critical approach to spirit communication, asserting that they had not cast off the authority of ministers and
corrupt religious institutions only to yield to the authority and influence of
spirits and their messages. These spiritual republicans followed Jefferson in
recognizing that the price of spiritual liberty was eternal vigilance. Still, their
defenses of selfhood and private judgment were suspiciously urgent and
frequent. Evidently, they were intensely aware of their departure from values
that they and non-Spiritualist Americans alike held dear.[83]

Indeed, lapses of republican vigilance were as recurrent as defenses of it.
Warren Chase, for example, argued in a lecture that spirit communications
were to be approached critically but then called them an "inspiration, from a
superior sphere" which mortals could "depend upon." Uriah Clark, too,
followed an assurance that spirits do not "seek to lead men blindly" with the
advice that "counsels and teachings" through "reliable and well-tried mediums" must "be heeded in spite of what would seem to be the best judgment
and reasons of mortals in the form." After all, he said, "directions and
instructions" from the spirits are "based on wisdom higher than mortals
know." John Shoebridge Williams was determined to subject spirit communication to "enlightened rules of criticism, reason, experience, nature
or common sense," but went so far as to counsel childlike trust and to believe
spirits "just because they say so." In language strikingly at odds with the
cultural premium on self-reliance, he confessed that he was "tired of guiding myself" and wanted spirits to tell him "what to do, when to do and
how to do."[84]

If Chase, Clark, and Williams experienced inner turmoil over the relationship between spirit ministry and self-reliance, reactions to John Murray
Spear's attempt to build a "New Motor" revealed tensions between some
Spiritualists and others over the issue. While his followers defended his behavior, other Spiritualists considered it immoderate and responded in ways
ranging from sympathetic pity to stern rebuke. Adin Ballou gently chided
him for his "false reliance on the taking place of some wonderful and un-
paralleled event, to be brought about mainly by Spirits, for the regeneration
and harmonization of the world," and lectured that human society would be
reformed in a "plain, uphill way." Others were more severe. Andrew Jackson
Davis sensed an "unreasoning faith" and "a frightful and pernicious tendency
to fanaticism." He called Spear "a modern follower of outward, arbitrary
authority" who had mistaken his own impulses for spirit impressions. J. H.
Robinson effectively questioned his manhood by commenting that "the
human mind was not *made* to be passive" and contrasting his "mental
slavery," which "sinks the manhood," with Davis's "rational mediumship"
and "active mind." Still, it is clear that Spear's critics shared his pessimism

about the human race and consequent revitalizing faith in the spirits, and were similarly prone to look outside the human race for comfort. The distance between Spear and the moderates was not as great as the latter imagined.[85]

Although Spear's machine was destroyed by a anti-Spiritualist mob after considerable public hostility, the unhappy fate of New York Supreme Court judge John W. Edmonds provides the best example of the threat that non-Spiritualist Americans sensed in spirit ministry. As a prominent official in a position of public trust that required critical and independent thinking, he came under especially intense fire for what detractors considered an excessive reliance on spirit guidance. Until he announced his conversion to Spiritualism in 1853, he enjoyed a distinguished career.[86] Born in 1799, he graduated from Union College in 1816, was admitted to the bar in 1819, and became a New York state senator in 1831. He was appointed prison inspector for the state in 1843, and became well known for his work in reforming methods of punishment and the treatment of prisoners. From 1845 to 1852 he served in the first New York circuit court, and in 1852 he was appointed to New York State Supreme Court. When he turned to Spiritualism, he was at the height of his career.

His wife's death in the late 1840s sparked an investigation of Spiritualism which, he would later insist, was characterized by careful observation and "obdurate skepticism." He became convinced nevertheless and developed into a medium soon after his conversion.[87] His public announcement of the fact, together with rumors that he claimed to have received counsel in his decisions from the spirits of dead jurists, caused a public outcry against his renomination to the Court. Edmonds retired under heavy public pressure, acknowledging that his new views were "obnoxious to a large portion of the public."[88]

One typical critic charged that his espousal of Spiritualism "constitutes an abandonment of all self-control, and a surrender of the supremacy of reason, as informed and enlightened by the senses, to the most nonsensical jugglery." The *New York Times* supported his decision to resign since his espousal of Spiritualism "must render the operation of his intellect utterly unreliable." A lawyer who had worked in his courts surmised that his experiences were "a vivid waking dream produced by opium, drink, and mental excitement." His compatriots questioned his sanity because he had overstepped the boundaries of what they considered "normal" behavior. Edmonds defended his sanity and masculinity, insisting that he had consulted "my own reason" in his decisions. Other Spiritualists likewise defended his "independence of charac-ter." But it was clear that the American public was troubled by, and labeled as deviant, any Spiritualist activity that seemed repugnant to independent self-hood, individual reason and judgment, and self-control.[89]

Still, Spiritualism and American ideologies of self-reliance cleaved more over means than ends. Spiritualists were committed to personal autonomy and consistently portrayed spirit intercourse as a means of promoting it. They believed, like Andrew Jackson Davis, that spirit ministry would make all people "sufficient guides unto themselves." Their reluctance fully to embrace individualism, too, resonated with the larger culture. Even Ralph Waldo Emerson, the apostle of self-reliance, declared in an early sermon entitled "The Limits of Self-Reliance" that "the origin of the self" lay in higher forces. The individual, he said, "did not make himself" but was "a mere effect of some other cause, and so a mere manifestation of power and wisdom not his own." In this belief he found, like the Spiritualists he opposed, "the perfect check, entire security." Spiritualists and their religious contemporaries shared a need, described by Richard Rabinowitz, for an "external standard to use as a check." They wanted to root "subjective probings at truth" in "the nature of all things." Spiritualists were not the only Americans who were "projecting [their] inner feelings as an extreme otherness" and "subjecting [themselves] to *its* authoritativeness." Rather, they joined their contemporaries in addressing the problem of anarchy created by the Protestant principle of private judgment and intensified by the democratization of authority in antebellum America. LaRoy Sunderland spoke for more than Spiritualists when he said that "in matters of faith, . . . there can be no sufficient AUTHORITY but SUPERIOR WISDOM." But most other religious Americans were unable or unwilling to recognize how similar the logic of Spiritualism was to their own.[90]

Spiritualists' disdain for existing churches and ministers, uncomfortable sense of an impersonal God, and feeling of loss at the passing of the nation's founders left them without clearly defined and tangible sources of spiritual guidance. Feeling liberated but alone, they coped with their fear of spiritual isolation and social chaos by reaching beyond themselves for cosmic companionship, restraint, and order. Like other religious Americans, they blended their commitment to democratized religious authority and individualized experience with a deep longing for spiritual community and attachment. The final two chapters will suggest that they created this feeling of community not only through their ideology but also through their practices.

◆I◆

6

The Structure of Spiritualist Practice

Portraits of Spiritualist Practice

On Sunday evening, April 24, 1853, John W. Edmonds gathered with physician George T. Dexter, Dexter's wife, and architect Owen G. Warren at the Dexters' home in New York City, as they had begun to do each Sunday. Dexter, the "best developed" medium of the group, soon entered a trance and, as the group believed, offered the usual pastoral greeting from the spirit of Emanuel Swedenborg: "In our circle, where the spirits of those we love most do congregate, are gathered together once, weekly, this number, and we celebrate what to us is the Sabbath day. . . . I this night greet you cordially, heartily, and truthfully, in the name of our heavenly Father." Spirit Swedenborg's "teachings" followed, after which he bid the circle good night. A few months later, spirit Francis Bacon announced the spirits' directions that the assembly "utter a prayer always" at the outset of the meeting, a proposal to which the group "expressed our assent." Meetings of this circle also included Edmonds' frequent symbolic visions, each designed to teach a religious lesson. Its gatherings, sometimes occurring as often as four times in a week, had an unmistakable and increasingly formal religious tenor.[1]

The members of the group developed a sense of community which they expressed by calling themselves the "Sacred Circle." The group expanded in June to include medium Elizabeth Sweet and her husband. Soon after, Edmonds' daughter Laura and niece Jane Keyes were "received as members of the circle." In December they became acquainted with Abby T. Hall and Helen Leeds, two Boston mediums who provided "occasional assistance." Edmonds and Dexter published the spiritual teachings received by the circle in a two-volume work called *Spiritualism*, which they proceeded to promote on a speaking tour, and in a monthly journal, called *Sacred Circle*, which they co-edited with Warren. All of the circle's members contributed to this journal, which first appeared in 1854 and continued into 1856. The group continued to meet regularly at least into late 1854 and probably longer.[2]

Another circle in New York City, formed in the wake of the Fox sisters' 1850 visit, was equally devoted to Spiritualist religious activities. This group included members and friends of the Fowler family, which had been involved with mesmerism, phrenology, and a variety of radical reform movements for several years and had established a publishing house, Fowlers and Wells, to promote their causes. Gathered around medium Edward P. Fowler were his brother Samuel J. Fowler, his sisters Charlotte Fowler Wells and Alvina Fowler, John Hunt, and Lewellyn Haskell. Like the sessions of the Sacred Circle, their weekly meetings, held each Saturday evening, were devoted to "further and more glorious developments of *Truth.*" Detailed reports of these meetings were prepared by Charlotte Fowler Wells from November 1850 to March 1851.[3] By the spring of 1851, Edward Fowler's mediumship began to attract such socially prominent New Yorkers as Edmonds, Dr. John B. Gray and his wife, wealthy match manufacturer Charles Partridge and his wife, and Dr. Robert T. Hallock and his wife. This group "wanted to keep their circle small and elite" and organized into the New York Circle in August 1851.[4]

Although the circle witnessed unusual physical phenomena, their activities were clearly religious and missionary. In November 1851, they began a series of weekly conferences "to which strangers at a distance could be admitted without the formalities attending more exclusive gatherings." Formally called the New York Spiritual Conference and meeting at Partridge's home, it was devoted to a sharing of séance stories and discussion of the spiritual philosophy. Although open at first by invitation only and confined in scope to the experiences of the New York Circle, the conferences grew from "semi-private . . . social gatherings" to "public though somewhat heterogeneous" affairs that included solicited reports from throughout the Northeast and Midwest. Eventually they attracted enough participants to require the rental of large public halls. In early 1852, the circle further expanded its activities by launching a weekly public lecture series designed to publicize their new religion. The first was given by S. B. Brittan on February 26 at Hope Chapel on Broadway, and later ones were given at Dodsworth Hall and the Stuyvesant Institute. The group also set up a committee that helped organize other circles throughout the city, calling itself The First Circle and assigning successive numbers to newer ones. It assumed a leading role in the movement, acting as a central office for mediums, a clearing house for information about the manifestations, and a center for advice and aid in organizing and operating circles. Perhaps more important than these activities was the introduction of Brittan, an energetic publicist who had lectured on psychology and harmonialism after editing the *Univercoelum*, to Partridge. The two men formed a prolific publishing partnership that produced the *Shekinah*, a high-toned monthly that first appeared in October 1851, and a series of books advertised as "Partridge and Brittan's Spiritual Library." Above all, in May 1852 they launched the *Spiritual Telegraph*, a newspaper-style weekly, in an effort to capitalize on the increasing public notice of the New York Circle. The *Telegraph* became the most widely circulated and longest lived Spiritualist periodical of the 1850s. Called by Hardinge "the first organic movement . . . established in connection with spirit communion," the New York Circle continued to meet "for some years."[5]

Parallel developments were taking place in Philadelphia. On October 9, 1850, a group of about a dozen "friends that had been before engaged together in . . . great moral and philosophical enterprises" began to meet every Sunday to explore Spiritualism. Encouraged by an entranced clairvoyant who offered "important directions in reference to the conduct of the members," these determined investigators began to witness spirit manifestations after four months of trying. When the public curiosity aroused by their meetings began to include the unwelcome attention of "some skeptical intruders," ten of them decided to organize a private circle which met for the first time on February 24, 1851, as "Philadelphia Harmonial Circle, A." The experiences of these "little gatherings," which were held on Saturday, Sunday, and Wednesday evenings from eight o'clock until ten-thirty, became "more and more intensely interesting." Physical demonstrations gave way to "a higher order of communications" of a religious and philosophical nature and a regular practice of opening with song before moving on to the evening's spiritual reading.[6]

Like the New York Circle, this group of experienced reformers and philanthropists balanced the private character of their circle with a missionary devotion to public outreach. They "instituted several new circles" in the city and "were in almost every case, in the formation of a new circle, called upon to visit them, to aid them by their experience, and encourage them onward in their labours of love and goodness." In March, their spirit contacts advised them of "your mission" to "assist the suffering" in accordance with "the command which Jesus gave to his followers." The result was the "Harmonial Benevolent Association of Philadelphia," a philanthropic organization formed "in obedience to the directions of our spiritual guides" and headed by a "Circle of Directors" drawn from Circle A and its associate circles. These Spiritualists, like those in New York, devoted increasing energy to their religious activities, one of them reporting that the activities of Circle A "for weeks occupied all their leisure time, and in fact often drew largely on that portion of it devoted to business." In 1851, the group produced a history of Spiritualism in their city addressed "to the skeptic" and aimed to achieve "your conversion." The book included detailed instructions on the "formation and management of circles." In 1853, their medium, E.C. Henck, compiled a book of spirit-dictated odes and hymns for the use of other circles.[7]

These portraits of Spiritualist practice reveal structural features both like and unlike those of conventional religious groups. They therefore confirm both sociologist James T. Richardson's argument for a tension between "emergent" religious movements and the structural features of "normative" churches and sociologist Roy Wallis's argument for the structural features of new religions.[8] Those who formed circles blended experimental new modes of expression with a retention of traditional ones to produce a satisfying religious alternative.[9] In their practice as in their ideology, they "came out" of objectionable institutions to enter suitably reconstituted ones that—for all their rebelliousness—looked remarkably conventional.

To be sure, their individualism was sufficiently strong to frustrate attempts at large-scale organization. Apart from broad agreement on the outlines of the Spiritualist ideology, spirit messages were as varied as Spiritualists themselves and therefore could not provide a basis for unity among large numbers of them. Their commitment to spiritual republicanism, moreover, militated against the establishment of a single authoritative leader or text that might have become the focus of a tightly organized religious sect; Andrew Jackson Davis could never achieve the status that Joseph Smith or Mary Baker Eddy did, nor could his *Principles of Nature* serve the same function as the *Book of Mormon* or *Science and Health*. Still, the formation of circles suggests that Spiritualists' individualism did not overwhelm their need for religious community. Robert Ellwood reminds us that ideology and structure in any social movement are closely connected and that "certain types of ideology tend to bring forth certain structures."[10] The Spiritualist ideology produced a system of practice in which many mediums attracted regular groups of religious seekers, resulting in the formation of small but more or less formal, well-organized, and centralized religious groups. Spiritualists' need for community found expression in the way they structured their séance rituals, in their creation of a structure of religious authority based on the crucial role of the medium, and in their (usually abortive) attempts to organize and institutionalize their new religious movement. In this and the next chapter we will examine these facets of Spiritualist practice.

The Religious Function of the Séance

Not all circles were as regular, ongoing, and formalized as the Sacred Circle, the New York Circle, and Circle A. Many groups of investigators sought only to satisfy their curiosity rather than to explore a new religion and stopped gathering after seeing or failing to see the sensational phenomena, concluding that the medium was fraudulent, or deciding to visit other mediums. But other groups met regularly in rituals called séances to commune with spirits through a favorite medium and to satisfy their spiritual needs. Statistical counts of how many circles assumed some degree of regularity are virtually nonexistent, and attempts at such counts highly problematic. The lack of sustained Spiritualist organizations in the 1850s frustrates any attempt to quantify the movement's scope—as Uriah Clark noted in his *Spiritualist Register* for 1860, "statistics are unavoidably incomplete as we have nothing like a sectarian organization or party to make official reports"[11]—and the private nature of the continuing circle further compounds the difficulty. Moreover, those most likely to gather statistics were moved by partisanship for or against the movement to inflate their numbers. Still, there is convincing (if sketchy and impressionistic) evidence that there were many more or less regular circles in the Northeast and Midwest (and elsewhere).

Since a thorough review of this evidence would violate considerations of space and reader patience, a few suggestive examples from different geographic areas will have to suffice. *Home Journal* editor Nathaniel Parker Willis estimated in the mid-1850s that there were about three hundred "magnetic circles" in New York City. Even allowing for inflation and a large number of short-lived circles, we can assume the existence of a substantial number of enduring circles there. In Philadelphia, meanwhile, a member of Circle A reported in 1851 that "between fifty and sixty circles" were "investigating the subject" there and that "several new circles were instituted" with Circle A's encouragement, most of which "have persevered and are doing exceedingly well." The author's references to "Circle E" and "Circle F" indicate that at least six were sufficiently enduring and structured to merit their names. In Boston, according to the *Telegraph*, circles were "quite numerous," one of them suggesting its formality by naming itself "the Olive Branch of Peace." In nearby Providence, Rhode Island, the *Union* reported that Spiritualists "have now regularly constituted societies in almost all our towns and cities" and "hold regular Sabbath services." Further west, the Cincinnati *Daily Times* reported fifty-nine séances "held nightly" in addition to the "hundreds of circles which are held occasionally, or by those who have just commenced experimenting." In Lake Mills, Wisconsin, according to one scholar, the formally named Circle of Progress "met regularly . . . like many other similar circles in other towns." A Spiritualist in La Porte County, Indiana, reported "several circles in our neighborhood." In Michigan in the 1850s, abolitionist and Spiritualist Lucy Coleman reported that Spiritualism was "rioting" and that "circles were the order of the day, and of the night." Late in the following decade, the Reverend Jonathan Harrison could report in a survey of liberal religion in the Midwest that "Spiritualism was almost everywhere active and powerful." It is evident that ongoing circles emerged with some frequency.[12]

These circles had an unequivocally religious function that went far beyond an interest in the phenomena of mediumship, scientific evidence of immortality, and conversation with lost loved ones. To be sure, not all of those who attended séances were searching for an alternative and satisfying form of religious experience. Some *were,* as other scholars have argued, simply seeking the tangible evidence that the growing cultural authority of science seemed to demand of religious belief. Some *were* resisting the all-too-common occurrence of early death in nineteenth-century America by trying to maintain ties with lost friends and relatives. And many others *were* drawn to séances by nothing more than an appetite for entertainment and a curiosity about strange phenomena and questions that seemed to exist on the frontiers of science. Such curiosity, a pervasive element of antebellum American culture that found expression in mesmerism and phrenology as well as Spiritualism, was fed by an accelerating pace of technological development that made anything seem possible and by the rise of entertainment that capitalized on the sensational.[13] It is no coincidence that the most popular Spiritualist newspaper of the antebellum period was called the *Spiritual Telegraph* or that showman P.T. Barnum promoted the Fox sisters during their extended stay at his hotel in New York City in 1850. Through their performances, both public and private, Spiritualist mediums reflected and contributed to the growing commodification of American culture and of American religion in particular. Often blending religion with other aspects of popular culture, they undeniably capitalized on Spiritualism's "stage possibilities."[14]

But Spiritualist leaders emphatically insisted on the deeper function of the séance, seeing phenomenal manifestations as needed empirical evidence of the existence of spirits that was otherwise of relatively minor significance. Anxious to dissociate Spiritualist religion from the sensational mediumship which attracted the curiosity of many Americans, Davis lamented the prevalence of the latter and identified "individual improvement and spiritual communion" as the main purpose of the circle. When one of the Philadelphia circles asked after six months of meeting whether it should "endeavor to obtain raps," they heard spirit voices respond that their "mission" was "not to amuse you" or to satisfy "idle curiosity" but "to assist you in your spiritual advancement." Spirit Swedenborg advised the Sacred Circle that it met "not for the purpose of showing to the world that spirits can confer with man" but "for the purpose of showing you the truths of your spirit-life." Even communication with the spirits of close friends and relatives often moved beyond mundane chatter about personal matters and expressions of solace to address highminded spiritual, religious, and moral themes. Many séance-goers sought to contact a higher spiritual and moral plane or, as Davis put it, to "recon-struct the internal mechanism, to properly arrange the secret springs."[15]

The movement's early publicists were particularly insistent upon this point. Uriah Clark advised readers of his *Plain Guide to Spiritualism* that the séance aims at "something more than a belief that spirits exist and communi-cate." Those whose "interest ends with the external manifestations or with the mere fact of immortal life demonstrated," he said, "have but a very dim view" of the meaning of the movement. William T. Coggeshall, a reformer and editor who investigated mesmerism and clairvoyance before discovering Spiritualism and publishing an account of its development in Cincinnati in 1851, likewise emphasized the religious function of the séance. Believers, he said, would be led from rappings, "the lowest order of manifestation," to higher "communings" that would "purify and elevate" their recipients. Emma Hardinge, a British-born singer and actress before becoming a popular medium, lecturer, and chronicler of the movement, confessed that she initially investigated séances because she "wanted amusement" and theater but emphasized how quickly and dramatically she became convinced of its religious value. After converting from Anglican orthodoxy to Spiritualism in 1856, she consistently contrasted the "steady faith and devoted adherence of *true Spiritualists*" with the "clamorous enthusiasm" of "wonder-seeking 'spiritists'" and with the "mere Spiritists" who had "simply advanced to the belief that spirits can and do communicate through phenomenal signs."[16]

Both Coggeshall and Hardinge indicate a trajectory from investigation to serious religious commitment. Once convinced of the reality of spirits, many investigators moved on to explore the religious truths they believed the spirits could offer or confirm. Philadelphia's Circle A, as we have seen, devoted its early meetings to producing physical phenomena but soon delved into Spiritualist philosophy and experienced a "higher order of communications" that stimulated it to missionary and benevolent activity. A Cleveland circle, according to the editor of that city's *Plain Dealer*, had "progressed so far as to dispense with the tedious tests" and were, "as they had reason to believe, actually taking lessons in philosophy from spiritual teachers." This develop-mental process was encapsulated in the procedures of a single circle that met regularly in Greenfield, Massachusetts. Each meeting opened with a brief visit from a "merry" spirit, followed by a more prolonged encounter with a "grave, earnest, and instructive" spirit. The purpose of the first was to "prepar[e] for the second, who is our teacher and guide, instructing us in wise philosophy and pure religious feeling."[17]

Even the famous "spirit room" run by Jonathan Koons in Athens County, Ohio, best known for its displays of sensational phenomena, was intended to do more than please a curious and entertainment-hungry public. Visitors were, to be sure, treated to quite a show, including concerts by invisible hands and "spiritual pyrotechnics" produced by electrical apparatus. But Koons wrote in 1853 that Spiritualism had carried him from "atheistical sentiments" to "religious faith." His spirits not only offered rousing concerts but "began to converse orally through the trumpets, sing, pray, lecture, draw charts of celestial scenery, diagrams of the spheres, and write long communications," many of which were "highly philosophical" and made a "deep and sublime impress . . . upon our minds." One attender commented on the Koons family's "intense faith and devotion to their angelic guides."[18]

For many visitors, too, the experience of the Koons spirit room was at least as much religious as theatrical. Seeking more than a spirit concert, one visitor who reported his experience to the Buffalo Spiritualist newspaper *Age of Progress* in 1854 asked for a significant communication. The message he received through Koons, that spirits visited circles to reveal "a higher condition of being than that of earth" and to direct mortals "into higher action," reinforced his and Koons's understanding of what Spiritualism was all about. The following year, Charles Partridge described in the *Spiritual Telegraph* not cacophonous concerts in a "spirit room" but a "sanctuary" in which he heard "songs of angels" that "seemed pregnant with holy sentiment, a "short lecture" of religious content spoken through the trumpet, and a benediction. One Thomas White, who was present with him, complained to him in 1859 that his subsequent visits to musical circles in the Midwest included "no speaking through the trumpet, no moral or philosophical lectures from ancient high and holy spirits, nor had we any sweet spirit singing." Many of Koons's guests evidently wanted and found more than good theater.[19]

In their religious (as well, perhaps, as their theatrical) function, Spiritualist circles sought to provide experiences much like those of the revivals which had become a familiar feature of antebellum life and "the single most effective religious ritual in American religious history." The circle reinforced the premium which evangelicals had placed on inner spirituality, personal experience, and direct contact with the divine. Both rituals were designed to foster religious revitalization and a sense of personal connection with the spiritual world. Both created an experience which anthropologist Victor Turner has called "communitas"; that is, they removed participants from the conditions of ordinary social existence so as to allow them an intense feeling of inward harmony with unseen and superhuman spiritual forces, resulting in a feeling of renewed spiritual selfhood. Indeed, many Spiritualist mediums and lecturers, like itinerant revivalists, traveled with the express purpose of promoting such religiosity.[20]

The similarity was not lost on Spiritualists, whose commitment to personal religious experience led them to combine their distaste for the excesses of revivalism with admiration for what they considered its positive aspects. Witnessing the experiential thrust of the 1857–1858 revival, John F. Gray was so struck by its "analogy to circle-sitting" that he expected it to produce "veritable manifestations." John F. Coles, meanwhile, found it easy to reconcile his new religion with his earlier enthusiasm for revivalism. "A convert to the previous revival" who had "helped to work the machinery himself," he now regarded the Spiritualist ritual as an extension of the revival, asking "what are our circles but efforts to secure the conditions which the prayer-meeting aims at?" Uriah Clark actually regretted that revivalism had "died out in the churches" and hoped that Spiritualism would as effectively "arouse the slumbering energies of humanity." A phrase in the table of contents of his *Plain Guide to Spiritualism* captured this hope: "genuine revivals needed." In a sense, then, the séance was a permutation of what had become a major form of religious expression in America.[21]

At the same time, however, Spiritualists clearly intended to put a new twist on the revival by discarding three elements of it that they deemed objectionable. First, they did not believe direct contact with an infinite Holy Spirit possible and aimed instead to establish mediated contact with the divine through finite spirits. The result was a new form of experiential religion that reconciled their need for personal connection with a higher realm with their uneasy sense of divine inaccessibility. Second, they rejected the orthodox theology that, in their estimation, turned the revival experience into an exploitation of fear rather than a celebration of love. Truman Woodruff, a former Methodist revivalist who used his talents as an itinerant exhorter to win converts to Spiritualism, attributed his success not only to the emphasis on direct experience which the two religions shared but also to the decisive doctrinal differences between them. Boasting to the *Telegraph* after an 1855 lecture in Wisconsin induced blissful visions of the spirit world in a hostile listener and the subsequent formation of a circle, he commented that his new religion preached "all love, no fear; all Deity, no devil; all heaven, no hell." Spiritualist emotionalism therefore involved "no groanings, no sighings, no weepings for poor sinners" but rather "a thrill of joy." Third, Spiritualists tried to moderate the emotional excesses that they associated with revivals by reducing ecstasy to order. Thus Emma Hardinge and the *Telegraph* responded ambivalently when Roulette, Pennsylvania, witnessed "one of [those] singular revival fevers" whose details seemed "closely allied to Spiritualism." They noted the similarities between the "phenomena of mediumship" and the "manifestations" that occurred in the presence of "itinerant Spiritualist evangelist" John Crapsey. These included speaking in tongues, uttering prophecies, prayers and exhortations by "entranced speakers," and an encounter by a Mr. Pendleton with "angelic beings" and "the spirits of dead persons." At the same time, they were relieved that this "outpouring" was eventually tamed under the calming influences of the spirits. "Its preternatural characteristics disappeared," Hardinge wrote, "the excitement subsided, and the orderly development of medium powers in and amongst Mr. Crapsey's congregation changed the fever into the normal and healthy tone of Spiritualism." She anxiously insisted that Spiritualism, unlike revivalism, was not a species of feverish religious insanity but a moderate and "orderly" religion that promoted a "normal and healthy" spirituality.[22]

The religious function of the séance, and its differences from revivalism, were powerfully underscored by its domestic setting. Conducted in the home of the (usually female) medium who led it, it was one of the many forms of ritualized devotional activity taking place in middle-class Victorian homes. Indeed, the home was the ideal setting for the Spiritualist circle, for it was regarded in the nineteenth-century ideology of domesticity as a morally wholesome and spiritually purifying bastion of order that served to counteract the disturbingly amoral and chaotic society outside it. It was a place where the small and intimate family group, led by the moral instruction of the father and (more especially) the mother, expressed its shared religious commitment in an appropriately quiet and subdued manner. It is not coincidental that Spiritualist religion, in which seekers sought wisdom from spirits considered parental and from the spirits of close friends and family members, emerged just as the home was becoming a widely recognized American sacred space and the family an important spiritual institution.[23]

The Structure of the Circle

Spiritualists conveyed their desire for structured religious practice above all by calling their groups "circles." A sacred symbol of cosmic order and harmony, the circle gave structure to their ritual as well as to their ideology. Thus Edmonds, Dexter, and Warren applied the name "Sacred Circle" to both their group and their journal. John Murray Spear, too, used the concept to link Spiritualism's cosmology with its ritual. Regarding the "formation of circles" as the "primitive lesson" of the coming new era, he said that these groups were organized "not primarily for the mere purpose of listening to unusual sounds" but to symbolize the "CONCENTRIC LAW" which he believed "pervades all things" and "holds things together which belong together."[24] The meeting of the circle, or séance, was the central and distinctive ritual of the new religion. It was "unchurched," usually taking place in the home, but was nevertheless structured by an unmistakable if loose order of ritual.[25] Like all religious rituals, it aimed at what sociologists of religion call the "routinization of faith." That is, it established regularized contact with a higher plane of reality in a controlled setting in order to provide continuing religious experience for a devoted group of believers. The circle was designed to summon the order and harmony of the cosmos to earth by replicating it in ritual. It gave participants the feeling, essential to harmonial religion, of being in tune with the infinite.[26]

Spiritualists' desire for a structured religious practice was especially apparent in the many sets of instructions on forming circles and conducting séances, usually quite detailed and exacting, which appeared during the movement's early years.[27] These instructions show that their circles, like any other religious ritual, were intended to affirm the underlying ideology and involved structure, method, and an unmistakable spiritual content. Few if any circles fully measured up to the ideals portrayed in such instructions, but the activities and behavior of circles like the Sacred Circle, the New York Circle, and Circle A suggest that Spiritualists took those instructions seriously as they designed their expressions of religiosity.[28]

The Spiritualists that celebrated "our little band" in a hymn called "Our Circle," written specifically for use in the séance ritual, suggested that circles often served their members as distinct if small-scale and "unchurched" religious communities (the typical circle consisted of perhaps a dozen people). They blended their commitment to spiritual autonomy with a promotion of intimacy and bonding, at least among small groups, as an important component of their religion. This feature of the circle reflected the centrality of small-scale community to republican ideology and Fourierist communitarian theory, Spiritualists' nostalgia for what they feared was a disappearing sense of community, and their belief, derived from Swedenborg, that the spirit world itself was structured in this way. Thus John Edmonds, guided by spirit George Washington, envisioned a large spirit society "divided into many smaller communities, and each one of them into others smaller still, till they are reduced to circles or bands of from twenty to fifty each." The hymn "Aspirations of the Circle" urged Spiritualists to replicate this social structure in their ritualistic gatherings: "Its meetings let us seek to make / Emblems of those on high." Spiritualists illustrate well that ideology calls forth structures of practice and that even individualistic religious sensibilities must provide some manner of social communion.[29]

As terrestrial replications of spiritual society and variations on the cultural theme of domestic religion, circles encouraged tight community and familial harmony among participants. This imperative recurs in published instructions on circle formation, descriptions of circle meetings, and Spiritualist songs. Davis called the séance a "spiritual association" and a "harmonial circle of friends" where "discord may not enter." The "intimate friends" who formed Circle A urged in the preface to their published collection of hymns and odes that the circle "should be gathered into one holy bond of union" since

CIRCLE. 8s & 7s.   J. B. PACKARD.

DESIGNED FOR THE OPENING OF CIRCLES.

1. Ho-ly Father, gently bless us, As we meet in love to-night, Let no earthly care oppress us, May we all be filled with light.
2. Lov-ing spir-its hov-er o'er us, Angels bright, in truth arrayed, Ope the path of life before us, Lead us on to cloudless day.

3. Let no jarring thought divide us, Sweetest harmony be ours; Wisdom's richest feast, provide us, As we pass these happy hours.

SECOND HYMN.

1	2
May the grace of Guardian Angels,	Thus may we abide in union
And the Father's boundless love,	With each other and the Lord;
With the Loving Spirits' favor,	And possess, in sweet communion,
Rest upon us from above.	Joys which earth cannot afford.

Illustration 5: The Spiritualist hymn "Circle." This hymn, written especially for the séance meeting, underscores the conventionality, structural nature, and communal aspects of Spiritualist practice.

harmony was "the essential principle of all associations." In another compilation of hymns, the one entitled "Circle" (see illustration 5) was intended to establish harmony and community at the outset of the ritual: "Let no jarring thought divide us, sweetest harmony be ours . . . thus may we abide in union with each other and the Lord; and possess in sweet communion, joys which earth cannot afford." The hymn which followed, written for the closing of the meeting, reaffirmed the thought: "We part in body, not in mind; our minds continue one; and each to each in love are joined, and hand in hand go on." Medium Semantha Mettler, a guest at a meeting of the Fowler circle, summarized this facet of Spiritualist religion in a phrase: "we should form a *whole*."[30]

The group identity of the circle typified the sociology of "excursus" religion. Although this type of religious practice is generally individualistic, involving a "personal subjective quest"—many messages received at circles were intended for specific individuals—it also encourages the formation of small and closely bound groups whose ceremonies confer "status in the group" and "demarcat[e] the group from outside society." Like other forms of religious excursus, the séance ritual "will define the set-apart order," "create an assembly with a special state of consciousness," and "form an intensive group or express the existence of one." It was not uncommon for Spiritualists who met regularly in circles to speak of themselves and others as "members" or, as Charlotte Fowler Wells and the Sacred Circle did, to distinguish those who "belong to the circle" from those who attended "by invitation" or "as visitors." The practice of naming their circles further cemented group ties and a sense of belonging. At least one circle, formed in

New York and called the "Circle of Hope," even adopted by-laws reminiscent of conventional religious organizations in its attempt to forge a congregational identity among its members. Such practices underscored the similarities between circles and formal church congregations. Attendance at a circle was not, as one historian has argued, entirely "unlike church attendance, which reinforced the worshiper's identity as a member of a congregation." As Ellwood reminds us, "any entitled group, however small, is very different from an individual religious quest."[31]

The desire to foster intimate religious fellowship and to replicate the harmony of cosmic society prompted at least some circles to adopt and recommend specific ritual, attendance, and membership practices. Sitting closely together in a circle "at equal distances" around a table and joining hands, an arrangement which allowed the participants to see each other and to establish physical contact, was virtually mandatory. This arrangement would "render harmony complete" and, by establishing what one author called "a complete circuit," promote rapport with a cosmos considered electrical in its operations. One Spiritualist even advised that small circles dispense with the table altogether if it prevented closeness. The instructions published by Philadelphia's Harmonial Benevolent Association further suggested "singing, reading, and cheerful conversation" in order to "promote a harmonious calmness and concert of feeling."[32]

As communal and quasi-familial gatherings, Spiritualist circles also promoted sociability, shared experience, and collective obligation. To be sure, scholars who portray séance attendance as "an intensely individual action" have a point. Spirit messages were often "private," intended for specific individuals rather than the entire group, and the cloistered mediumship of John Shoebridge Williams underscored the atomistic potential of Spiritualist practice. But the circular and intimate seating arrangement and the joining of hands suggest that the séance was intended to be something more than a group of individuals expressing private spirituality in a common setting. One circle was advised that "your feelings, your views, and your desires . . . should be interchanged during the sitting" and later urged to "open your thoughts to one another, and to mingle your affections and aspirations together." Furthermore, Spiritualist writings often emphasized a theme of collective obligation and the primacy of the group over the individual. The Philadelphia circle was told to "meet for the good of the whole; and not each member merely for his own good" and the members of the Sacred Circle were to "individually ask the question of themselves, Have I, by my feelings, retarded my own and the circle's advance?" Even the religious vision, usually an individual experience, became on several occasions a joint experience for Sacred Circle members Laura Edmonds and Helen Leeds. Like church worship, the séance was at least as much a social affair as it was a private one.[33]

Also essential to religious community was regular and frequent attendance at séance meetings. Spiritualist writers counseled circles to "meet regularly, if possible" since "by frequently meeting together, mental harmony is increased, which renders the conditions favorable for communicating." Circle A recommended meeting "at least, once in each week" (but actually, like the Sacred Circle, met more often), while Davis suggested no more than two weekly gatherings since meetings held too often might become "deprived of their sanctity, and hence also of their power to benefit the assembled individuals." Lax attendance could elicit strong rebukes, as members of the Sacred Circle learned when turnout dwindled in June 1852. Speaking for spirit Swedenborg, George Dexter lectured his coreligionists that "any breaking in the harmony of a full circle always retards the character of the manifestation, and the subsequent circles are shorn of some of their proportions." The lesson was clear: "Nothing should prevent the members of a circle being present at its meetings but sickness, or unavoidable occurrences which detain them." Not all circles maintained this kind of regimen, of course; many circles formed spontaneously and met irregularly if they met more than once. But religious Spiritualists considered attendance a weighty matter.[34]

Community bonding was further strengthened by insulation and exclusivity, which added to the members' sense of belonging to a special group. Coming together amidst concerns of privacy, the members of Circle A agreed "to say but very little, out of the circle, of what transpired within it" and believed that their "little gatherings became more and more intensely interesting" as a result. John Shoebridge Williams heard spirit Eliza urge "the necessity, of little bands harmonizing themselves, without the influence of the world." This "enjoined seclusion" was meant "to harmonize you as efficiently as may be." Circles desiring to expand, like the New York circle, were cautioned by the spirits to be selective; while "it would be well" to add new members, they were not to admit "those of contragenial natures" and to "be very careful in deciding who are contragenial." Davis likewise counseled that the circle's integrity required that each member "be temperate in all his habits, free from intoxicating or stimulating beverages." Such practices, reminiscent of the covenanted congregations of Puritan New England, served to create, maintain, and protect that sense of separate and special identity so important to a small group whose religious beliefs were often ridiculed or persecuted by the larger society.[35]

Exclusivity and insulation proved problematic, for they might easily undermine Spiritualists' missions of moral uplift and publicizing their religion. A Philadelphia circle trying to heed spirit advice to "keep thyself pure" was forced to choose between purity and charity when their meeting was attended by "a person . . . whose moral character rendered him . . . unharmonious." Some of the group "felt constrained to withdraw to another room," where the spirits counseled them to "avoid the influence of the dark in spirit" while striving to "assist them when it is possible." In this instance, insularity got the better of benevolence. Philadelphia Circle A confronted a different problem when it began to face "charges of selfishness and exclusiveness" from would-be investigators. Another of the Philadelphia circles resolved this dilemma in a way that its members hoped would satisfy the requirements of both privacy and publicity. Although they usually "adhered to our rules of meeting in privacy" under the belief that allowing "strangers" would compromise "harmony and unity of feeling and aspiration," they agreed to admit a select committee of outside witnesses to some of their meetings. This decision did not come easily—one member feared that the presence of "so many strangers" would make it difficult for the medium to communicate—and they carefully distinguished between the "union circle," at which this committee was present, and the "private circle" composed only of the circle's regular members. They protected their group identity by ensuring that during union meetings "the members of the circle sit near and opposite the Medium, that she may not be unfavorably influenced by the spheres of the strangers present." The New York Circle similarly balanced exclusivity with outreach and publicity by maintaining a restrictive membership policy while opening up its weekly conferences. While Spiritualists encouraged open investigation, then, it is not true that "Spiritualist leaders made no attempt to . . . exclude casual observers from their central ritual." On the contrary, they were often reluctant to admit outsiders and cautious when they did.[36]

The sober tenor of instructions on circle formation and emphasis on the integrity of the gathering suggest that circle meetings were not only thoroughly structured but also decidedly solemn affairs. There was a clear seriousness of purpose, requiring a setting and deportment that were meant to set the circle apart from mere entertainment and from the rhythms of everyday life. Churchlike tranquility and dim lighting were particularly important to the creation of the necessary mood. Davis advised that circles meet in a "darkened" place "retired from all noise and interruption" so that participants could avoid diversion by "external things" and "more easily concentrate their thoughts upon the *object* for which they have met together." The home, like the church widely regarded as a tranquil refuge from the chaos of surrounding society, served this function well.[37]

A properly reverent state of mind was also necessary. Those who consulted Uriah Clark's *Plain Guide to Spiritualism* were reminded that spirit communication was "a solemn as well as a joyous thing" that "requires some preparation of mind, heart, and life." Davis agreed that circles would receive "*good* and *lofty* communications" only if their "thoughts and intentions be also *good* and *elevated*" and the meeting was "conducted with a religious dignity and harmony." One set of instructions urged that circles should "meet together in cheerfulness," but "avoid levity." The Sacred Circle was warned that "many circles fail" to achieve the "full circulation of the magnetism" because of "frivolity of conduct" and "carelessness of manner." In preparation for one of Edmonds' visions, spirits instructed the circle in a tone suggestive of the discipline of children: "Now the circle will keep silence, and be as still as possible. The teaching will be of much importance. Therefore let each one be seated most comfortably, so as not to disturb the vision." While such reminders and instructions indicate that perfect dignity was not always maintained, Spiritualists took them seriously. When A. E. Newton was told to approach the spirits "with elevated thoughts and purity of purpose," he felt compelled to "act in accordance with instructions so proper."[38]

Gender-conscious membership and seating were also required to replicate and harmonize with an androgynous cosmos. Since, as Spear taught, "the Divine mind itself, from which all organizations flow, is both male and female," Spiritualists took care to include both "female" and "male" (or, in electrical terms, "negative" and "positive") components (see illustrations 6 and 7). Sometimes this required the presence of both men and women. Uriah Clark's *Plain Guide to Spiritualism* recommended "an equal number of each sex." Other instructions advised that men and women sit in alternating positions to facilitate the flow of spiritual influences, and most illustrations of circles depict such arrangements. "Male" and "female" sometimes referred less to biological sex than to personal characteristics culturally identified with one or the other gender. Davis wrote that his "distinction of *male* and *female*" was "not so essential with regard to *sex*" as it was with regard to a proper balance between "the *feminine* attributes of character which are *negative* and *affectionate*" and the "*masculine*," or "*positive* and *intellectual* temperament." Another set of instructions suggested that optimal "electrical conditions" required an equal number of "those of grossness and masculinity of nature, whether male or female," labeled "positive," and "those more refined, and feminine in their natures, organization, and developments," called "negative." "Positive" and "negative" persons were to sit alternately and opposite each other for maximum effect.[39]

Such technical precision indicates that rapport with the cosmos required a ritual not only carefully gendered but also scientifically and technologically engineered. Spiritualists' worshipful attitude toward science and technology resulted not only in a religious devotion to technology, as in Spear's New Motor project, but also in a technology of religious devotion. Davis, for example, understood the ideal circle to be essentially an electrical circuit. It should consist, he said, of twelve individuals in addition to the medium, six people of "electrical temperament . . . who possess a mild and loving disposition" sitting on the medium's right, symmetrically balanced by six "magnetic" individuals who are "positive and intellectual" on the left. Davis

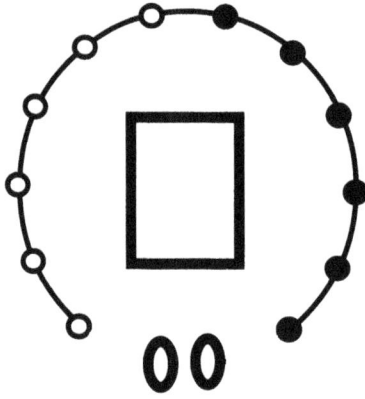

The séance circle. Illustration 6 is Andrew Jackson Davis's diagram of a model circle. This abstract diagram perfectly illustrates the Spiritualists' scientific approach to religious ritual. Illustration 7 (Courtesy Bettmann Archive, New York City) depicts another model circle. Notice the circular arrangement, the alternate seating by gender, and the physical contact which Spiritualists considered essential to religious community and cosmic harmony. Notice also the basket of knitting materials to the medium's left, suggesting the domestic setting of the séance and the cultural definition of mediumship as a "feminine" practice.

also advised that the sitters hold, at least for the first hour or so of the ritual, a "magnetic cord" consisting of steel and copper wire wrapped around a silk- or cotton-covered rope. Doing so to "establish and preserve an *equilibrium* of vital electricity and vital magnetism throughout the entire circle," the group could put it aside once the necessary "equilibrium" was achieved and join hands to maintain harmony. Davis illustrated his recommended arrangement by means of an abstract diagram resembling those commonly used in contemporary textbook discussions of electricity and magnetism (see illustration 6).[40]

The scientifically designed séance exemplifies a nineteenth-century strain of religiosity that has been called "technical religion." That is, Spiritualists joined other Americans in a search for the best technical means of producing religious feelings. Davis used case studies to suggest that conformity to his specifications would elicit not only spirit communications but also mediumistic trances, clairvoyance, prophecy, and speaking or writing in tongues. By suggesting that the proper scientific conditions might induce such phenomena and employing case histories for empirical support, Davis gave substance to Spiritualists' ideological promise of a scientific approach to religious experience. Like LaRoy Sunderland and revivalist Charles G. Finney, he believed that rapturous communion with the spiritual world could be scientifically controlled.[41]

While Spiritualists believed that these new, alternative, and unchurched rituals would help them achieve their experiential goals, they were reluctant to abandon all that was familiar. Constructing a cosmology largely on Christian foundations, acquainted with conventional Christian expressions of devotion and community, and evidently convinced that some of those practices effectively met their religious needs, they forged a ceremony that looked in many ways like those they had left behind. Meetings of the Sacred Circle, we have seen, opened with such invocations from the spirits as "I give you my spirit blessing, and greet you in God's name"; closing benedictions, such as "good-night, and our Father be with you" were also a regular element in their order of worship. Spirit mediums also transmitted homiletic messages that, like sermons in more traditional Christian congregations, were aimed at the entire circle and constituted the central feature of the ritual.[42]

Many Spiritualists also retained the practice of prayer as an instrument of cosmic connectedness. One set of instructions recommended that circle meetings open with "serene silence, meditation, interior prayer, and the singing of appropriate hymns." The Sacred Circle complied with "the directions of the higher spirits" by agreeing to "utter a prayer always before we commence the duties of the evening." In publishing a series of Spiritualist prayers in the *Sacred Circle* under the title "Devotion of Spiritualism," this circle underscored their kinship to "devotionalism," a mid-nineteenth-century American religious style which emphasized prayer as an important form of expression.[43]

The importance of prayer to Spiritualist religiosity is well illustrated by Robert Hare, whose attraction for the practice stands in striking contrast to his earlier aversion to it. As a young man, he had been sufficiently non-devotional to elicit comment from his devout friend and fellow scientist Benjamin Silliman, and as a believer in the inviolability of natural law he doubted that prayer could alter the course of events. Though he continued to harbor that doubt, the older and more obviously religious Hare that embraced Spiritualism decided that prayer served deeper needs. He approvingly quoted a contemporary Swedenborgian-Transcendentalist work entitled *The Rambles and Reveries of an Art-Student in Europe*:

> Prayer is a simple and natural method of becoming *en rapport* with higher beings and a higher world. . . . prayer is one of the most holy, beautiful, and useful of things; it is the earnest asking of the soul for comfort . . . and by the exaltation of feeling, we rise up from the earth-life into the higher spiritual planes, and become harmonized by the indwelling harmonies of those spheres. Prayer is aspiration. Prayer is the desire to embrace the Infinite.

The "light of Spiritualism had begun to dawn in the mind of the author," Hare said, and "his language respecting prayer is in strict conformity with the doctrine of Spiritualism." Hare's religion offered him no promise that a distant deity could hear him, but it met his need to embrace the cosmos. And when Edmonds noted "the union of the minds of the circle" upon a prayer he uttered, he suggested that Spiritualists considered it not only an individual and personal act but a shared expression that enhanced religious community.[44]

Song was another familiar element incorporated into the séance ritual. A group activity considered essential to the creation of harmony, it was consistently suggested in instruction manuals. It was present from the inception of the movement. As early as 1849, Charles Hammond sang "several . . . pieces of sacred music" in a sitting with the Fox sisters. Singing was sufficiently important to Spiritualist devotion to occasion the publication of such hymnals as Circle A's *Spirit Voices* (1853) and *The Spirit Minstrel* (1855). These compilations contained both traditional Christian tunes, sometimes with lyrics adapted to Spiritualist ideology, and entirely new hymns written for séances. Both new and adapted pieces fostered religious identity not only by encouraging shared expression but also by celebrating the basic tenets of Spiritualist belief. Spiritualists singing "Aspirations of the Circle," "Freedom," "I'm a Pilgrim," "The Guardian Angel," "Angel Guides," "Ministration of Angels," "Influence of Angels," "Spirits Bright Are Ever Nigh," "Mission of Mediums," and "The Spirit Home" articulated their new ideology and affirmed their commitment to it (see illustration 5).[45]

At least one circle spotlighted a potential that Spiritualism had but never developed by engaging in regular readings from Davis's *Principles of Nature* and *Great Harmonia*. Despite the frequent Spiritualist counsel against treating any given religious text as authoritative, this Philadelphia group evidently looked to Davis's writings in much the same way that members of other religious groups look to their own sacred texts. They were only following what they considered explicit instructions from the spirits. Asking "What shall the exercises of the circle be?" they were told to "read Davis's Revelations and sing." Davis's status was elevated even further by this circle when the spirits told its members that they "must *only* read Davis's Spiritual Revelations" [italics mine].[46]

The Spiritualist ritual even involved a sacred object, namely the table (usually circular) around which the group met. Although it was a focus of ridicule for critics who dismissed Spiritualism as a trite fascination with such strange phenomena as "table-tipping," Spiritualists made it a symbol of their spiritual values and conferred on it a special religious significance. For Cincinnati medium Mrs. G. B. Bushnell, it was essential to the proper functioning of the circle. Asked how a group of individuals might form the "battery" required for obtaining communications, her answer was "by sitting around a table." Emma Hardinge considered it the altar for a ritual whose most important setting was the home. She noted many who came to the séance table "for mere curiosity" arose from it "startled by the conviction that the humble domestic board had become the family altar, at which the beloved immortals had been the ministering spirits." Robert Hare thought it "a great error to consider our tables as less sacred than our firesides" since it was a focal point of domestic life; "even when not excited by hunger, we value the social meeting which takes place around it." The table was also a symbol of law and order. One Spiritualist suggested that sitting around a table was "very convenient" for the "preservation of order," and Hare noted that "at tables, conferences are held, contracts and deeds signed, and decrees, statute-laws, and ordinances are written." Finally, it served as a symbol of American republicanism. Hare pointed out with pride that the Declaration of Independence had been signed at a table and that "in Trumbull's picture of its presentation to Congress a table is made to occupy a conspicuous position." The table, in short, represented not only spirit intercourse but also piety, domesticity, community, harmony, freedom, order, and republicanism. It symbolically linked Spiritualist ideology and practice.[47]

Religious séance attenders believed that a successful recreation of cosmic harmony around the table could produce awesome experiential results. At a circle held in Bridgeport, Connecticut, Davis beheld with his "spiritual perceptions" not only eighteen spirits in the room but also "a large congregation of friendly spirits" located "about thirty miles above the atmosphere of our earth" who "directed a mighty column of vital electricity and magnetism, which current, penetrating all intermediate substances, passed through the roof and walls to the apartment where we were seated." Joining spirits and mortals in a single cosmic congregation, the column of electricity linked the spiritual and material realms and symbolized the function of the séance. Davis used the scientific vocabulary of antebellum culture to depict the séance room as a sacred space removed from the ordinary world and the column of electricity as a cosmic axis along which the sacred order of the spirit world dramatically broke in upon the profane chaos of earth. This feeling of cosmic connectedness left participants feeling different, better, spiritually richer, than they had before. It gave them the renewed sense of harmony with the universe that constituted the fundamental aim of harmonial religion.[48]

The Structure of Spiritualist Experience

Davis's powerful description should not obscure the fact that the séance experience, like most religious rituals, was highly routinized. Mistrustful of the enthusiasm of the revival, Spiritualists imposed order and regularity on their religious expressions. One way they did this was to set strict, even rigid, times for meeting and spirit communication that stood in sharp contrast to the less structured and often more extended revival meeting. Thus a spirit voice kept its promise to a Cincinnati circle to entrance its medium in precisely "two minutes and a half" and, after departing for exactly one hour, announced its return by means of a promised signal. Spirit encounters were eminently predictable, and Spiritualists were often surprised when the spirits failed to keep their scheduled appointments. Mortals, too, were expected to "be prompt as to the time." Circle A agreed to meet from eight o'clock until ten-thirty and its members considered it a religious duty to show up at the "appointed time." The medium resisted extending the meeting, a fact that must have been frustrating to those who were not ready to return to ordinary life at ten-thirty. At least one member of the circle was disappointed that the spirits sometimes signed off "in the midst of most interesting responses and manifestations." One joyful séance participant requesting an extension received the chilling response that "you must apply for it before it is near out. It was your own proposal to close at that time, and now you must abide the result." Another circle found the spirits and the medium unwilling "that the time should be altered, as all arrangements are made to meet with you on these evenings." Mediums and spirits presumably led busy lives in which sacred time had to be sharply circumscribed and separated from ordinary time. Indeed, one of Circle A's members wrote that appointed times were set "so that the process shall not interfere with the ordinary vocations of the mediums." But the joy of spontaneous religious experience did not always mesh well with such regimented practice. Rapture and order sometimes worked at cross purposes, perhaps leading some Spiritualists to appreciate the less structured revival.[49]

The tension between spontaneity and the séance is suggested even more strongly by John Edmonds's spirit-inspired visions. Both their form and substance suggest the order, structure, and symmetry that characterized the Spiritualist imagination. Unlike the ecstatic visions so often characteristic of intense religious experience, Edmonds's were systematic, sequential, and logically connected, and came only after he and the circle had been prepared for them. After one vision, for instance, the medium explained to the circle that Edmonds had just experienced "the first in this series" and then previewed the content of the next.[50] Furthermore, Edmonds was fully conscious during his experiences, narrating them as he went along, sometimes conversing with the other members of the circle and answering their questions. He understood spirit contact much as Charles G. Finney understood the conversion experience, namely as something "not supernatural, but in compliance with fixed laws." Edmonds's ecstasy was structured by logic, tamed by science, and subdued by reason.

Indeed, he conveyed little feeling of mystic rapture in describing his visions. Rather, his tone, very much in the tradition of Swedenborg, was rational and sober. The spirit of Francis Bacon, a frequent visitor to séance circles and to most nineteenth-century Americans a representative of empirical method, informed the Sacred Circle that the visions involved not "your own imagination" but "the absolute reality of living fact." Consider one typical vision in which Edmonds beheld, "high above me in the heavens, a very massive and magnificent temple." His description of the building, a perfect example of Spiritualists' moderate approach to religious experience and concern for order and symmetry, is worth quoting at length.

> The order of architecture was unlike anything I had ever seen, but it was so perfect in its construction, that it was indeed pleasurable to look upon, and so just in its proportions, that I was unaware of its vastness until I measured it by a comparison with my own dimensions. It was built around four sides of a parallelogram, leaving an area inside, uncovered overhead, and capable of containing many thousand persons.
>
> On three sides of the building were rooms devoted to the residence of

spirits. There were three stories of these rooms and galleries running around those three sides on each level. At the other end was a platform, ascended by a flight of steps, interspersed with smaller platforms or landing-places. I counted the steps in the several flights. They were 3, 5, 7, 9, 7, 5.

Edmonds certainly maintained a firm grip on his powers of observation and discernment during these "pleasurable" moments. Indeed, he sometimes doubted that his mind was "sufficiently under the control of the spirits" during his visions and wondered "whether by this preservation of my self-hood I did not interfere with this part of the teaching." Davis, too, brought technical precision and measurement to bear on his blissful visions. In one, for example, he observed a gathering of spirits "about thirty miles above the earth's surface" and surrounded by a visible aura "of glory and beauty" which stretched "in every direction about twenty feet."[51]

Despite the close similarity between mediumship and mystic illumination, then, Davis and Edmonds underscored a small but important distinction between them. Living in what they considered the scientifically enlightened nineteenth century and concerned to tailor their religion to meet the demands of reason and republican individualism, American Spiritualists showed a tendency, lacking among earlier religious luminaries, to dissect their visions and to resist ecstatic absorption in a higher reality. Their religious experiences also differ sharply from the exuberant and unrestrained behavior Spiritualists associated with the revival "fever." Edmonds could not have emphasized more clearly the centrality of emotional restraint to Spiritualist religiosity. For him and his peers, religious experience involved the head as much as it did the heart; reason was not to be overwhelmed by emotion. Spiritualist séances, occurring beneath the vaulted arches of their architecturally ordered cosmos and in scientifically structured circles, were as quiet and controlled as they were intense.

Once Edmonds received a vision, it was cast into a form which could be preserved and reproduced for all Spiritualists to share. "Write out the vision," Bacon told Dexter, "as a general teaching." Dexter obeyed and added "some things . . . written in explanation" as Edmonds narrated.[52] The result was a routinization of the experience, a transmutation of its immediacy and vitality into a formulaic verbal presentation. The same can be said of the more general practice among Spiritualists of presenting spirit communications in oral, written, and published form. Their descriptions of their rapturous contacts with a higher reality, particularly the plain and matter-of-fact prose style that Edmonds modeled on the writings of Swedenborg, exemplify the ordered ecstasy of Spiritualist religion. Far from understanding their experiences in accordance with Otto's description, that is as inherently nonrational episodes incapable of being examined and conveyed in print, they considered reason and careful recording essential lest their religion threaten the critical acumen and self-control that their culture demanded of them. They were convinced that preserving the relevance of things spiritual in a culture increasingly respectful of science required that religious rapture be made to conform to their notions of law and order.[53]

None of this means that Spiritualists did not enjoy satisfying and intensely religious experiences. Edmonds's admittedly rational visions resonated with the currents of devotionalism in American religious culture. Devotionalists' desire for a personal interaction with the divinity within, Richard Rabinowitz points out, led them to revolt against an earlier religious disdain for the visual, the use of imagination, and the reverie. It also created a propensity for withdrawal as an element of religious experience. "The religious culture," he comments, "seemed to authorize these inner episodes of projecting oneself into imaginary situations." In fact, Spiritualists pushed this trend further than other devotionalists, joining Shakers and Mormons in believing that God or the spirits might extend special revelations through graphic visions and dreams. Edmonds's visions are only one example of the Spiritualist use of reverie and imagination. Others include the visions and solitary rambles of Andrew Jackson Davis, who noted in his autobiography that his characteristic propensity to daydream and to find religious solace by retiring into himself was apparent even during his childhood; John Shoebridge Williams's reclusive seeking of visions and his extended dialogues with Eliza; and Robert Hare's enthusiastic assessment of *The Rambles and Reveries of an Art-Student in Europe,* whose author related frequent visions and musings of the imagination. Above all, the Spiritualist description of the spirit world in graphic and pictorial terms, usually as a more colorful but entirely recognizable version of earth, constitutes a playful if restrained use of imagination.[54]

While the circle indulged the imagination and provided an emotionally fulfilling religious expression, its defining features were order, structure, symmetry, and a grounding in the scientific and technological developments of the period. It aimed through strictly controlled and repeatable procedures to create and recreate the intense experience which Spiritualists were unable to find elsewhere while satisfying their intellectual allegiance to scientific empiricism. It wed emotion and intellect, religion and science, rapture and reason.

The Ministry of the Medium

At the center of any Spiritualist circle was the medium's special contact with the spirit world. While most Spiritualists believed that democratized mediumship and spiritual equality would eventually be achieved, spiritual republicanism recognized a "natural aristocracy." Even the most vocal advocates of a democratized mediumship recognized that not all who sought contact with spirits succeeded on their own and that some people, especially but not solely women, seemed particularly sensitive to spiritual influence and therefore naturally suited for mediumship. Some went further, arguing in the vein of Swedenborg and the New Church that the practice was dangerous and ought to be tightly controlled and limited to those who had been specially trained and prepared for it. Although Robert Ellwood has noted a discrepancy between the restrictive mediumship of strongly group-oriented religions and the individualistic religious quest characteristic of American excursus religion, Spiritualist religion combined them by democratizing mediumship in theory while often restricting it in practice. Some Spiritualists, like Williams, discovered their own mediumship, abandoned the circle, and embarked on lone voyages of inner discovery. But far more experienced a group excursus by forming small circles gathered around one or more mediums through whom they enjoyed vicarious contact with the spiritual realm.[55]

As representatives of advanced spirits for those unable to establish a direct connection, mediums transmitted spirit ministration to the members of the circle. They therefore held a position of de facto authority in Spiritualist religious practice much like that of ministers and charismatic leaders in other denominations and sects.[56] Believing in a parallelism between the physical and spiritual realms, Spiritualists believed in a dualistic ministry of spirits and their mortal representatives. It was not uncommon, nor was it a contradiction, for them to refer explicitly to mediums, like the spirits, as "ministers," or to look to them for religious inspiration and leadership. John Shoebridge Williams referred casually to the "medium, priest, pastor, or whatever name mediums may be known by." R. P. Ambler called well-disciplined mediums "ministers of truth" who had been "selected" by the spirits "to perform the work of enlightening and elevating the race." A Universalist minister before becoming a medium, he looked back in 1852 upon his career up to that point as one of "spiritual ministry" and regarded his mediumship as a continuation of the work he had begun as a clergyman. Thomas Lake Harris, who favored inspiration over education as the basis of ministerial authority, likewise considered the "spiritual seer" to be "a legitimate teacher of religion."[57]

To be sure, aversion to clerical despotism kept Spiritualists well aware that the status of the medium was derivative. They granted special status to their mediums only because, as Harris suggested, they believed them to have been naturally prepared and empowered by authoritative spirits rather than by merely artificial religious institutions. But the voices of the mediums, however derivative, were the ones directly heard in the séance. Like all religions, Spiritualism required tangible channels through which spirituality was believed to flow. Anxious both to discard a mortal ministry and to establish links between the terrestrial and spiritual planes, Spiritualists had it both ways. Moreover, once convinced of a medium's authenticity and of the inherently gentle and unobtrusive nature of spirit authority, they sometimes carried their notions of mediumistic authority to great lengths. John Murray Spear thought that "harmonic relations" with an all-pervasive "Grand Concentrative Element" which "moves, guides, influences, [and] controls nature" qualified the medium to become "a governor of others" who "controls them as he will."[58]

The Spiritualist medium therefore resembled the religious mystic, connecting with the spiritual world and passing higher wisdom to a circle of followers who sought enlightenment. Spiritualists themselves noted the similarity. "To be a medium," said A. E. Newton, "is only to be what prophets, seers, and apostles have been—what Christ himself was—channels through which Divine light and goodness can be poured into the minds of men." A feeling of kinship with earlier mystics led Spiritualists to laud Davis as the latest in a long line of "seers," inspired the *Shekinah* to run a series of biographical sketches of such "Ancient and Modern Seers" as Pythagoras, Jesus, and Swedenborg, and motivated Partridge and Brittan to publish an American edition of Justinius Kerner's *Seeress of Prevorst,* an account of a clairvoyant German girl of the early nineteenth century. These models of Spiritualists' practice constituted their pantheon of heroes.[59]

Mediums also resembled shamans in traditional religions. If the function of the shaman is to assert human mastery over the mysteries of the spiritual realm, antebellum Spiritualists reduced the mysteriousness of spirit not only by probing its nature and asserting the humanity of their spirit contacts but also by developing repeatable procedures by which the medium could bring the spirits into their presence at will. In other words, the circle took possession of the spirits just as surely as the spirits took possession of mediums. Similarly, mediums were often examples of what Robert Ellwood called "the modern magus" or the "shaman-in-civilization." "The transformative catalyst he becomes for the circle around him is more important than what he says or does, in itself. The most significant feature of the charismatic figure, the magus, is that he becomes a symbol in the minds of others—a symbol powerful enough to effect a reordering of the disciple's mindset, to raise or lower the threshold of the unconscious."[60]

Indeed, the medium-qua-shaman led the circle through a religious ritual akin to a rite of passage. As Robert C. Fuller has observed, the experience of the trance followed the rite of passage step for step. It separated individuals from their accustomed identity, temporarily induced a paranormal state of consciousness understood as an avenue to otherwise inaccessible truths, and returned experientially invigorated persons to ordinary life with new insight.

While only mediums experienced the trance or vision, other members of the circle enjoyed a vicarious experience in which they left the ordinary behind in the special setting of the séance room, established indirect contact with a higher reality, and returned to daily life strengthened by new spiritual wisdom.[61]

Even some non-Spiritualists, like popular writer and *Home Journal* editor Nathaniel P. Willis, were struck by the medium's aura of clerical authority. At a trance lecture by Cora Hatch, Willis noticed her "clergyman's attitude of devotion" and commented that her "tone and manner were of an absolute sincerity of devoutness which compelled respect." A "church full of people," he noted, seemed to agree, for they were "listening attentively while she prayed!" Tammany politician and would-be heckler Issiah Rynders was moved to tears by his experience at her lecture. "Her prayer" seemed to him "beautiful, her theory profound, and her language eloquent." He had "never heard so beautiful and touching an exhortation from any pulpit."[62]

The medium's central religious role and the natural inequality of mediumistic talent meant that the structure of authority in the Spiritualist circle closely resembled that of most other religious groups, particularly tightly centralized ones (such as the Mormons) that involved strong charismatic leadership based on contact with the spirit world. John Murray Spear described mediums as "prominent persons" gifted with a "concentric principle" that enables them to "call others around them." This "true religious teacher," he said, "becomes the focal mind, the religious brain, the emotional mouthpiece" of the circle. His recognition that "Americans have been taught to abhor" such a monarchical system did not dampen his enthusiasm for it (either religiously or politically), for it was like the human organism and the cosmos itself in being a "beautiful structure under a high, controlling mind." Spirit voices urged John Shoebridge Williams to avoid involvement with a group of Spiritualists whose "radical defect" was trying to base their practices "upon the democratic platform or on the common level or independent sovereignty of all the members." The order of these Spiritualists, he believed, was "not the order of Heaven," which was "a kingdom" rather than a democratic republic. In the natural order, "every circle has a center" and therefore "every circle of spirits [has] its central member or medium of the functions proper to its members." Like the Puritans of early New England, Spear and Williams envisioned a theocratic government that promoted religion and spirituality as essential to order. So would the structure of religious authority remain until the realization of spiritual equality in the indefinite future.[63]

Less zealous Spiritualists like LaRoy Sunderland envisioned a similar structure of religious authority. Even after he became disillusioned with mediumship, he advised those "little attracted to the usual places of sectarian instruction" to form "circles for spiritual culture" and to look for leadership to a "head," "parental," "teacher," and "minister" who "has the most wisdom, by which others would be likely to be attracted around him." This figure "presides in all the public meetings, . . . performs the usual offices of a presiding officer," and "serve[s] the same function as is similarly done by the wise Parent." Above all, this leader "preserves order. . . . he must give direction, he is the Form and Order of all that is done." To be sure, Sunderland had a distaste for "complicated machinery," including "appointing officers, adopting constitutions, by-laws, &c." But his desire for a structured order of religious observance is clear. Spiritualism, like other "excursus" religions, had not a network of institutionalized churches but a large number of "intensive centers" in which "the real focus is the charisma of the mediumistic minister."[64]

In fact, many Spiritualists frankly suggested that mediums constituted a special clerical class. Spear's criticism of the clergy, for instance, called not for its elimination but its improvement. Democratized mediumship would eventually obviate the need for distinct religious leaders, he believed, but since only "a few persons have become qualified" as mediums and "arrived at this high wisdom state" so far it was "needful that teachers should be raised up." Even Adin Ballou, a critic of Spear's activities and an opponent of excessive mediumistic authority, echoed him on this point. He favored the idea "that God has ever so inspired some human beings, above the generality, as to make them reliable media of fundamental principles to the rest" over the democratic idea "that every human being is naturally so inspired as not to need the aid of any such select media." This pattern of behavior was typical of excursus religious practice, which tends toward an undemocratic belief that trances are dangerous and ought to be tightly controlled or limited to a small body of experts. Moore has correctly pointed out that Spiritualist publications "fairly consistently discouraged systematic attempts to develop a mediumistic potential that had not appeared spontaneously."[65]

Spiritualist religion therefore provides abundant support for Nathan O. Hatch's point that the democratization of religious authority in the early republic encouraged antidemocratic developments. In Spiritualism, as in other new religious movements of the period, self-proclaimed prophets and spiritual leaders claimed special inspiration and authority and attracted followers into strictly and autocratically controlled religious groups. Like such mystics and prophets as Swedenborg, George Fox, and Joseph Smith, Spiritualist mediums not only represented individualistic rebellion against existing religious institutions but became foci of new religious communities.

Every sustained circle exhibited this tendency, but the most pronounced and colorful instances involved Spear and Williams. To be sure, they drew harsh criticism from other members of the movement. Ballou lamented the "hallucination, extravagance, credulity, fanaticism, semi-insanity, abnormal absurdity, and spiritual confusion" as well as the authoritarian tendencies of mediums who considered themselves "super-excellent and highly favored." The *Telegraph* compared some mediums' "excess of bombast and positive assertion" with what they considered the inflated claims of William Miller and Joseph Smith. But figures like Spear and Williams only accentuated the broader Spiritualist tendency toward charismatic leadership and centralized structures of authority among small groups.[66]

Spear's mediumistic activities were inspired by Andrew Jackson Davis's statement that the spirits had selected twelve individuals on earth to advance the welfare of the human race through teaching and healing the sick. Spear believed himself to be one of these apostles of Spiritualism, a naturally empowered spiritual leader in the tradition of Christ, and set out in 1852 on a mission of benevolence that was modeled on early Christianity and included healing by virtue of spirit power. Inspired by what he considered the "especial supervision and immediate direction of . . . spirit friends," he appointed twelve "Teachers" or "Apostles," five women and seven men, to labor for Spiritualist religion and reform with the goal of constructing a "new, living, and rational *Church*." He ritualistically initiated new members of his group and consecrated them to their work.[67]

Consider, for example, his recruitment of medium Semantha Mettler of Hartford, Connecticut. An impulse from the spirit world, he believed, sent him to Hartford as part of his missionary travels. There he recounted to a group of friends his own enlistment by the spirits. He then entered a trance, explained his commission "to wisely instruct this woman for a high purpose," and arranged to initiate Mettler into his circle of disciples in a ceremony at ten o'clock the following morning. At the rite, Spear announced on bended knee that "this fondly loved one shall be consecrated to the charities" and gave her the special name "Charity" to establish her new religious identity. Then, with the words "receive now this blessed power," he breathed on Mettler's hand. "This hand shall be unfolded to dispense blessings. . . . It is done." Emma Hardinge described the experience of hearing Spear's "conversion" narrative and passing through his ritual as "something akin to the passionate emotions of a great revival season." Another of Spear's followers, Cleveland lawyer and radical abolitionist John M. Sterling, observed that obedience to his spirit-inspired commands involved considerable hardship, self-sacrifice, and a "most severe discipline." Spear attempted to form, in short, a dedicated, well-ordered, and tightly controlled band of missionaries.[68]

This aspect of Spear's mediumistic practice, like so many others, was criticized by Spiritualists in the name of spiritual republicanism. The editors of the *Spiritual Telegraph* lamented that his followers had "sunk their personality and manhood in a deplorable subservience to a doubtful authority." Even one of his "apostles," Chicago abolitionist Thomas Richmond, eventually opted for individualism over discipleship. He was initially impressed by Spear, who sought him out, "consecrated me, and gave me a name." But by the end of 1858 Richmond's faith had been shaken. He related his confusion to Spear, asking "what is the instrument I am to use to discern the true or the false? . . . I know of no other than to look within myself." He evidently decided to break with the Spear entourage; there is no further record of his support for it. Still, many other disciples remained devoted to him. John M. Sterling retained an "unshaken faith" that led him and Spear's other followers to defend their favorite medium from the *Telegraph*'s charges and to continue to obey what they considered his spirit-inspired instructions.[69]

John Shoebridge Williams, meanwhile, attempted to use his mediumship to transform his dysfunctional family into a tightly controlled religious patriarchy grounded in his role as minister, his reading of the Old Testament, and his conception of cosmic order. He feared that his family would scatter under a democratizing process which had encouraged his grown children to make decisions for themselves and his wife (from whom he was divorced) to challenge his governance. He therefore urged on his children his doctrines of "family concentration" and "patriarchal order." Over sixty years old and feeling distant from a family over which he had lost control, he declared his authority as "the orderly medium of truth to his children" and the family's "divinely constituted head." He complained that the "true family order" of the Old Testament, in which children consulted their fathers before making decisions, had been undermined in America, "where republicanism is gone to seed." Instead, his society had mistakenly encouraged the "democratic plan" in which uppity wives and children increasingly resisted patriarchal control.[70] Family concentration required that children feel not independent but rather thankful to parents for having been created, "dependent upon others, or something superior to himself," and cognizant that "one is nothing of himself and is only any thing as he receives from those able and appointed to give." He urged men to grow beards as essential conduits of spirit influence and symbols of authority that create "a patriarchal venerable look" and enhance fathers' resemblance to "the good Patriarchs and saints of old." Furthermore, "females cannot half so easily feel beardless men as their fathers and protectors as they can those with full grown beards." His children, particularly his sons Robert and Joseph, resisted in the name of freedom; Joseph insisted that he must act "according to his own understanding." An embittered Williams eventually gave up his attempt, reminiscent of Joseph Smith's, to restore ancient religious patriarchy in antebellum America. He spiritualized his hopes through a belief that a family of spirits would cluster around him, "grow up together as one acknowledging you as their father," and "look on you as the center of influence from on high."[71]

The examples of Spear and Williams offer a counterpoint to the usual emphasis on the religious authority and empowerment of women in Spiritualist practice. To be sure, women could easily achieve the special status of the medium because Spiritualists considered the characteristics attributed to them by the nineteenth-century ideology of domesticity—passivity, nervous sensitivity, and moral purity—essential to effective mediumship. Taking place in the medium's home, moreover, the séance was set in what was widely regarded as "women's sphere." Women therefore far outnumbered men as mediums and Spiritualist religion opened a unique opportunity for them. Many female mediums ventured beyond the confines of the home, setting out on regional or national speaking tours and lecturing from the trance state on a variety of such controversial religious, moral, and social issues as slavery and women's rights. Some were emboldened by their success as trance speakers to address audiences while in the "normal" state. Ann Braude has persuasively demonstrated that women found in mediumship an avenue to practical authority and a public role in American religious life.[72]

But Spiritualist religion also encouraged patriarchal mediumistic practices. Its identification of spiritual causality and power with masculinity in a gendered cosmos and its corollary that even male mortals were "feminine" recipients of spiritual influence from "masculine" forces above meant that a replication of the natural order of the cosmos in terrestrial spiritual and social relations could easily become an ideological basis for strong forms of male religious authority. Spear may have believed that the "central persons" who possessed the "concentric principle" and attracted followers were "generally . . . females" and that the perfect social order "will place WOMAN at its head, or, rather, in its centre." But while he assigned women leadership roles in his utopia and prominent positions in his group, he maintained a status above that of his followers and never elevated a woman to equal status with himself. The androgynous Williams, meanwhile, did not even envision a social state run by women, and considered the subordination of women to men in his patriarchal order perfectly natural.[73]

Williams and Spear dramatized the practical results of mediumistic authority in Spiritualist religion. Like John Humphrey Noyes and Joseph Smith, they claimed contact with a higher authority and became (or, in the case of Williams, tried to become) nuclei of new communities characterized by strong centralized authority. Ministers in mainline Protestant denomina-

tions, too, based their authority not simply on education or formal ordination but on a special relationship with a higher spiritual reality. Spear and
Williams throw into relief the resemblance between their religion, which
replaced conventional ministers with mediums as de facto leaders, and the
others on the antebellum landscape. Above all, they remind us that Spiritualists avoided as much as they embraced the atomizing implications of religious
democratization. Their religion aimed not to drive Jacksonian Americans
apart but to bring them together in a new configuration of community and
order.

⊷⊶

7

The Structure of Spiritualist Society

The Organization of Spiritualist Society

In his autobiography, Andrew Jackson Davis recalled with terror that his entranced mind, freed to roam inner space, drifted to "thoughts of disorganization." He found security in his belief that, in the beginning, his deity had reduced a primordial chaos to order and made organization a fundamental characteristic of nature. He and his audience believed as strongly that Nature and its deity knew best as that formal institutions potentially threatened the values of spiritual republicanism. Reminding readers of the *Shekinah* that "nature performs her operations by organized action," S. B. Brittan counseled them that the threat posed by organization was potential only; "we should not fear organization," he said, simply "because some have made it the engine of oppression." Adin Ballou agreed that "organic despotism" was to be avoided but suggested in "Individuality vs. Organization" that abuse of power characterized individuals rather than institutions as such. His leadership of the heavily law-laden Hopedale community during the 1840s and 1850s, criticized by some as excessively authoritarian, indicates his willingness to act on this conviction. Joel Tiffany saw no inconsistency between his commitment to individual freedom and his advocacy of noncoercive organizations based on a "natural affinity" that attracted like-minded members together. Even Mary F. Davis, whose strongly anti-organizational sentiments were mentioned in chapter 3, feared by the late 1850s that some members of the movement "are disposed to cut loose from all restraint, scatter to the winds all traces of order and system, and fly off to the extreme limit of individual independence and arrogance!" These Spiritualist republicans felt that religion required as strong a commitment to organization, community, and group life as to individual self-realization.[1]

They expressed their need for religious attachment not only in their circles but also in their frequent if often controversial attempts to create communities and institutions that extended beyond them. To be sure, Spiritualism lacked an institutional definition, especially during the 1850s. Those organizations that did appear failed to provide unified direction to the movement's variety of adherents, and many Spiritualist leaders played down institutional loyalty in both rhetoric and practice. Some studies have therefore concluded that the movement was hostile to organization. In fact, however, Spiritualists' desire to encourage both individual freedom on the one hand and religious community and order on the other resulted in complex and ambivalent attitudes toward formal structure. Far from shunning organization altogether, Spiritualists debated its merits and many of them tried to stake out a middle ground. Even strong defenders of individual conscience against perceived institutional constraint were as concerned to avoid excessive individualism as excessive centralism. Some Spiritualists considered themselves "no-organizationists," but most accepted organizations as natural entities that had to be monitored.[2]

Spiritualists' patterns of organization reflected their desire to replicate in their religious lives a hierarchically arranged spirit world in which innumerable tightly knit circles based on affinity were combined into increasingly broad centralized entities. Williams's vision of cosmic social structure was typical in its combination of centralized and decentralized structure. "There are central mediums," he explained, "and around these as order is perfected will other mediums cluster. Those who cluster around the primary centers will themselves be centers for more outer circles." At the center of his spiritual cosmos was Christ, "the great central medium of all mediums."[3]

Andrew Jackson Davis likewise understood the spirit world as a well organized place. In August 1852 he experienced a vision of a "Spiritual Congress" at the tower atop High Rock, the same sacred site at which Spear would later attempt to build the New Motor (see illustration 4).[4] This "Congress" was decidedly American and Christian in nature. It had both republican characteristics, including its name, its engagement in "calm debate," and its skill "in the divine art of self-government and individual culture," and more centralistic ones, including its division into such aristocratically titled bodies as the "Royal Circle of the Foli." The Congress was arranged "into harmonious groups and circles, as if to systematize their number." The movement as a whole similarly tended to blend centralized and decentralized structural patterns as Spiritualists formed countless small circles and sometimes larger institutional structures.[5]

Spear's activities exemplify this pattern. Inspired by Davis's belief that the "Spiritual Congress" would work for "the general welfare of our common race," he led an organized reform effort modeled on his understanding of the structure of spiritual society. Like Davis, he understood the "Grand Central

Mind" as "an ORGANIZER" and believed that "organization exists in nature [as does order]." His spirit world was therefore a "group-world" dedicated to institutionalized missionary activity on earth. He imagined that the "Spiritual Congress" had appointed a "General Assembly" which authorized him to arrange his followers into seven groups replicating seven spirit "associations" (called Beneficents, Electricizers, Elementizers, Educationizers, Healthful-izers, Agriculturalizers, and Governmentizers). The leader of each group was expected to attract followers, resulting in a series of departmental subcircles overseen by Spear and his spirit contacts and devoted to religious, reform, educational, scientific, medical, and political enterprises.[6]

The Spiritualist pattern of small-scale organization, highlighted by Spear's example, led Adin Ballou to fear that Spiritualists, like Protestants, would form as many small and mutually hostile sectarian groups as there were charismatic mediums who could attract followers. Spear himself lamented Protestantism's centrifugal potential and called for unity. Defending "associa-tion" against "bald individualism," he called Protestantism a religious "vol-cano" or "whirlwind" that had too often "thrown men off into ragged fragments." A church based on the principles of nature, he said, "gathers up these fragments, smooths the rough corners; again they associate, come to-gether, and are one." But Spiritualist individualism discouraged that possibil-ity. Despite Spear's hopes, he and many other mediums became centers of sometimes mutually mistrustful religious subcommunities within the move-ment. Like Protestantism, Spiritualism combined centrifugal and centripetal tendencies and therefore encouraged the formation of many small and well-structured groups that one scholar has called "Spiritualist denominations." Having experienced sectarian quarrels, Ballou must have taken a wry satisfac-tion in being right.[7]

But other Spiritualists openly defended a "denominational" configuration as the only hope for religious order. Explaining that belief in spirit communi-cation was an insufficient basis for organization, a writer for the *Telegraph* advocated "spiritual platforms" adopted by small groups as a foundation of harmony and community among those that voluntarily accepted it. The re-sult would be a well organized if decentralized movement in which believers could enjoy religious community without the coerced conformity which Spiritualists associated with existing institutions. Religious pluralism, in short, meant to this Spiritualist not chaos and contention but organization, order, and fellowship among like-minded believers. This writer did not convince all Spiritualists but had the satisfaction of approving what had become a *fait accompli* not only among Spiritualists but in American religious life as a whole.[8]

The same concern for order led some Spiritualists to favor a centralized ecclesiastical polity over such decentralist visions. Once a member of the

Society of Friends, Edmonds still accepted its individualistic doctrine of the inner light but criticized its lack of centralized organizational structure. The Quakers, he said, had mistakenly "refused to have any presiding or controlling power anywhere, as if order was not Heaven's first law." Born in opposition to a dominating religious hierarchy, Quakerism had run to the opposite extreme of "hostility to all order or religious government" and as a result had "almost vanished from among us." By contrast, he pointed out, the tightly organized Methodist hierarchy, overseeing the largest denomination in antebellum America, had learned the "lesson of government taught by nature" and enjoyed spectacular success. Edmonds hoped that Spiritualism would "profit by the example." Uriah Clark agreed that too many Spiritualists, "rejecting false authorities, false restraints," tended "to reject all authority, all restraint, and run rampant into a liberty in danger of leading to anarchy and licentiousness." Like Edmonds, he sensed a "danger of rejecting . . . all religious order." For Edmonds, Clark, and many others in the movement, a centralized religious organization seemed the only guarantee against chaos.[9]

Spiritualism's organizational pattern helps to explain its appeal to some of the Shakers, whose sect was a model of orderly organization. To be sure, Shakers and Spiritualists found much to criticize in each other's movements; many Shakers disapproved of the sensationalism and perceived materialism encouraged by the fascination with séance phenomena, while Spiritualists condemned what they considered the excessive authoritarianism of Shaker life. It is also true that the appeal of Spiritualism for Shakers lay chiefly in its emphasis on spirit communication, with which antebellum Shakers were quite familiar. Many Shakers heard the "mysterious knockings" which began just as the Shaker spiritualism of the 1830s and 1840s waned, Spiritualist mediums sometimes visited Shaker villages, and Shakers sometimes visited Spiritualist séances. Hervey Elkins, for instance, commented after moving from Shakerism to Spiritualism that "I was, and continue to be a firm believer in spiritual entity and spiritual influence," and Edmonds reported the attendance of two Shakers from the Mount Lebanon community at a meeting of the Sacred Circle. Still, the Spiritualist circle's centralized structure aroused the interest of prominent Shaker leader Frederick W. Evans, who contributed a number of friendly articles to the *Spiritual Telegraph* between 1853 and 1856. In "Mediums and Circles," Evans echoed Spear and Williams: "every circle should have a head to govern and direct it." He added that this leader might change from time to time and could be either male or female, but insisted that "every perfect circle will always have for the time being, a head, hands, feet, and every other member necessary to make it a perfect body, and to preserve perfect order." Spiritualism and Shakerism were evidently more alike than Spiritualist critics of the Shaker organization admitted.[10]

Nor is it surprising that some Spiritualists were attracted to the institutionalization, centralization, and structured religiosity of the Catholic church despite their tendency to share the American bias against its perceived authoritarianism and spiritual monarchy. Like Edmonds, John Shoebridge Williams began his religious life as a Quaker but "could not see enough in friends forms to bind me." His search for a more structurally substantial religion led him from the Society of Friends to Swedenborgianism to Spiritualism, from which he launched his exploration of the Catholic church. Mary Gove Nichols and her husband Thomas Low Nichols experienced a similar spiritual pilgrimage. Raised as Quakers, they considered themselves radical individualists for a time, but "individuality began to recede as a concern" and "collective harmony became prominent" around the time they became involved with Spiritualism in 1854. Despite their opposition at that time to any "Spiritual Church Organization" that would "have its Bishops, and perhaps its Cardinals and Popes," they embraced Catholicism in 1857 after receiving spirit revelations from St. Ignatius Loyola and St. Francis Xavier. By 1864, Thomas had shrugged off his flirtation with a Spiritualist movement which he deemed "chaotic" and "disorderly." For Edmonds, Williams, and the Nicholses, Spiritualism was part of the trajectory from individualism to centralization that defined not only their personal religious lives but also an American culture in transition from a mood of "boundlessness" to one of "consolidation."[11]

Some Spiritualists considered even spiritual individualism and democratized mediumship compatible with such organized forms of group devotion as churches and congregations. Averse to the religious solitude of a Williams, they looked to the Quaker meeting as a model combination of individualism and community. Convinced that "we need not break up existing church meetings and pull down church edifices," Charles Partridge envisioned a "Church of the Future" that would discourage the abuses of "a hired priesthood" and encourage individual expression. He wanted a meeting "edified by the spontaneity of thoughts" in which "each person will contribute from time to time" under the inspiration of spirits. The "Educational Church" contemplated by Spear would work much the same way. Its meetings would open with "a season of profound silence" broken when a person "impressed" by the spirits posed some important spiritual question "addressed generally to the assembly." "Deliberative waiting" would follow until another participant was impressed to reply. The assembly would then meditate on the reply until someone offered another question. These ideal religious meetings were democratic but also orderly, institutionalized, and communal. The religious life sought by Spiritualists like Spear and Partridge was structured and literally "churched."[12]

This tendency toward formal organization makes the appearance of Spiritualist churches, which began in the late 1850s and accelerated thereafter, entirely comprehensible.[13] Lacking centralized leadership and an authoritative set of writings, their churches were "distinctly congregational," with authority resting at the local level. Their services, which like the circle usually included an invocation, prayers, hymns, and a sermon or lecture, resembled those of more conventional Christian groups except for the reception of spirit messages through a medium. In smaller locales, a local medium acted as the minister and delivered the lecture, but in larger towns and cities this function was more likely to be performed by a leading figure in the movement.[14] A product of some Spiritualists' desire to forge bonds of community beyond what was possible in the circle, the congregational-style Spiritualist church underscores the broader Spiritualist pattern of creating small religious communities.

The organizing impulse and the desire to expand religious community found expression in other Spiritualist religious activities as well. In 1853, Spiritualists began to hold regular formalized public Sunday services that transferred the comforting features of the small private circle to a larger public setting. Boston Spiritualists flocked to the Melodeon and their New York counterparts to the Stuyvesant Institute, then Hope Chapel, and finally Dodworth's Hall. Like the circle, these meetings varied somewhat in their proceedings but involved a general order of ritual, had a religious tone and content, included spirit communications, were punctuated by inspirational music, and generally began with an opening prayer. But they also included elements not typical of the circle meeting, including selected readings from Spiritualist works, periods of spontaneous prayer (reminiscent of Partridge's "Church of the Future" and Spear's "Educational Church"), and a featured speaker, female or male. In large cities, one might hear Andrew Jackson Davis or his wife Mary, editor S. B. Brittan, or such famous mediums as Cora Hatch and Emma Hardinge. In smaller locales, an itinerant lecturer or local medium was more common. By offering shared religious experience, these meetings created ties of spiritual fellowship which were looser than those forged in the more intimate setting of the circle but encompassed larger numbers of people.[15]

The outdoor summer camp meeting was another practice which brought together large numbers of Spiritualists—in this case thousands of them—in an institutionalized setting. Camp meetings like Spiritualist churches were largely a postbellum phenomenon (they became especially popular during the 1870s), but they too first appeared during the late 1850s. Unlike Spiritualist churches and Sunday meetings, the summer camp involved an environment more festive than solemn and therefore bore only a remote resemblance to the extended outdoor revival. Private consultations with mediums, moreover, seem to have been more common than the more communal religious practices of holding circles or formal religious services. But to the extent that they highlighted shared Spiritualist beliefs, they enhanced bonds of community and "provided an important sense of coherence and cohesion."[16]

Spiritualists also created, or attempted to create, institutions designed to carry on the day-to-day business of Spiritualist religion. Uriah Clark, for example, was as opposed to religious tyranny as any Spiritualist but recognized "a need for such organizations as are expedient to form orderly circles, obtain places for public conferences and lectures, procure suitable speakers and mediums, raise means for meeting expenses and maintain certain legal rights." And Spear was not the only Spiritualist who felt that effective reform, missionary, and benevolent activity required organized effort; witness Circle A's formation of the Harmonial Benevolent Association and the endeavor of arch-individualist John Shoebridge Williams to create a Society for the Protection of the Defenseless Oppressed.[17]

Consistently with other aspects of Spiritualist practice, attempts to create such institutions were most successful when they were small in scope. Spiritualists succeeded during the 1850s in creating "an uncountable number of local societies," organizations in most states, and in some cases regional associations. More ambitious efforts were more problematic. Consider, for example, an October 1854 attempt by a convention of Spiritualists at the Boston Melodeon to establish a broad organization. Recognizing the value of a centrally organized enterprise and dominated by such followers of Spear as S. C. Hewitt and A. E. Newton, this gathering approved of Newton's call for a "central institution," based on an earlier suggestion by Hewitt, to serve as a focal point for Spiritualist mediums and a center or "nucleus" for the movement. Lacking time to develop a mature plan for such an institution, the convention's Committee on Organization adopted a general resolution that the "principle of co-operative effort" required at least the formation of a "Unitary Home" for the support of Spiritualist mediums. J. H. Robinson opposed the idea, identifying the chief obstacle to large-scale organization among Spiritualists when he argued that every individual was a "nucleus."[18]

The most controversial attempt at organization came in June 1854 when John Edmonds and other prominent New York Spiritualists launched the Society for the Diffusion of Spiritual Knowledge (SDSK), intended to be national in scope, and established *The Christian Spiritualist* as its official periodical. Designed to preserve "Christian" Spiritualism against the movement's rationalistic wing and to bring together an important subset of the movement, its founding sparked a flurry of debate in the Spiritualist press about the relative merits of organization and individualism. Opponents feared that its centralized authority would endanger freedom, while its defenders looked to it for "a hope of order and system, where all has heretofore been like the disjointed matter in space awaiting the voice of God to speak it into active and useful existence."[19] The SDSK eventually folded, as pointed out in chapter 3, because its socially topheavy leadership, outspokenly Christian orientation, and potential threat to individual spiritual autonomy alienated many Spiritualists. But by underscoring the movement's organizing thrust, the fact that the SDSK was created at all tells us as much about Spiritualist religion as does its ultimate failure.

One of the controversies surrounding the SDSK shows that Spiritualists were averse less to organization per se than to large scale centralizing efforts, and could indeed be fierce defenders of organizational localism. When Society members Uriah Clark, P. B. Randolph, and *Christian Spiritualist* editor J.H.W. Toohey tried late in 1854 to swallow an emerging Brooklyn society by transforming it into an SDSK auxiliary, Tappen Townsend, a member of the Brooklyn association and occasional contributor to Edmonds's *Sacred Circle,* defended the smaller local organization against what he perceived as the SDSK's tendency toward excessive concentration of power. Townsend was no radical individualist or anti-organizationist—he praised his local institution for allowing "the largest liberty of individual action consistent with order"—but he feared that this attempt at "spiritual annexation" would offend those "not willing to admit the assumptions of that society" and "opposed strongly to the idea of spiritual centralization." His defense of local autonomy against central authority failed, convincing only Clark, but the attempt typified the Spiritualist pattern of steering a middle course between centralization and atomization through the creation of relatively small religious structures. His defeat, meanwhile, underscores the power of the movement's centralizing impulses.[20]

A final way in which Spiritualists sought to extend organization and community beyond the circle was through the creation and circulation of periodicals. At least eighty titles, most of them very short-lived, appeared during the dozen years between the inception of the movement and the Civil War, suggesting that their establishment was a matter of considerable importance. Financing and editing Spiritualist periodicals was not remunerative, but Spiritualists persisted in the face of repeated failure because of the crucial function that their periodicals served. Without large-scale institutions, Spiritualism lacked many of the means of achieving cohesion and disseminating information available to other American sects and denominations. The Spiritualist press filled this gap by fostering what journalism historian David Nord has called "reader communities," that is, "groups of geographically separated but like-minded individuals who learn of each other's existence and maintain contact through the columns of newspapers."[21] They established communication and solidarity among their readers, whose beliefs often isolated them from others in their towns. Such titles as

Spiritual Telegraph and *Spirit Messenger*, then, had a double meaning, signi-
fying the communication not only between Spiritualists and spirits but also
among Spiritualists themselves. Similarly, the title of the *Medium* suggests
that that periodical was intended to serve as a central source of spiritual
enlightenment for its "circle" of readers.

Spiritualist periodicals were information centers that published not only
spirit communications, essays, and editorials but also reports of the travels and
engagements of itinerant mediums and lecturers, advertisements for mediumistic services, accounts of the movement's progress in different locales,
and the proceedings of meetings and conventions at the local, regional, and
national levels. The *Telegraph*, for example, included such regular features as
"The Principles of Nature," which offered extended religious and philosophical essays, "More Table-Moving Facts," which reported the latest
manifestations, "Home and Foreign Items," which kept readers abreast of the
most recent developments in the movement, and "Business Notices," which
informed readers of the availability of lecturers, mediums, and circles in their
area. Some periodicals, such as the *Shekinah*, included reviews of relevant
books and new odes and hymns for use in the séance ritual. Newspapers also
affirmed Spiritualist identity and ideology through such titles as *Spiritual
Telegraph, Sacred Circle, Medium, Spiritual Universe*, and *Spirit Guardian*
as well as through mastheads which invariably symbolized higher authority
and wisdom, centralized power, and community.[22]

In keeping with the antebellum Spiritualist pattern of small-scale religious
community, Spiritualist periodicals (particularly those of the 1850s) often
fostered solidarity among small groups and subcommunities within the
movement. To be sure, some papers, particularly the *Telegraph*, the *Banner of
Light*, and others emanating from such major centers of activity as New York
and Boston, linked Spiritualists all over the nation, finding subscribers, cor-
respondents, and contributors from the South and far West as well as the
Northeast and Midwest. Still, the appearance of a number of local papers
suggests a felt need to create reader communities on a smaller geographic
scale. In addition to New York and Boston, then, Spiritualists of the 1850s
established regional and local periodicals in Buffalo, Cleveland, Cincinnati,
Detroit, Milwaukee, St. Louis, and New Orleans, not to mention the states of
Maine, Vermont, Indiana, Illinois, Iowa, Arkansas, Georgia, and California.
The appearance of the *Spiritualiste de la Nouvelle-Orleans* indicates that
language and ethnicity as well as locality could become the basis for small-
scale religious community within the movement.[23]

Reader subcommunities were defined by ideology as well as geography
and language. While the most successful papers, such as the *Telegraph* (or,
later, the *Religio-Philosophical Journal* and the *Banner of Light*), achieved
relatively high circulation and long life by avoiding ideological extremes and

controversies, others were more slanted and appealed to smaller but more intensely like-minded audiences. Boston's *New Era,* for example, edited by S. C. Hewitt, defended Spear's radicalism against the more moderate *Telegraph.* Another paper, *Disclosures from the Interior and Superior Care for Mortals,* likewise catered to the small group that gathered around charismatic mediums Thomas Lake Harris and James L. Scott in Auburn, New York, and became a frequent target for other Spiritualist periodicals. Such radical newspapers as the *Social Revolutionist* and the *Vanguard* similarly attracted fewer subscribers than the *Telegraph*'s five thousand, but their supporters, like those of *New Era* and *Disclosures,* constituted more ideologically coherent reader communities.[24]

If Spiritualist newspapers became centers of reader "circles," they also provided their editors with roles of religious leadership comparable to those of mediums. Addressing their readers on a regular basis in order to spread the gospel of Spiritualism, editors tended to view the roles of themselves and their newspapers in ministerial terms. When Charles Partridge took over as sole editor of the *Telegraph* in 1857, he made this function as well as the domestic setting of Spiritualist religion clear enough by adding the words "and Fireside Preacher" to the original title. Other periodical titles, such as *Spiritual and Moral Instructor,* similarly indicate this clerical function. The religious leadership exercised by editors was especially important to Spiritualist men, who constituted the majority of the movement's editors and writers and the minority of its mediums. There were, of course, some male mediums who became strong religious leaders, and some female Spiritualist editors, such as Mrs. H.F.M. Brown of Cleveland's radical *Agitator* and Harriet N. Greene of the *Radical Spiritualist,* whose positions contributed to the expansion of women's leadership roles. But because male mediumship was more the exception than the rule, there is some truth to the claim that "publishing a newspaper was the closest thing to ministry that the new faith offered to male advocates."[25] Many of the movement's chief male figures, including Brittan, Edmonds, Partridge, Ballou, Newton, Clark, Thomas Lake Harris, W. S. Courtney, and Joel Tiffany, achieved their status in the movement at least in part through their editorial activities. Finally, editorship linked its often upper-middle-class practitioners, who made up a important segment of the movement's leadership, to at least those of its rank-and-file members who read its periodicals.

Spiritualists' cosmology, circles, rituals, meetings, churches, associations, and periodicals provide abundant evidence that Spiritualist practice was not consistently antithetical to institutionalization and organization. It is misleading, then, to argue that Spiritualism's "inherent antinomianism predisposed believers against all structures of authority" or that its "insistence on individual freedom in all things prevented its adherents from establishing formal structure, organization, or leadership of any kind."[26] Rather, Spiritualists replaced older religious forms with newer ones that involved group experience and organized activity. One finds nothing comparable among Transcendentalists, who were more individualistic in practice and produced far fewer structured expressions of spirituality. In their practice as in their ideology, Spiritualists sought order and community as assuredly as they sought freedom and autonomy.

Spiritualist Communitarianism: The Mountain Cove Episode

In July 1851, James L. Scott experienced what he believed was an inspiration given him by spirits. Its content was not unusual in the context of Spiritualist ideology or of the broader cultural impulses toward moral reform, social reform, and communitarian experimentation that marked the antebellum period. He was told, so he claimed, to find an appropriate location for a colony of Spiritualists seeking a communal alternative to the perceived selfishness and moral corruption of contemporary American life. By October, he and about a hundred Spiritualist followers had migrated from Auburn, New York, an early hotbed of Spiritualist activity, to the mountains of Fayette County, Virginia (now West Virginia), to establish a cooperative agricultural community. They were convinced that the spirits, using Scott as their medium, had issued a "call to the mountain." The Mountain Cove community, a turbulent and short-lived attempt at utopia led by Scott and Thomas Lake Harris, was the result.[27]

The Mountain Cove episode is best understood as an experiment in structuring spiritual society and therefore as a particular form of Spiritualist practice. In its inception, formation, operation, and, finally, its dissolution, it provides a case study of the Spiritualist ideology at work, highlighting both its basic tenets and its inner tensions. On the one hand, it constituted an extension or large-scale version of the Spiritualist circle, aiming to forge bonds of community through shared experience, a common mission, and a commitment to moral purity through the practice of spirit communication and a belief in spirit activity on earth. Like the circle, the community was an attempt to structure its members' religious lives and establish sacred connection and harmony between them and the cosmos. The central features of Spiritualist religion thus served as Mountain Cove's social glue and foundation of community life. On the other hand, at Mountain Cove as in other facets of Spiritualist culture, mediumistic authority and commitment to cosmic community ran up against the imperatives of spiritual republicanism as the dual commitments of Spiritualism to freedom and order came to blows.

Embracing both a principle of individual sovereignty and a belief that spiritual mediums exercise an authority derived from their presumed contact with spirits, Spiritualists found the establishment not only of viable religious institutions but also of utopian communities to be highly problematic. An examination of how the inner tensions of the Spiritualist ideology played themselves out at Mountain Cove brings together the themes discussed in the previous chapters and serves as a fitting way to conclude our analysis.[28]

While both the Spiritualist and communitarian movements were prominent and familiar features of the antebellum cultural landscape, the direct joining of the two—that is, the creation of communities based on Spiritualist principles—was a relative rarity. To be sure, many Spiritualists had close connections with utopian experimentation. Conceiving of the spiritual universe in communal terms and determined to counteract social atomization and economic individualism by applying their cosmic vision to earthly society, they were apt to join communitarian ventures. Like other religious participants in what has been called the "communitarian culture" of the nineteenth century, they intended to establish bastions of moral and spiritual virtue apart from and as examples to the larger competitive society. Many of them had supported Charles Fourier's plan of "associationism" during its American vogue of the 1840s, and in the early 1850s they figured prominently in Adin Ballou's Hopedale and in Modern Times, a Long Island community whose guiding lights, Josiah Warren and Stephen Pearl Andrews, flirted with Spiritualism. Still, communities grounded in the Spiritualist ideology were few and far between.[29]

Communitarian activity and belief in spirit communication were closely intertwined in antebellum America well before the advent of the Spiritualist movement. Mormon leader Joseph Smith claimed to have received his ideas concerning the economy and politics of the kingdom of God, which he tried to implement in Kirtland, Ohio, during the 1830s, in revelations from the invisible world. The dedication of the Mormon temple in Kirtland was said to have been accompanied by an outburst of spiritual manifestations, suggesting the Mormons' desire for spirit sanction of their communitarian practices. The spiritual manifestations among Shakers during the late 1830s and 1840s, meanwhile, appeared in part as a response to the erosion of social and moral order in Shaker communities. In a function encouraged by the Shaker leadership, spirit messages bolstered order and strengthened group bonds by urging renewed commitment to Shaker ideas and ideals. For John Humphrey Noyes, who established the Oneida community in 1848, a broadly defined "Spiritualism," or belief in communication with the spirit world, was essential to the "religious theory" of community. He called "communication with the heavens" the "palladium of conservatism in the introduction of the new social order."[30]

Spiritualists put the spirits to similar communitarian uses. Their invisible ministers preached and practiced the virtues of community, rejected the moral status quo, emphasized cooperative modes of living, and held up social arrangements in the spirit world as a model for mortals on earth. Adin Ballou and Josiah Warren recognized spirit authority and looked to the spirits for advice, approval, and confidence in their respective efforts at Hopedale and Modern Times.[31] But the Mountain Cove community, lasting from 1851 to 1853, was different from these others not only in its members' shared belief in Spiritualist religion (Spiritualists and non-Spiritualists commingled at Hopedale and Modern Times), but also in that spirit communication was both a central and a continual element of community experience and bonding (unlike communities of Shakers or Mormons, where spirit communication was important but not continual). At Mountain Cove, in short, contact with spirits was uniquely essential to the communitarian method and experience. An application of Spiritualist ideology to communitarian practice, Mountain Cove was an example of "Spiritualist communitarianism," both reflective of and distinct within the larger utopian culture. Placing spirits and mediums at the center of community life, the Spiritualists of Mountain Cove both highlighted and brought to a focus a larger cultural connection between spirit communication and communitarianism during the antebellum period.[32]

Since Spiritualists' resistance to institutional restraints on the individual ran counter to an important element of communitarian practice, an unqualified emphasis on their individualism and anti-institutionalism leaves Spiritualist communitarianism unexplained.[33] It is essential to recognize that spiritual republicanism involved a dual commitment to freedom and order, to individualism and community, and that Spiritualists believed their cosmology to have prescriptive application for human society. Since the harmonious organization of the spirit world above—called by Catherine L. Albanese a "metaphorical encodement of a utopian vision for society"—was supposed to have a correspondential counterpart on earth, the Spiritualist ideology encouraged the formation of intentional communities just as surely as it did circles.[34]

Nor is it surprising that Spiritualist communities were established by charismatic mediums of pronounced antidemocratic tendencies, such as John Murray Spear and Thomas Lake Harris. Early Spiritualist historians like Emma Hardinge interpreted the Mountain Cove episode as one of the "darker shades of the spiritualistic history," dismissed it as one of the "follies and fanaticisms" that "deform the sacred name of Spiritualism," and attributed its troubles to the personal mediumistic "idiosyncrasies" of "Pope Harris and Cardinal Scott," but it was in fact a natural byproduct and a legitimate expression of Spiritualist religion.[35]

It was by no means a long theoretical step from the séance circle, itself a structured religious community centered on authoritative spirits and their mediumistic representatives, to a Spiritualist utopian community based on spirit authority and the medium's charismatic and even authoritarian leadership. The close conceptual connection between them was made explicit when communitarian experimenter Josiah Warren attended a séance in New York City with the Fowler family. Anxious for advice concerning Utopia, his communal venture located near Cincinnati, and facing a shortage of capital, Warren consulted with the spirit of John P. Cornell, a recently deceased Spiritualist and attorney. Echoing Swedenborg and Fourier, spirit Cornell explained to Warren that Utopia lacked "a spiritual element upon which society must be founded" and advised him that the successful community began with the circle. Indeed, except for the numbers involved, Cornell's instructions for establishing society on the "spiritual principle" were virtually indistinguishable from those given for the successful formation of circles.

> Those who wish to obviate the evils of society, can do so . . . by forming into circles, at first admitting but few, and gradually increasing in number to as many as twelve or twenty-four or forty-eight. . . . Let them on first meeting join hands, which will equalize their spheres. All care should be thrown aside, and their minds should be perfectly calm and composed, otherwise an equilibrium cannot occur, but when all is quiet and calm, and no improper feelings disturb and retard the soul from holding sweet inter-communion with congenial spirits, then shall man intuitively read the thoughts of man, and a sympathetic communion and union and an inconceivable harmony will be the result.

Cornell further told Warren to circulate his ideas at first among a small number of sympathetic private individuals rather than broadcasting them before a larger and spiritually underdeveloped public, as he had previously done. Here, he forged the direct link between the circle and the utopian community: "Should you form yourselves into a circle based on the spiritual principle, the [financial] means would come. You would draw others within your spheres, and thereby your community would become enlarged gradually but firmly." Like the successful circle, then, the successful community was essentially spiritual in nature and modeled on the architecture of the cosmos.[36]

At the same time, the Spiritualist utopian community was more than an expanded circle. The circle met periodically, for a few hours at most, carefully and purposefully set apart from everyday life in order to perform a shared religious ritual. But while the utopian community was a shared experience, set apart from the larger society and to a large extent religiously motivated, its members were in continual social contact and forced to confront the realities of everyday life in an effort to survive. The relationships among them, therefore, were economic and political as well as religious. Spiritualist communitarians, then, faced strains and challenges that the circle did not, and their leaders carried a heavy burden of responsibility. These practical differences were at least as important as the theoretical and structural similarities.

The Mountain Cove episode suggests that the movement from circle to utopian community was as short a practical as it was a theoretical step, for it was a direct outgrowth of a circle in Auburn, New York. Auburn was a center of Spiritualist activity virtually from the start. Located near Hydesville, where the rappings began in the home of the Fox family in the spring of 1848, its first spirit manifestations broke out soon after, when Margaret Fox moved to the town to live with an older brother. For several weeks in the autumn of 1849, furthermore, Kate Fox held frequent séances during a stay at the Auburn home of the early Spiritualist publicist E. W. Capron. Among those who discovered their own mediumistic powers in the subsequent wave of Spiritualist activity was Ann Benedict. Her claim to contact with the spirits of the apostles and ancient prophets attracted a small group of ex-Millerites who had become Seventh-day Adventists. This group, which grew with time, called itself the "Apostolic Circle" or, alternatively, the "Auburn circle." The story of Mountain Cove began here.

In 1850, the exalted spirits of the Apostolic Circle sent Benedict to Brooklyn to call on the Reverend James L. Scott of the Seventh-day Baptist Church. Scott had been a pastor in Richburg, New York, until moving West in 1842 to perform missionary work that included establishing churches, conducting revivals, distributing tracts, and opposing slavery, alcohol, Catholicism, Mormonism, and "infidelity." He then returned east, continuing to lead revivals, and was back in New York by 1850.[37] There Benedict ordered him in the name of the spirit of the apostle Paul to move to Auburn. Convinced, Scott obeyed what he regarded as spirit instructions. By 1851 he established himself as the charismatic leader of the Auburn circle, claiming privileged contact through Benedict with the circle's spirit directors. Under Scott, the circle grew into what many of its followers called a movement.

Thomas Lake Harris, an ex-Universalist minister, became the other of the circle's two leaders. He had briefly associated with A. J. Davis and evangelized on behalf of the *Univercoelum* and the harmonial philosophy before going on to lead a liberal independent Christian congregation, composed mostly of spiritualistically inclined Swedenborgians, in New York City. There he received his "spirit instructions" to go to Auburn. The growth of the circle accelerated in his powerful presence.

Harris remained only briefly before returning to the metropolis to organize public meetings and new Apostolic circles, but Scott stayed and established a firm spirit-based autocratic control over the Auburn group. His spirit-inspired sermons, given three nights per week, were attracting several hundred listeners by the spring of 1851, and by summer more than three hundred men and women identified themselves with the movement. He insisted that any communication received through any medium other than Benedict be legitimized by the sanction of the spirit of the apostle Paul, whose secret sign only he knew. And he and Harris maintained a tight editorial control over *Disclosures from the Interior and Superior Care for Mortals,* a periodical "dictated by spirits out of the flesh" and established in Auburn in February 1851 as the voice and glue of the budding "apostolic movement." They claimed that "the circle of apostles and prophets," acting "under direction of the Lord Supreme," conducted it and held "control over its columns."[38] Their autocratic authority over their followers was well established by the time Scott received his "call to the mountain" in July 1851.

Guided by spirit ministers and their mediumistic representatives, Mountain Cove was supposed to be, quite literally, an American restoration of Eden. Upon arrival, Ira S. Hitchcock, who accompanied Scott to Virginia in October 1851, reported to the Oneida *Circular* that the group had found the actual garden of Eden and would establish there a focal point for the redemption of the human race. Scott and his disciples were told by their spirit guides to "flee to the mountains whither I direct" in order to "come out" of a sinful society.[39] The "Holy Mountain" was to be, like the spirit world and the Victorian home, the moral reverse of an unpalatable social order, emphasizing communal values over individualistic ones. The participants attempted to create a utopia in imitation of spirit society under the direction of spirits exercising their divinely sanctioned authority through Scott and Harris. Once convinced that they had found the right spot, the group purchased farms and a printing press. Eventually, "schools were to be established, and different branches of business instituted." Scott sent word back to Auburn, and by winter about 100 of the faithful had arrived.

A pair of articles in the *Mountain Cove Journal and Spiritual Harbinger,* another closely controlled periodical which the communitarians established in 1852, set forth the community's mission and identified its Spiritualist ingredient. Mountain Cove's purpose differed little from those of other communitarian ventures of the period except in the important roles assigned to spirits. Christian principles, said the *Journal,* had "no binding and legal recognition" in American society but would serve as the basis of a "MORAL COMMONWEALTH" that could "only be established through institutional organization and practical operation of the law of love." The "call to the Mountain," the *Journal* continued, "is the invitation to the Christian Man to co-operate with Holy Angels in practically founding Society on Earth according to that form in which Society is organized in Heaven." As John Murray Spear, another Spiritualist communitarian, put it, "in order to introduce the true 'kingdom of heaven' upon the earth, that which exists in the heavens must, correspondentially, be brought down to earth; or, better, earth must be *heavenized*." He put a Spiritualist twist on this basic communitarian idea when he said that the perfect society would constitute "a full and perfect Union of the Earth-Life with the Spirit-Life." For him and other Spiritualists, the structure of the spirit world was the blueprint for an earthly utopia.[40]

As ex-Millerites, many of the Mountain Cove Spiritualists were even more pessimistic about human improvement than most of their peers, exhibited especially pronounced premillennial tendencies, and were therefore particularly attracted by the idea of spirit aid in achieving social perfection. They believed, in fact, that the spirits heralded a sudden and catastrophic divine intervention in human affairs and the consequent millennium. Early Spiritualist historian Eliab W. Capron reported that the original nucleus of the Auburn circle consisted of "two or three men . . . strongly imbued with the second advent faith" and looking to spirit communication to confirm their belief in the "speedy termination of all mundane affairs by a general conflagration." He also noted that communications through Benedict were pervaded by the "peculiar phraseology of the second advent advocates." The *Mountain Cove Journal* was similarly infused with the rhetoric of premillennialism. One article, for instance, warned:

> The crisis that shall end the old kingdom of misrule is darkening upon us. That fearful Era when the Crime of ages shall be finally made manifest and judged and swept away before the face of the Lord; that Era long prophecied, long expected, long prayed for by the suffering child of God, now comes as in the dead hour of the night.

Since human reason was "inadequate to the construction of Harmonic Society upon the fallen Earth," spirits would help hapless mortals put their affairs in order.[41]

The role of spirits in Spiritualist communitarianism can be best understood through a brief glimpse into Harris's spiritual philosophy, typical of Spiritualist religion and summarized in an 1852 *Telegraph* article called "Authority of the Ideal." The "primal law" of his spiritual universe was the familiar one of "impartation," by which "each receives wisdom, goodness, beauty and energy of life from the ministry of those above, and in turn imparts of his fulness to those below." The result was that "ideas of truth and principles of wisdom descend from the world of Glorified and Redeemed Spirits to outer expression on our terrestrial globe." By "divine necessity," the "omnipotent" ideal of social harmony flowed from God into the ordinary world through the advanced spirits and angels who inspired mortals on earth. The "ideal" was closer to realization in the spirit world than on earth, and human history was continually "moving forth under the pressure of Spiritual Forces, and in obedience to Spiritual Laws." This philosophy had important communitarian implications, for it reinforced the basic communitarian idea that social life and organization should be patterned on a perception of absolute truth and suggested that spirits actively inspired the communitarian. Not merely passive exemplars of community, spirits were thought to point out and lead mortals along the path to utopia. Scott and Harris claimed to establish and direct the Mountain Cove community under the influence of the "Ideal" and, more directly, of the spirit ministry that acted in its behalf.[42]

As it turned out, life in this new Eden was far from ideal. The community not only faced the persistent hostility of Virginians who associated Spiritualism with northern radical reform and unwelcome doctrinal innovation,[43] but was also plagued by discord, decreasing confidence in Scott and Harris, and diminishing membership. Not all of those who supported the movement in Auburn had sufficient faith in its leaders to follow Scott to Virginia—only about one hundred of what had been "as many as two or three hundred" open "supporters of the cause" answered the "call" to Mountain Cove—and those who did migrate found their faith taxed almost from the start. Virtually immediately a crisis of confidence in Scott's leadership prompted changes in the structure of authority. The crisis was first sparked by a sexual scandal. By December 1851, within two months of the original settlement, Scott was accused by a community member of "licentiousness and adultery." A public meeting, attended by only a few, was called to explore the matter. Although an entranced Scott declared that he would "stand firm" and the investigation ended, his accusers continued their agitation. An inside "informant" told Spiritualist chronicler E. W. Capron of persistent "strife and contention" from this time forward. Scott's response was to attempt autocratic control over the community in the name of God and the spirits. In December 1851, he dispensed with Benedict's mediumship and claimed appointment as "medium absolute" by "high spiritual power." He added a defensive warning designed to protect his status and community order against challenges to his leadership: "Whoso seeketh the destruction of this medium, appointed of Heaven . . .*warreth with God,* and not the medium." Although his claims were acknowledged, at least at first, by most residents, his tone betrayed his weakness. Like the circle, his community depended for its stability on confidence in the medium, but it was now beginning to unravel.[44]

Although Scott's move against Benedict was prompted by an immediate crisis, it provides another example of the larger patriarchal forces at work in the Spiritualist movement. While mediumship provided religious empowerment and leadership roles for women in the circle and the lecture hall, Spiritualist communities (like virtually all utopian communities in antebellum America) were run by men. Once the Auburn circle became the Mountain Cove community, and a purely religious mediumship merged with the political and economic leadership considered by many mid-nineteenth-century Americans to be properly exercised only by men, Benedict's authority was suppressed.

Scott's theocratic, "spiritocratic," and autocratic control extended to the community's property arrangements. Soon after declaring his divinely authorized control of community affairs, he demanded that residents resign their property to God, Scott's spirit directors, and their earthly representative "James, the medium." Addressing a general statement to this effect to believing Spiritualists everywhere, he also announced his policy through a number of individual epistles issued to sympathizers throughout the country. This centralistic policy met with the disapproval of some and intensified the unrest at Mountain Cove. At least one disaffected resident later complained that members of the Auburn circle had been promised individual property and businesses before the migration, and a vigorous defense of Scott's policy in the *Journal* suggests that the opposition may have been considerable. It certainly indicates tension between economic individualism and centralized community authority. Describing the "True Principle of Human Association," the *Journal* insisted, much like many other antebellum communitarians, that human beings hold their possessions in stewardship for the Lord:

> The Christian Man acknowledges that the Savior is his Lord, Lawgiver and Director. He claims no exemption. His time, talents, influence, possessions, are all held in trust. He lives as one who must finally render account of his stewardship. In this his motive and his movement is the opposite or inversion of that of the Man of the World. The latter has one maxim, namely, "to do as he likes with his own." Virtually and practically he is in a state of rebellion against his Lord. He usurps control of his Master's goods. He denies his accountability to the Ruler of the Universe. He is a traitor to the Law of Love.

Clearly, the divine social order that the spirits were working to establish through Scott could tolerate individual property no more than it could any other form of "rebellion."[45]

Rather, declared another *Journal* article, the keynote of that order was a spirit-inspired communalism.[46] Such "unfallen intelligences" as "spirits of just men made perfect" desired "no individual and isolated possessions" but were, rather, "mutual in existence, mutual in inheritance," and therefore "harmoniously existing" in God's universe. It was only "fallen beings" who, "by reason of sin, in virtue and moral purity detached from the universe of spirituality, individualize themselves, and seek independent and separate possessions." Thus spirits became advocates, representatives, and exemplars of an alternative communal economic and social order (symbols, in short, of community). They held out the promise of social, economic, and spiritual security to those troubled by the individualism and competition of American society. Replicating the spirits' communal living arrangements would strengthen community members' "spiritual relations to the universe of embodied and disembodied spirits." Alienated by the status quo, these Spiritualists looked to Mountain Cove as "a city of refuge," "a hiding place and a shelter," and "an asylum for the afflicted." Still, while some of the communitarians embraced the centralization of property as a means of social and spiritual connectedness, others resisted Scott's stewardship as inconsistent with their vision of utopia. Against the latter, Scott invoked the spirits as symbols of divine impatience with "rebellion."[47]

Scott's authority was further corroded, and the tension between individualism and community further underscored, when some community members used their critical reason to discern inconsistencies in his alleged revelations. This development occurred "before the lapse of many weeks," with the result that "a number of families" withdrew "in about three months," or in the early months of 1852. The imperatives of spiritual republicanism, then, pitted reason against faith and widened the cracks in Scott's spiritual fortress.[48]

Events at Mountain Cove took another turn for the worse in February 1852, when Scott and his community failed to meet the payments on the holy mountain. The land was returned to its seller and "several families" left "on account of the contention and want of confidence in the movement." His authority and the order of the community again threatened by a crisis, Scott called an emergency meeting, only the second known community meeting in what had become an autocracy. The community's spirit guides explained through an entranced Scott that "James must go to New York, to seek new minds to carry on the Lord's work." There he enlisted Harris's aid in convincing several families, including some of substantial wealth, to join the venture and to help finance the repurchase of the land. The new communitarians, among them Harris, arrived in the spring of 1852 to augment the "some half a dozen families" that remained. Upon his return, meanwhile, Scott had bought back the land and, in an attempt to preserve his crumbling authority and ensure what he considered social harmony, banished dissenters.

The newly arrived Harris established a joint mediumistic leadership with Scott and attempted to ground their authority in Spiritualist ideology. He explained their status as a reflection of the hierarchical social and spiritual order of the universe, and expected community residents to acknowledge what he called in an April *Journal* article "the due dependence of the inferior on the superior, as the child to the parent, the governed to the governor in authority of right." But in May, the two men issued a joint "epistle" that carried their claims and the implications of Spiritualist belief beyond what most Spiritualists would have considered acceptable mediumistic practice.

They declared themselves perfect and infallible mediums transmitting "truth absolute," Harris explaining in lectures given around the time that Spiritualism provided access to "an interior source that never errs, that never falsifies, that never misjudges, never misconceives, never mistakes, and never misdirects." They warned that any medium who challenged their leadership would be either silenced or taken over by evil spirits. Only those who followed and obeyed them, they insisted, had hope of redemption.[49]

Scott and Harris sometimes claimed, moreover, not only to communicate with the "circle of apostles" but to be in direct contact with God. Bypassing spirit mediators, they overstepped the definitional boundaries of Spiritualism and accentuated the close similarities between their religious movement and the other charismatically led sects of antebellum America. They also further alienated many of their followers. One resident later complained of their claim that "the infinite God communicates with them directly, without intermediate agency."[50] Even their earlier claim to contact with the apostles was more lofty than those of most Spiritualists, who tended to communicate with spirits of humbler status. From the start, then, the Mountain Cove Spiritualists were much closer than were their peers to other charismatic religious and communitarian movements on the antebellum scene. The excesses of Scott and Harris made it possible for other members of the movement, as champions of spiritual republicanism, to dismiss the Mountain Cove affair as an expression more of authoritarianism and religious fanaticism than of Spiritualism. But because spirits linked humanity and deity in Spiritualist theology, and because mediums could aspire to contact with increasingly advanced spiritual beings in proportion to their own moral development, it was conceivable for a Spiritualist to make mediumship practically identical with the direct divine inspiration and sometimes authoritarian leadership commonly claimed by other contemporary religious and communitarian leaders.

Moreover, until Scott and Harris did so they were within the bounds of Spiritualism even if they exaggerated its defining features. Existing evidence strongly indicates, furthermore, that the community retained its defining Spiritualist features; that is, residents still believed spirits to occupy important positions of intermediary authority in its operations and that belief was still important to community bonding. Scott and Harris claimed, for example, that the epistle establishing their infallibility and divine inspiration had been issued by "The Circle of Apostles and Prophets to the Auburn Circle of Disciples." Its opening sentences suggest spirit authority:

> The especially appointed and commissioned spirits, through whom superior wisdom has approached and instructed mortals, dictate unto you the present epistle in the light of understanding, in the purpose of

counsel, and in the desire of harmonious interprocedure of love. They review your works, declare their directed purposes, and seek to guide your feet in the way of peace.

The spirits then proceeded to review their role in the establishment of the community. Residents were reminded that Scott's instructions to create it came "by direction absolute from the interior through the appointed vehicles therefor" and that the spirits had determined "to resume the disclosure of his truth" by replacing Auburn's *Disclosures from the Interior* with the *Mountain Cove Journal.*[51]

Faced with mounting challenges to their authority, Scott and Harris resorted to increasingly forceful measures to retain it in the name of God, the spirits, and community order. After reporting in the summer of 1852 the spirits' announcement that the land containing the community buildings must be leased to them in God's name, they began to persecute dissenters, resulting according to Capron in still more "slander, discord and contention." Scott and Harris finally did what members of some other American primitivist groups did when faced with persistent opposition: they issued thinly veiled threats against those they perceived as perpetuating error. They declared in the autumn of 1852 that they were the two witnesses spoken of in the eleventh chapter of Revelation and possessed the power described there, including destroying their enemies by fire, causing droughts and plagues, and turning water to blood.[52] Such actions probably did little more than to betray the instability of their leadership, further undermining the confidence of wavering community members and accelerating the dynamic of dissent. Not all residents, to be sure, lost their faith and declared their independence of Scott and Harris. One skeptical community resident reported that those still accepting their authority "were kept in awe of these self-appointed 'anointed of the Lord' by the constant asserting of the awful power" described in the book of Revelation. Nevertheless, the community collapsed in 1853.[53]

The published exposé of I. S. Hyatt, an alienated follower, provides a rare and unfriendly glimpse into the authoritarian Spiritualist experience at Mountain Cove and highlights the role of ideological tensions between freedom and authority in causing dissent and the community's resulting demise. Hyatt had been the editor of the *Spiritual and Moral Instructor,* a short-lived and closely monitored Auburn paper dedicated to the "apostolic movement."[54] Arriving from Auburn "unwavering in my faith" in December 1851, he quickly learned of the accusations against Scott and suggested that they be investigated. Before long he began to question Scott's authority. He left the community in the spring of 1852, "about four months" after his arrival and at about the time that Scott ordered dissenters to leave. His exposé, suppressed in Mountain Cove over his objections, appeared in October in the *Telegraph*, which had established itself as a defender of a free press and a critic of mediumistic excess. He wrote a second article for the *Journal of Progress* (it also appeared in the *Telegraph*) the following summer, as the Mountain Cove episode was drawing to its unhappy close.[55]

As a spiritual republican, Hyatt charged that Scott had threatened private property by insisting on communalism and undermined individual sovereignty and judgment by claiming infallibility. Instruction by advanced apostolic spirits had been supplanted and caution in dealing with the spirits had been jettisoned, the medium claiming "entire infallibility" and "Divine inspiration, in its most unequivocal sense." This abuse of mediumistic authority had destroyed individual freedom in the community since "all the principles and rules of practice—whether of a spiritual or temporal nature—which govern the believers in that place" were "dictated" by Scott and Harris. Community members were denied "the privilege of criticizing, or in any degree reasoning upon, the orders and communications uttered" and "forbid the privilege of having any reason or conscience at all, except that which is prescribed to them by this oracle." Hyatt urged vigilance, noting that his own reason had led him to detect inconsistencies in Scott's communications and to conclude that "the controlling power . . . which I had believed to be Divine, originated in a source perhaps partly spiritual and partly human, but which in no case was entitled to absolute confidence." That "the 'inspiration' conformed itself to . . . the opinions of those whose support was most requisite for external success," furthermore, suggested a corrupt leadership and further undermined Hyatt's confidence in Scott. His agitation was apparently successful; he reported that the dictatorial actions of the community's leaders had

> awakened, in the minds of more reasoning and reflective members, distrust and unbelief, which has caused some, with great pecuniary loss, to withdraw from the community, and with others, who remain, has ripened into disaffection and violent opposition; and the present condition of the "holy mountain" is any thing but that of divine harmony.

Invoking images of tyrannical monarchy to foment a rebellion, this spiritual patriot won recruits by insisting that the "ruling power" should be "conceded to be absolute or else completely dethroned."[56]

Hyatt, then, reflected Spiritualism's antiauthoritarian and individualistic impulse, just as Harris and Scott reflected its centralizing impulse. The dispute, in other words, emblemized the larger ideological divisions and tensions in antebellum Spiritualism, communitarianism, and religious culture generally. Although Hyatt rejected Scott and Harris, and thus Spiritualism's authoritarian potentialities, he reaffirmed his commitment to Spiritualist ideology, which he considered compatible with individual sovereignty. Having objected to the claims of Scott and Harris to communicate directly with God, he continued to look to spirit mediators for religious authority, complaining to Capron that it was "understood that there was to be no dictator in the movement; but the whole was to be under the direction of the spirits." As the editors of the *Telegraph* observed, Hyatt had dissociated himself only from fanaticism while remaining "a firm believer in a rational Spiritualism."[57]

The *Telegraph*, defending individualism against mediumistic excess, was anxious to marginalize the Mountain Cove episode. Its editors introduced Hyatt's second article with the comment that they had "never regarded the claims of Messrs. Scott and Harris with favor" and that those continuing to reside in the community were "deluded" by Scott's "absurd pretensions." Scott denied Hyatt's charges in a "counter-statement," also published by the *Telegraph*, but he seems to have changed few minds. John Humphrey Noyes, himself a charismatic communitarian leader, later dismissed Scott's rebuttal as "special pleading" and emphasized that "all the information that we have obtained by communication with various ex-members of the Mountain Cove community, goes to confirm the substance of the preceding charges." He concluded that this and all other Spiritualist communities of the period failed because of "the superior tenacity of the[ir] devotion to the great antagonist of association, Individual Sovereignty." While this explanation does not account entirely for the demise of Mountain Cove, Noyes did pinpoint a fundamental obstacle in Spiritualist ideology to communitarian commitment and, indeed, to many forms of institutionalized religious expression.[58]

The Mountain Cove episode accentuates the underlying similarities between Spiritualism and other religious philosophies that spawned communitarian efforts: a vision of a highly structured cosmos, a tendency to regard that vision as a pattern for human society, and an encouragement of charismatic leadership. It also suggests that Spiritualist and non-Spiritualist communitarians alike faced the perennial problems of moral scandal, financial instability, tension between individual freedom and centralized authority, and a potential for abuse of power. Despite the crucial difference between Spiritualist communitarianism and the rest of antebellum communitarian culture, then, Mountain Cove failed not because of an inherent Spiritualist antistructuralism but in large part because of problems characteristic of all intentional communities.

Another problem at Mountain Cove was that Spiritualist ideology, aiming like many other religious systems to maximize both spiritual autonomy and cosmic oneness, provided no easy way to distinguish subjective whim from objective spirit voices. This dilemma, hardly unique to Spiritualism, was exacerbated by the cultural power of spiritual republicanism in antebellum America. Thus while some members of the Mountain Cove community looked at Scott and Harris as vehicles of the spirits, others like Hyatt saw little more than two men grasping at temporal power. The result was an explosive battle between freedom of judgment and mediumistic claims to special authority much like that over the question of whether ecclesiastical government and the institutional organization of their religion were desirable. Only relatively small groups of Spiritualists, like those that formed circles or congregational-style churches, were able to overcome this dilemma and achieve the kind of harmony that permitted sustained expressions of religious commitment. If Spiritualist communitarians were to use notions of spirit contact, spirit authority, and human mediumship to forge bonds of community while preserving the requirements of spiritual republicanism, they would have to agree on what voices originated with spirits; only in this way could they protect individual freedom by containing mediumistic excess and abuse. Other antebellum religious utopian efforts and the continuing loyalty of some Mountain Cove residents to the leadership of Scott and Harris illustrate that communities based on charismatic religious authority had the potential for long life.[59]

Understanding Spiritualist communitarianism requires a recognition of the ideological complexity of both Spiritualism and the larger culture. Spiritualism's antistructural and antiauthoritarian thrust explains its failure to create viable large-scale religious institutions, including utopian communities, during the antebellum period. The equally potent structural impulse, meanwhile, explains the development of such small-scale institutions as the circle and the attempt to establish larger organizations and the Mountain Cove community. The uneasy coexistence of these counteracting impulses explains how the same Scott who inveighed against Catholicism as an itinerant evangelical in the early 1840s could be branded "Cardinal Scott" by a disapproving Emma Hardinge in her history of the movement. It is no coincidence that as the intensity of individual sovereignty within the Spiritualist movement declined during the decades after the Civil War, more viable large-scale Spiritualist organizations and communities began to appear.[60]

The same ideological tension that divided the Spiritualist movement and sundered the Mountain Cove community would soon lead Harris himself, whose later communitarian endeavors were to be far more successful, to renounce his involvement in the episode. Addressing an audience of Spiritualists in May 1854, he warned against allowing spirits and mediums "to become our spiritual rulers." He confessed that his earlier position of mediumistic infallibility had been "untenable." "In admitting, therefore, a ministry of the spirit, we must see that it is kept free from a dogmatic element, free from absolutism. . . . Not even the angels," he concluded, "are infallible."[61]

Conclusion

Attempted contact with spirits is a perennial feature of human religious expression, but the emergence of Spiritualist religion in antebellum America made particularly good sense. Despite the bewilderment of contemporary cultural commentators like George Templeton Strong, it was a logical response to religious, social, and economic developments which had combined by the 1850s to produce an acute spiritual malaise among many Americans. A religion based on contact with spirit mediators allowed Spiritualists to both resist and accept these developments. Feeling that God transcended their concerns and was indifferent to the human experience, they found a personal and human spiritual presence and the warmth of a cosmic community; questioning conventional structures of religious authority, they found new ones on which they could rely; sensing the centrifugal potential in the democratization and individualization of religious experience, they found the hope of religious unity; losing their faith in humanity just as it was becoming a focus of attention in their religious circles, they found renewed confidence; and fearing that economic individualism would spawn social and moral chaos, they found a new basis for order.

It is simply not true that the ideology of Spiritualism "had very little to do with the appeal of the movement." Many Americans attended séances for scientific proof of an afterlife, for reassurance in the face of death, for satisfaction of curiosity, or simply for fun, but many others did so as part of a religious and philosophical quest. These Spiritualists participated in a broad search among antebellum Americans for both freedom and order, autonomy and authority, independence and community, self and Other. As American society shifted, in the words of one historian, "from classical republican values to those of a vulgar democracy and entrepreneurial individualism," they joined their contemporaries in applying the American Revolution's promise of ordered freedom to spiritual matters. As with the other "democratic sects" of the period, the voices of the spirits "offered themselves as cures rather than helps to nineteenth-century individualism." Their voices were the voices of antebellum American culture.[1]

Since the spiritual malaise persisted, the Spiritualist ideology endured even as the movement itself increasingly fell prey to its sensationalistic tendencies and consequent debunking during the decades after the Civil War. Indeed, the growth of liberal theology and evolutionary gradualism created a religious and intellectual environment in some ways friendly to it. Works on Spiritualist religion and philosophy, elaborating a spirit-centered cosmology and the doctrine of spirit ministry, therefore continued to appear in the late nineteenth and early twentieth centuries. The perceived tension between individualism and spirit ministry persisted; Mary F. Davis was still warning Spiritualists in 1875 to consult spirit guides as friends and teachers rather than as leaning posts that might compromise spiritual selfhood.[2]

But the individualistic element of spiritual republicanism, derived from the culture of Jacksonian America, eroded after the Civil War, removing the crucial check on Spiritualism's organizational impulse.[3] Not surprisingly, then, efforts at national organization intensified in the 1860s and culminated in the founding of the National Association of Spiritualists in 1893. The number of Spiritualist churches climbed as well. These developments, which established formal institutional structures for the Spiritualist religion, constituted not so much departures from the situation of the 1850s as a strengthening of tendencies already present. Once the individualism that had frustrated attempts at formal structure waned, Spiritualism followed other emergent religious movements down the path from liminality to bureaucracy. This development, familiar enough in religious history, was even less surprising in a religion born amid a cultural shift from the exuberance and individualism of "boundlessness" to the conservatism, caution, and concern for order associated with a mood of "consolidation."

Antebellum Spiritualists who watched the evolution of their movement in the latter decades of the nineteenth century seemed less concerned with its intensifying organizational thrust than with the growing dominance of sensational mediumship over religious ideology. Indeed, religious Spiritualists looked to organization to save their religion from "mere Spiritism." To the likes of A. J. Davis and others, fascination with such marvels as cabinet materializations, in which visiting spirits were believed to take on visible form, seemed to have obscured the deeper religious meaning of spirit communication, mediumship, and the séance. Sensational mediumship resembled entertainment rather than mystical illumination and elicited increasing suspicion among the original Spiritualist leaders, particularly amid the wave of exposures of fraudulent séance practices that discredited the movement in the 1870s.

As early as 1857, Davis began to separate his "harmonial philosophy" from Spiritualist sensationalism by creating the New York Spiritualist Association, and he established the *Herald of Progress* in 1860 with a similar mission in mind. But the "phenomenalists" took over the New York organization as well as most other Spiritualist organizations of the 1860s and 1870s. Davis redoubled his efforts with the publication in 1870 of the intensely polemical *The Fountain, with Jets of New Meaning.* The book was so hostile toward contemporary mediumship that Davis was charged with having "recanted" and "gone back on Spiritualism." Although he insisted to his detractors in the movement that he was a truer Spiritualist than they, he declared a divorce between the increasingly sensationalized Spiritualist movement and his harmonial philosophy when he omitted the term "Spiritualist" from the name of his First Harmonial Association of New York, established in 1878. He could only conclude that his philosophy was "incompatible with the superstition and magic which prevailed among the mass of Spiritualists." A disillusioned S. B. Brittan, meanwhile, lamented that the festive atmosphere at Spiritualist summer camp gatherings of the 1870s had overwhelmed all concern with human spiritual and moral betterment. Such disappointed prewar devotees of Spiritualist religion as Davis and Brittan dissociated themselves and their belief systems from the movement and disappeared from it during the 1860s and 1870s.[4]

Other Spiritualists of the 1850s, looking either for firmer standards and structures of religious authority than Spiritualism could provide or simply for new religious frontiers, found in the movement only a temporary resting place and moved on. Indeed, just as threatening to the Spiritualist religion as its association with sensationalism was the emergence in the 1870s of such similar and competing ideologies as Christian Science and Theosophy. Like Spiritualism, they drew on Swedenborgian and, in the case of Christian Science, Transcendentalist ideas to create alternatives to conventional Christianity. Like Spiritualism, they offered religious seekers new ways to understand their inner spirituality and to achieve oneness with the cosmos. Thus they attracted those whose religious search had already led, or might have led, to Spiritualism. Still other Spiritualists died, remaining like Davis dedicated to their beliefs to the end. Whether they left the movement to escape sensationalism, to find greener spiritual pastures, or to enter the invisible world they had long imagined, they remained committed to their search for freedom, order, and a home in the universe.

◆┼◆

NOTES

✦✦✦

1. Introduction

1. Emma Hardinge, *Modern American Spiritualism: A Twenty Years' Record of the Communion Between Earth and the World of Spirits* (New York, 1870), 561.

2. Allan Nevins and Milton Halsey Thomas, eds., *The Diary of George Templeton Strong*, 4 vols. (New York, 1952), II: 244–45; Robert S. Ellwood, *Alternative Altars: Unconventional and Eastern Spirituality in America* (Chicago: University of Chicago Press, 1979), 12.

3. See Higham, *From Boundlessness to Consolidation: The Transformation of American Culture, 1848–1860* (Ann Arbor: William L. Clements Library, 1969), 17–18.

4. The apprehensiveness of antebellum Americans has been explored in Fred Somkin, *Unquiet Eagle: Memory and Desire in the Idea of American Freedom* (Ithaca: Cornell University Press, 1967).

5. Jon Butler, *Awash in a Sea of Faith: Christianizing the American People* (Cambridge: Harvard University Press, 1990), 225–56.

6. Carroll Smith-Rosenberg, *Disorderly Conduct: Visions of Gender in Victorian America* (New York: Knopf, 1985), 87, 90; Robert A. Abzug, *Cosmos Crumbling: American Reform and the Religious Imagination* (New York: Oxford University Press, 1994), 8; Shomer Zwelling, "Spiritualist Perspectives on Antebellum Experience," *Journal of Psychohistory* 10 (1982): 3–25; William L. MacDonald, "The Popularity of Paranormal Experiences in the United States," *Journal of American Culture* 17 (1994): 35, 36, 41. Smith-Rosenberg and MacDonald continue the tradition of interpreting Spiritualism as a product of social and economic change. Still, as explained below, the explanations for developments in antebellum religious culture are not entirely reducible to explanations focusing on the admittedly powerful and unsettling social and economic transformations of the period.

7. Higham, *From Boundlessness to Consolidation*, passim., esp. 24–25; Robert Wiebe, *The Opening of American Society: From the Adoption of the Constitution to the Eve of Disunion* (New York: Knopf, 1984); Ann Braude, *Radical Spirits: Spiritualism and Women's Rights in Nineteenth-Century America* (Boston: Beacon Press, 1989); John C. Spurlock, *Free Love: Marriage and Middle-Class Radicalism in America, 1825–1860* (New York: New York University Press, 1988). Spurlock's discussion includes many allusions to Spiritualism.

8. Anthony F. C. Wallace, "Revitalization Movements," *American Anthropology* 58 (1956): 264–81. William G. McLoughlin applies Wallace's theory to American religious life in *Revivals, Awakenings, and Reform* (Chicago: University of Chicago Press, 1978), treating the antebellum period in ch. 4.

9. Mary Farrell Bednarowski, *New Religions and the Theological Imagination in America* (Bloomington: Indiana University Press, 1989), ix–xi, 1–2. Bednarowski did not include Spiritualism in her analysis of America's new religions.

10. Sydney Ahlstrom, *A Religious History of the American People* (New Haven: Yale University Press, 1972), 1019; Sacvan Bercovitch, "The Problem of Ideology in American Literary History," *Critical Inquiry* 12 (1986): 635. Religious scholar

George Lawton asserted that Spiritualism "presents as elaborate, definite and as nearly articulated a system of religious beliefs and practices as can be found anywhere in the history of thought," [*The Drama of Life After Death* (New York: Holt, 1932), ix], but R. Laurence Moore emphasized the lack of uniformity in Spiritualist writings and denied the existence of a coherent belief system [*In Search of White Crows: Spiritualism, Parapsychology, and American Culture* (New York: Oxford University Press, 1977), 42]. Moore is correct insofar as he is suggesting that Spiritualism lacked a uniform creed, but I believe that there was nevertheless a fairly well-defined ideology. So do Ann Braude, *Radical Spirits*, 6, 32–55; Bednarowski, "Nineteenth-Century American Spiritualism: An Attempt at a Scientific Religion" (Ph.D. diss., University of Minnesota, 1973), 4, 22; and Alex Owen, *The Darkened Room: Women, Power, and Spiritualism in Late Victorian England* (Philadelphia: University of Pennsylvania Press, 1990), xviii. Moore's position reflects his larger argument that Spiritualism was dominated by sensational séance phenomena; but he admits that many Spiritualists sought "assurance of a purpose behind life," that they "did speculate about many theological questions," and that they reached something of a "consensus" on such matters (*White Crows*, 43, 51–61).

11. Here, I employ Clifford Geertz's now classic definition of culture: "an historically transmitted pattern of meanings embodied in symbols." See Geertz, "Religion as a Cultural System," in *The Interpretation of Cultures* (New York: Basic Books, 1973), 89.

12. Victor Turner, *The Ritual Process: Structure and Antistructure* (Ithaca: Cornell University Press, 1977).

13. Moore, *White Crows*, and Braude, *Radical Spirits* emphasize Spiritualism's democratic, antistructural and anti-institutional features. Stephen Prothero's recent article, "From Spiritualism to Theosophy: 'Uplifting' a Democratic Tradition" [*Religion and American Culture* 3 (1993): 197–216], suggests that this view is not only commonly accepted but taken for granted. This incomplete view of Spiritualism characterizes most broader studies of American culture; see, for example, Smith-Rosenberg, *Disorderly Conduct*, 135, 141, and McLoughlin, *Revivals*, 121. Nathan O. Hatch offers a similar interpretation of early-nineteenth-century American religious culture as a whole in *The Democratization of American Christianity* (New Haven: Yale University Press, 1989). Braude's concern with women, who were largely excluded from American institutions and thus critiqued them, and with the women's rights movement, which had some of its roots in a philosophy of individual rights, perhaps understandably led her to focus on this aspect of Spiritualism; but according to Nancy F. Cott, *The Bonds of Womanhood: "Women's Sphere" in New England, 1780–1835* (New Haven: Yale University Press, 1977), the women's rights movement was grounded as much in notions of community and "sisterhood" as in a philosophy of individualism.

14. Stein, "Liberty, Equality, and Community: Shakerism and Republicanism in the Early Republic," unpublished paper presented at the 1991 annual meeting of the Organization of American Historians, Louisville, Kentucky, esp. 15 (I have quoted from 7–8); idem, "Shaker Gift and Shaker Order: A Study of Religious Tension in Nineteenth-Century America," *Communal Societies* 10 (1990): 102–13 (I have quoted from 106).

15. See Hatch, *The Democratization of American Christianity*.

16. For comparisons between Spiritualism and Mormonism, see Davis Bitton, "Mormonism's Encounter with Spiritualism," *Journal of Mormon History* 1 (1974): 39–50; Michael W. Homer, "Spiritualism and Mormonism: Some Thoughts on the Similarities and Differences," *Dialogue: A Journal of Mormon Thought* 27 (1994): 171–91; R. Laurence Moore, "The Occult Connection? Mormonism, Christian Science, and Spiritualism" in Howard Kerr and Charles L. Crow, eds., *The Occult in*

America: New Historical Perspectives (Urbana: University of Illinois Press, 1983), 135–61; and idem, *White Crows*, 5, 47, 50, 235. Homer emphasizes the differences between them, pointing out that while the two religious movements shared a belief in spirit communication, the similarities between them are in the final analysis superficial. Homer also notes, correctly, that the idea and practice of spirit communication was far more central to Spiritualism than it was to Mormonism (190).

17. On the connections between the Shakers and the Spiritualist movement, see Stephen J. Stein, *The Shaker Experience in America* (New Haven: Yale University Press, 1992), 199, 223, 225, 320–28; Hardinge, *Modern American Spiritualism*, 27.

18. On the connection between Spiritualism and Swedenborgianism, see Mary Farrell Bednarowski, "Nineteenth-Century American Spiritualism," 72–76; Moore, *White Crows*, 9–10, 56; and Scott Trego Swank, "The Unfettered Conscience: A Study of Sectarianism, Spiritualism, and Social Reform in the New Jerusalem Church, 1840–1870" (Ph.D. diss., University of Pennsylvania, 1970), 162–313.

19. Stephen J. Stein's comment that what occurred among the Shakers in the antebellum period should be called "spiritism" rather than "spiritualism" since spirit communication "was only one aspect of their faith" rather than its central element, is far more accurate than Richard Kyle's statement that "the Shakers were the first Spiritualists." See Stein, *Shaker Experience*, 321, and Kyle, *The Religious Fringe: A History of Alternative Religions in America* (Downer's Grove, Ill.: InterVarsity Press, 1993), 76.

20. Andrew Jackson Davis, *The Philosophy of Spiritual Intercourse* (New York: Fowlers and Wells, 1851), 122n; Jon Butler, "The Dark Ages of American Occultism," in *The Occult in America*, 72. A relevant discussion appears in Janet Oppenheim, *The Other World: Spiritualism and Psychical Research in England, 1850–1914* (New York: Cambridge University Press, 1985), 105–107.

21. On the primitivist impulse in American religion, see Richard T. Hughes and C. Leonard Allen, *Illusions of Innocence: Protestant Primitivism in America, 1630–1875* (Chicago: University of Chicago Press, 1988), and Richard T. Hughes, ed., *The American Quest for the Primitive Church* (Urbana: University of Illinois Press, 1988). On primitivism in the context of the antebellum democratization of American Christianity, see Hatch, *Democratization*, 167–70. Puritan primitivism is considered in Theodore Dwight Bozeman, *To Live Ancient Lives: The Primitivist Dimension of Puritanism* (Chapel Hill: Published for the Institute of Early American History and Culture by the University of North Carolina Press, 1988), and Mormon restorationism is discussed in Jan Shipps, *Mormonism: The Story of a New Religious Tradition* (Urbana: University of Illinois Press, 1985).

22. Sandra Sizer Frankiel, *California's Spiritual Frontiers: Religious Alternatives in Anglo-Protestantism, 1850–1910* (Berkeley: University of California Press, 1988), xiff. See also J. Stillson Judah, *The History and Philosophy of the Metaphysical Movements in America* (Philadelphia: Westminster Press, 1967), 12–13.

23. Rudolf Otto, *The Idea of the Holy,* trans. John W. Harvey (London: Oxford University Press, 1923); Mircea Eliade, *The Sacred and the Profane: The Nature of Religion,* trans. Willard R. Trask (New York: Harcourt and Brace, 1957). The quotations in the text are taken from Otto, 33, 147. Davis's description appears in Andrew Jackson Davis, *The Present Age and Inner Life; A Sequel to Spiritual Intercourse* (New York: Partridge and Brittan, 1853), 82.

24. Spiritualist religion was analyzed at length by George Lawton in *Drama of Life After Death* (1932), but he considered it in the abstract rather than in its American cultural context.

25. Moore, *White Crows*.

26. Oppenheim, *The Other World*; Braude, *Radical Spirits*; Alex Owen, *The*

Darkened Room; Logie Barrow, *Independent Spirits: Spiritualism and English Plebe-ians, 1850–1910* (London: Routledge and Kegan Paul, 1986).

27. Prominent examples of this historiography are Geoffrey K. Nelson, *Spiritual-ism and Society* (London: Routledge and Kegan Paul, 1969), and Whitney Cross, *The Burned-Over District: The Social and Intellectual History of Enthusiastic Religion in Western New York, 1800–1850* (Ithaca: Cornell University Press, 1950). Other works in this category include Gilbert Seldes, *The Stammering Century* (New York, 1928; reprint, New York: Harper and Row, 1965), and Alice Felt Tyler, *Freedom's Ferment: Phases of American Social History from the Colonial Period to the Outbreak of the Civil War* (Minneapolis: University of Minnesota Press, 1944). Moore has discussed the limitations of explanations involving social and economic disruption in *White Crows*, 102–103.

28. Robert Abzug, *Cosmos Crumbling*, similarly emphasizes the religious motiva-tions of antebellum reform and avoids "the modern trend toward psychological and material reductionism" (p. viii).

29. See, for example, Hardinge, *Modern American Spiritualism*, 207–208, and E. W. Capron, *Modern Spiritualism: Its Facts and Fanaticisms, Its Consistencies and Contradictions* (New York: Partridge and Brittan, 1855), 131, 220.

30. R. Laurence Moore has questioned the usefulness of the categories "main-stream" and "fringe" for analyses of American religious culture in *Religious Outsiders and the Making of Americans* (New York: Oxford University Press, 1986). See also Moore, *White Crows*, xii–xiii.

31. See, for example, Lawton, *Drama of Life After Death*, viii–ix; Robert W. Delp, "Andrew Jackson Davis: Prophet of American Spiritualism," *Journal of American History* 54 (1967): 51; Cross, *The Burned Over District*, 347–49, Ernest Isaacs, "The Fox Sisters and American Spiritualism," in *The Occult in America*, 80; Scott Trego Swank, "The Unfettered Conscience," 169–70; and Michael A. O'Sullivan, "A Harmony of Worlds. Spiritualism and the Quest for Community in Nine-teenth-Century America" (Ph.D. diss., University of Southern California, 1981), 143–44.

32. Butler, *Awash*, 255. See also Braude, *Radical Spirits*, 28.

33. Lewis O. Saum, *The Popular Mood of Pre–Civil War America* (Westport, Conn.: Greenwood Press, 1980), 47–53; Braude, *Radical Spirits*, 28–31. See also Moore, *White Crows*, ch. 1.

2. American Spiritualism and the Swedenborgian Order

1. Andrew Jackson Davis, *The Magic Staff; An Autobiography of Andrew Jackson Davis* (New York: J. S. Brown, 1857), 363–66.

2. Burton Gates Brown, "Spiritualism in Nineteenth-Century America" (Ph.D. diss., Boston University, 1972), 6; Ernest J. Isaacs, "A History of Nineteenth-Century American Spiritualism as a Religious and Social Movement" (Ph.D. diss., University of Wisconsin, 1975), 7.

3. On Swedenborg, see Cyriel Odhner Sigstedt, *The Swedenborg Epic* (New York: Bookman Associates, 1952); Signe Toksvig, *Emanuel Swedenborg, Scientist and Mystic* (New Haven: Yale University Press, 1948); George Trobridge, *Swedenborg: Life and Teaching*, 5th ed. (New York: Swedenborg Foundation, 1992); and George F. Dole and Robert H. Kirven, *A Scientist Explores Spirit* (New York: Swedenborg Foundation, 1992).

4. The anthropocentric and social nature of Swedenborg's spiritual world, and his "thick description of heaven" which influenced the Spiritualists' own conceptions of

the afterlife, are explored in Colleen McDannell and Bernhard Lang, *Heaven: A History* (New Haven: Yale University Press, 1988), 181–227, 292–306.

5. On mesmerism, see Robert Darnton, *Mesmerism and the End of the Enlightenment in France* (New York: Schocken Books, 1970), and Robert C. Fuller, *Mesmerism and the American Cure of Souls* (Philadelphia: University of Pennsylvania Press, 1982). On the association between Spiritualism and mesmerism, see Bednarowski, "Nineteenth Century American Spiritualism," 64–67; Moore, *White Crows,* 9; and Fuller, *Mesmerism,* 95–100.

6. On Fourier's thought, see Nicholas Riasanovsky, *The Teaching of Charles Fourier* (Berkeley: University of California Press, 1969), Jonathan Beecher, *Charles Fourier: The Visionary and His World* (Berkeley: University of California Press, 1986), and Carl Guarneri, *The Utopian Alternative: Fourierism in Nineteenth-Century America* (Ithaca: Cornell University Press, 1991). Guarneri discusses the connection between Spiritualism and Fourierism on 348–53.

7. On the connection between Spiritualism and Transcendentalism, see Bednarowski, "Nineteenth-Century American Spiritualism," 67–69; Moore, *White Crows,* 25, 52–54; and Braude, *Radical Spirits,* 44–46. On that between Spiritualism and Universalism, see Bednarowski, "Nineteenth-Century American Spiritualism," 70–72; Moore, *White Crows,* 49, 56; Braude, *Radical Spirits,* 46–48; Neil B. Lehman, "The Life of John Murray Spear: Spiritualism and Reform in Antebellum America" (Ph.D. diss., Ohio State University, 1973), 19–20, 54–59; and Frank Podmore, *Modern Spiritualism: A History and a Criticism,* 2 vols. (London: Methuen, 1902), I: 217–20. On that between Spiritualism and Quakerism, see Braude, *Radical Spirits,* 12–15, 64ff.

8. For biographical information on Davis, see Robert W. Delp, "The Harmonial Philosopher: Andrew Jackson Davis and the Foundation of Modern American Spiritualism (Ph.D. diss., The George Washington University, 1965); idem, "Andrew Jackson Davis," 43–56; idem, "Andrew Jackson Davis's *Revelations,* Harbinger of American Spiritualism," *New York Historical Society Quarterly* 55 (1971): 211–34; Brown, Jr., "Spiritualism," 16ff.; Isaacs, "A History," 26ff.; and Davis, *The Magic Staff.*

9. George Bush, *Mesmer and Swedenborg; or, the Relation of the Developments of Mesmerism to the Doctrines and Disclosures of Swedenborg* (New York: John Allen, 1847), 169–217.

10. *USP* I (Dec. 4, 1847): 8–9.

11. On Harris, see Herbert W. Schneider and George Lawton, *A Prophet and a Pilgrim: Being the Incredible History of Thomas Lake Harris and Laurence Oliphant; Their Sexual Mysticisms and Utopian Communities Amply Documented to Confound the Skeptic* (New York: Columbia University Press, 1942); Arthur A. Cuthbert, *The Life and World-Work of Thomas Lake Harris* (New York: AMS Press, 1975 [Glasgow, 1909]); Swank, "The Unfettered Conscience," 207ff.; and Isaacs, "A History," 244. On Chase, see his *The Life-Line of the Lone One; or Autobiography of the World's Child* (Boston: Bela Marsh, 1857) and *Forty Years on the Spiritual Rostrum* (Boston: Colby and Rich, 1888), as well as Moore, *White Crows,* 91ff., Swank, "The Unfettered Conscience," 283ff., and Isaacs, "A History," 121ff. and 241ff.

12. Moore, *White Crows,* 12–13; Braude, *Radical Spirits,* 34–35.

13. Lawton, *The Drama of Life After Death,* xii.

14. See, for example, Isaacs, "A History," 8.

15. Hardinge, *Modern American Spiritualism,* 233. Robert S. Ellwood has pointed out that even Shaker spiritualistic practices were enhanced by familiarity with the works of Swedenborg on the part of informed Shakers like Frederick Evans; see *Alternative Altars,* 77–78.

16. *SH* 1 (1852): 119.

17. Ibid., 105; Andrew Jackson Davis, *The Principles of Nature, Her Divine Revelations, and a Voice to Mankind* (New York: S. S. Lyon and W. Fishbough, 1847), 589–91, 675–76; Robert Delp, "Davis's *Revelations*," 214, 223–24; *ST 7* (June 12, 1858): 67; *JSW*, 3:2:234 (in this and all future references to the Williams manuscripts, the first number refers to volume number, the second to book number, and the third to page number); *ST 7* (Jan. 8, 1859): 366.

18. *AC*, 2886; Samuel Warren, *A Compendium of the Theological Writings of Emanuel Swedenborg* (New York: Swedenborg Foundation, 1875), 272; HH, 39, 391. References to Swedenborg's works are not to page numbers but to the numbers with which Swedenborg himself punctuated his text.

19. *AC*, 50, 905; Warren, *Compendium*, 278, 383, 617, 622–623; *AE*, 1182; *SD*, 1647; *HH*, 258.

20. *SD*, 1622; NJ, 311–19; *AC*, 3670, 9809, 9989; Warren, *Compendium*, 431.

21. Warren, *Compendium*, 132–33, 622–23; *SD*, 1625; *HH*, 265–66, 314; *AC*, 5121.

22. See Lawton, *The Drama of Life After Death*, 112–13n90.

23. See Hatch, *Democratization*.

24. On this point, see Lawton, *The Drama of Life After Death*, 28, 35; Mary Farrell Bednarowski, "Nineteenth-Century American Spiritualism," 29–30; and James Turner, *Without God, Without Creed: The Origins of Unbelief in America* (Baltimore: Johns Hopkins University Press, 1985), 79, 82, 84.

25. Lehman, "Life of Spear," 24–25.

26. Ahlstrom, *Religious History*, 485.

27. John B. Wilson, "Emerson and the Rochester Rappings," *New England Quarterly* 41 (1968), 249–50, 251; Emerson, "Swedenborg; or, the Mystic," in Robert E. Spiller, ed., *Selected Essays, Lectures and Poems of Ralph Waldo Emerson* (New York: Washington Square Press, 1965), 142, 149, 155.

28. *ST 5*: (Sept. 6, 1856): 150; *SH 1* (1852): 105–19.

29. *BJM 3* (July 1851): 10; Robert Hare, *Experimental Investigation of the Spirit Manifestations* (New York: Partridge and Brittan, 1855); Davis, *Spiritual Intercourse*. On Spiritualism's scientific dimension, see Moore, *White Crows*, 19–39, and "Spiritualism and Science: Reflections on the First Decade of the Spirit Rappings," *American Quarterly* 24 (1972), 474–500; Bednarowski, "Nineteenth Century American Spiritualism"; James Turner, *Without God*, 104–109, 164–65. Herbert Hovenkamp, *Science and Religion in America, 1800–1860* (Philadelphia: University of Pennsylvania Press, 1978), and Walter H. Conser, Jr., *God and the Natural World: Religion and Science in Antebellum America* (Columbia, S.C.: University of South Carolina Press, 1993), are useful for providing context. On the Baconian character of antebellum American science, see George H. Daniels, *American Science in the Age of Jackson* (New York: Columbia University Press, 1968); Spiritualism is specifically addressed on 133–34. On the Baconian character of religious thought in this period, see Theodore Dwight Bozeman, *Protestants in an Age of Science: The Baconian Ideal and Antebellum American Religious Thought* (Chapel Hill: University of North Carolina Press, 1977).

30. See Moore, "Spiritualism and Science," 484, and *White Crows*, 18; Wilson, "Emerson and the Rochester Rappings," 248–49.

31. Emerson, "Swedenborg," 149; Edward Waldo Emerson, ed., *The Complete Works of Ralph Waldo Emerson*, centenary ed., 12 vols. (New York: Houghton Mifflin, 1903–1904), II: 65.

32. On this last point, see Arthur Cushman McGiffert, *Young Emerson Speaks* (Boston: Houghton Mifflin, 1938), 110, 237n4, 237n8, and 237–38n9.

33. *JSW*, 1:1:169.

34. George Bush, *Prof. Bush's Reply to Emerson on Swedenborg* (New York: John Allen, 1846), 1, 16, 17; *NJM* 8 (1834–35): 243–45; Isaacs, "A History," 118–20.

35. New Church leaders disagreed on the issue of Swedenborg's authority, some considering his writings plenarily inspired and hence infallible and others maintaining the higher authority of the Scriptures. See Marguerite Beck Block, *The New Church in the New World: A Study of Swedenborgianism in America* (New York: Holt, Reinhart, and Winston, 1932), 191–92.

36. Swank, "The Unfettered Conscience," 240ff.; Block, *New Church,* 133, 142–43; Rev. John Jewett to John Shoebridge Williams, 11 May 1857, in *JSWP;* "A Layman," *The Nineteenth Century; or the New Dispensation: Being a Brief Examination of the Claims and Assertions of Emanuel Swedenborg,* 2nd ed. (New York: John Allen, 1852), 311–18. See also *The Pythonism of the Present Day: The Response of the Ministers of the Massachusetts Association of the New Jerusalem to a Resolution of that Association Requesting Their Consideration of What Is Usually Known as Modern Spiritualism* (Boston: George Phinney, 1858).

37. *ST* 5 (June 21, 1856), 59; SC 1: 8; *ST* 2 (Jan. 28, 1854): 156; *JSW,* 2:2:198; *ST* 7 (Jan. 8, 1859), 366; *ST* 1 (Oct. 16, 1852): 1; *ST* 2 (Apr. 15, 1854), 197; *ST* 5 (Mar. 7, 1857): 357.

38. On the New Era movement, see Swank, "The Unfettered Conscience," 197–239.

39. Ibid., 199; Block, *New Church,* 127.

40. *ST* 5 (Jan. 17, 1857): 300.

41. George Bush and B. F. Barrett, *"Davis's Revelations" Revealed; Being a Critical Examination of the Character and Claims of that Work in its Relations to the Teachings of Swedenborg* (New York: John Allen, 1847).

42. Swank, "The Unfettered Conscience," 264–68; Isaacs, "A History," 50; John R. Hibbard, *Necromancy; or, Pseudo-Spiritualism Viewed in the Light of the Sacred Scriptures, and the Teachings of the New Church* (Chicago: Whitemarsh, Fuller, 1853); *The Pythonism of the Present Day.*

43. Swank, "The Unfettered Conscience," 198, 204–205, 230–31, 238–39, 250, 273–74.

44. LaRoy Sunderland, *Book of Human Nature: Illustrating the Philosophy (New Theory) of Instinct, Nutrition, Life; with Their Correlative and Abnormal Phenomena, Physiological, Mental, Spiritual* (New York: Stearns, 1853), 323.

3. Spiritualist Republicanism

1. *SM* 1 (May 31, 1851): 337–40; Davis, *Magic Staff,* 190–91; *AP* 2 (July 12, 1856): 1.

2. *SA* 1 (July 4, 1857): 38; Robert T. Hallock, *The Child and the Man: or, Anniversary Suggestions, by Dr. R. T. Hallock* (New York: Ellinwood and Hills, 1856), 26.

3. *SC* I: 268; Hatch, *Democratization.* On radical individualism, see Braude, *Radical Spirits,* esp. 56–81, and Lewis Perry, *Radical Abolitionism: Anarchy and the Government of God in Antislavery Thought* (Ithaca: Cornell University Press, 1973), 213ff. See also John L. Thomas, "Romantic Reform in America, 1815–1865," *American Quarterly* 17 (1965), 656–81; idem, "Antislavery and Utopia," in Martin Duberman, ed., *The Antislavery Vanguard: New Essays on the Abolitionists* (Princeton: Princeton University Press, 1965).

4. On the importance of republicanism and the Revolutionary legacy to religious

thought and life in the early republic, see Hatch, *Democratization,* esp. 3–46. On the republican ideology, see Bernard Bailyn, *The Ideological Origins of the American Revolution* (Cambridge: Harvard University Press, 1967).

5. Uriah Clark, *Plain Guide to Spiritualism,* 4th ed. (Boston: William White, 1863), 76–77. On the identification of independence with manliness, see E. Anthony Rotundo, *American Manhood: Transformations in Masculinity from the Revolution to the Modern Era* (New York: Basic Books, 1993), 15–16.

6. Hallock, *The Child and the Man,* 17; Davis, *Beyond the Valley; A Sequel to the Magic Staff: An Autobiography* (Boston: Colby and Rich, 1885), 63; idem, *The Penetralia; Being Harmonial Answers to Important Questions* (Boston: Bela Marsh, 1856), 258.

7. John W. Edmonds and George Dexter, *Spiritualism,* 2 vols. (New York: Partridge and Brittan, 1853–1855), II: 448–49; *PC* 14 (July 16, 1853): 23; Hallock, *The Child and the Man,* iii–iv. Spiritualists looking to spirits in this way replicated an important element of many traditional religions. In both Spiritualism and the "central morality religions" described by anthropologist I. M. Lewis, the spirits contacted are "sternly moralistic" and act as conservative "censors of society" whose "task is to uphold and sustain public morality." See I. M. Lewis, *Ecstatic Religion: An Anthropological Study of Spirit Possession and Shamanism* (Hammondsworth: Penguin Books, 1971), 34.

8. *SC* 1: 573–76; see George Forgie, *Patricide in the House Divided: A Psychological Interpretation of Lincoln and his Age* (New York: W. W. Norton, 1979), 13.

9. Davis, *Beyond the Valley,* 321, 323–26. On the fusion of republicanism with millennialism, see Ruth Bloch, *Visionary Republic: Millennial Themes in American Thought, 1756–1800* (New York: Cambridge University Press, 1985).

10. *PC* 14 (July 16, 1853): 23; Edmonds and Dexter, *Spiritualism,* II: 448–49; Spear, *Twelve Discourses on Government: Purporting to Have Been Delivered in Boston, Mass., December 1853, by Thomas Jefferson, of the Spirit World, through John M. Spear, Medium* (Hopedale, Mass.: Community Press, 1853), 15–18; *ST* 5 (June 14, 1856): 6; Hallock, *The Child and the Man,* iii–iv.

11. Richard Rabinowitz, *The Spiritual Self in Everyday Life: The Transformation of Personal Religious Experience in Nineteenth-Century New England* (Boston: Northeastern University Press, 1989), 65; *ST* 7 (January 22, 1859): 381; Davis, *The Penetralia,* 286–88, 303–304; *ST* 6 (June 20, 1857): 60. Spiritualists' anti-institutionalism is discussed in Moore, *White Crows,* 13–14; Braude, *Radical Spirits,* 163ff.; and Bednarowski, "Nineteenth Century American Spiritualism," 41. The connection between Spiritualism, radical individualism, and women's rights has been persuasively argued in Braude's *Radical Spirits.*

12. *ST* 3 (August 5, 1854): 53; Hallock, *The Child and the Man,* 9; *ST* 6 (June 20, 1857): 60. Explaining the religious appeal of Spiritualism, Lawton has pointed out that established religious systems tend to "become codified, formal, impersonal and—irrelevant" (*Drama of Life After Death,* 396).

13. *ST* 5 (May 2, 1856): 3; *ST* 2 (July 9, 1853): 37; *ST* 1 (July 10, 1852): 2nd page. See Hughes and Allen, *Illusions of Innocence,* 103–108.

14. The concepts of republicanism used in this and the following paragraphs are elaborated in Bailyn, *The Ideological Origins of the American Revolution.*

15. *PC* 14 (June 18, 1853): 14; Edmonds and Dexter, *Spiritualism,* II: 61; *ST* 1 (December 4, 1852): 1; *ST* 8 (September 10, 1859): 235.

16. R. P. Ambler, *Elements of Spiritual Philosophy; Being an Exposition of Interior Principles* (Springfield, Mass.: R. P. Ambler, 1852), 13; S. C. Hewitt, *Messages from the Superior State; Communicated from John Murray, through John M. Spear* (Boston: Bela Marsh, 1853), 152–53; William H. Fish, *Orthodoxy versus Spiritualism and*

Liberalism (Hopedale, Mass.: Community Press, 1857), 15, 17; *PC* 13 (January 29, 1853): 78; *PC* 14 (December 17, 1853): 65.

17. Hewitt, *Messages,* 138; *ST* 7 (May 8, 1858): 16; *SM* 1 (May 31, 1851): 338.

18. *ST* 2 (April 22, 1854): 201; *ST* 3 (August 5, 1854): 54. The latter comment in the text was signed "F.," a frequent contributor to the *Spiritual Telegraph.*

19. The best source of information about Ballou's life is still his own *Autobiography of Adin Ballou,* ed. William S. Heywood (Lowell, Mass.: Vox Populi Press, 1896). See also Philip Sidney Padelford, "Adin Ballou and the Hopedale Community" (Ph.D. diss., Yale University, 1942).

20. Fuller, *Mesmerism,* xi–xii, 30; Hughes and Allen, *Illusions of Innocence,* 108; Moore, *White Crows,* 40–69, and Braude, *Radical Spirits,* 56–81.

21. *ST* 3 (October 14, 1854): 93; Chase, *Life-Line,* 209–10.

22. See Isaacs, "A History," 227ff.

23. *ST* 3 (August 5, 1854): 55; *NI* 2 (August 12, 1854): 2. For other reactions against the Society, see *ST* 3 (August 19, 1854): 61 and *ST* 3 (September 16, 1854): 77.

24. Charles Hammond, *Light from the Spirit World; The Pilgrimage of Thomas Paine, and Others, to the Seventh Circle in the Spirit World* (Rochester: D. M. Dewey, 1852), 194; John S. Adams, *A Letter to the Chestnut St. Congregational Church, Chelsea, Mass., in Reply to its Charge of Having Become a Reproach to the Cause of Truth, in Consequence of a Change in Religious Belief* (Boston: Bela Marsh, 1854), 14; Edmonds and Dexter, *Spiritualism,* I: 9; Hughes and Allen, *Illusions of Innocence,* 3, 21, 137.

25. *SC* 1: 287–91; Davis, *Spiritual Intercourse,* 169.

26. *ST* 4 (May 19, 1855): 9; *ST* 7 (May 15, 1858): 26; Thomas Wentworth Higginson, *The Unitarian Autumnal Convention* (Boston: Benjamin B. Mussey, 1853).

27. R. P. Ambler, *The Spiritual Teacher; Comprising a Series of Twelve Lectures on the Nature and Development of the Spirit* (New York: R. P. Ambler, 1852), 91–92; Hammond, *Light,* 114; *ST* 1 (July 3, 1852): 3rd page. The Spiritualist rejection of Calvinist orthodoxy is discussed in Braude, *Radical Spirits,* 32–55, and Moore, *White Crows,* 40–62.

28. On "come-outerism," see Perry, *Radical Abolitionism,* 92ff.; Ruth Alden Doan, *The Miller Heresy, Millennialism, and American Culture* (Philadelphia: Temple University Press, 1987), 121–25; Braude, *Radical Spirits,* 61; Lehman, "Life of Spear," 132.

29. I. M. Lewis, *Ecstatic Religion,* 18–36; Clarke Garrett, *Spirit Possession and Popular Religion: From the Camisards to the Shakers* (Baltimore: Johns Hopkins University Press, 1987).

30. See Swank, "The Unfettered Conscience," 197–239, and Stephen J. Stein, *Shaker Experience,* 165–90. On Mormonism in the context of religious democratization, see Hatch, *Democratization,* 113–22. Ruth A. Doan has commented that "emerging notions of subjective experience" conflicted with clerical power, church discipline, and the claims of religious structures to authority. "The individualistic and egalitarian implications of evangelicalism," she continues, "had always posed a threat, though often latent, to existing structures of authority. In the 1840s, a flurry of challenges to such structures demonstrated just how tenuous their hold had become" [Doan, "Millerism and Evangelical Culture," in Numbers and Butler, eds., *The Disappointed: Millerism and Millenarianism in the Nineteenth Century* (Bloomington and Indianapolis: Indiana University Press, 1987), 134]. The case of Spiritualism suggests that the experiential emphasis of the Second Great Awakening could stimulate not only new and more democratic forms of religious authority but also

doctrines far less orthodox than those held by the "mainline" denominations. This point has been made by Michael A. O'Sullivan, "A Harmony of Worlds," 37.

31. John Murray Spear, *The Educator: Being Suggestions, Theoretical and Practical, Designed to Promote Man-Culture and Integral Reform with a View to the Ultimate Establishment of a Divine Social State on Earth* (Boston, 1857), 432; Fish, *Orthodoxy versus Spiritualism*, 15, 17; *ST* 5 (March 7, 1857), 357.

32. On Williams's involvement with the New Church, see Swank, "The Unfettered Conscience," 312n77.

33. Braude, *Radical Spirits*, 10–13; *JSW*, 2:1:40.

34. Isaacs, "A History," 138; Braude, *Radical Spirits*, 47–49; Moore, *White Crows*, 46.

35. Adams, *Letter*, 10, 47, 49.

36. A. E. and Sarah J. Newton, *Answer to Charges of Belief in Modern Revelations, Etc. Given before the Edwards Congregational Church, Boston, by Mr. and Mrs. A. E. Newton* (Boston: Bela Marsh, 1856), 2; idem, *The "Ministry of Angels" Realized. A Letter to the Edwards Congregational Church, Boston*, 3rd ed. (Boston: A. E. Newton, 1853), 25; *ST* 2 (January 21, 1854): 150. As Braude points out (*Radical Spirits*, 43), excommunications of Spiritualists were relatively rare since spirit communication contradicted no basic Christian tenets; those that did occur resulted, as in the case of the Newtons, from the unorthodox conclusions concerning religious authority which often followed an espousal of Spiritualism. Moore discusses the threat posed by Spiritualism to the authority of the Bible in *White Crows*, 46–49.

37. Adams, *Letter*, 6, 18, 28.

38. Braude, *Radical Spirits*, 56–57.

39. *ST* 6 (May 2, 1857): 1; *JSW*, 2:4:202.

40. Edmonds and Dexter, *Spiritualism*, II: 59–60; *ST* 2 (August 20, 1853). See Bednarowski, "Nineteenth Century American Spiritualism," 48–58.

41. Isaac Post, *Voices from the Spirit World, Being Communications from Many Spirits, by the Hand of Isaac Post, Medium* (Rochester: C. H. McDonell, 1852), viii; *SC* 2: 291. See also Lawton, *Drama of Life After Death*, 584–85, and Braude, *Radical Spirits*, 56–57.

42. Williams, *Nature and the Bible Have One Author, Demonstrated by Their Coincidences and Common Sense, Without Reference to History or the Opinions of Men* (Cincinnati: Wrightson, 1861): back cover (a copy of this pamphlet may be found with *JSWP*); *JSW*, 2:1:2, 3:3:241–42, 3:4:83. Williams discusses his scuffle with New Church officials in a four-page circular inserted in volume 4, book 1 of *JSW*.

43. Williams, "Synopsis of Spiritual Experience," in *An Address to the Officers and Citizens of the United States, Recommending a Manifestation in Favor of the Bible* (Baltimore: Sherwood, 1854), 1–2; *JSW*, 1:1:138.

44. Ibid., 1:1:113, 1:3:10.

45. Ibid., 2:2:129, 2:4:16, 1:4:235.

46. Ibid., 3:2:251, 2:1:94; John Humphrey Noyes, *History of American Socialisms* (1870; reprint, New York: Hillary House Publishers, Ltd., 1961), 540.

47. *SC* 1: 447; *SC* 2: 8; *ST* 6 (March 20, 1858): 383; Joel Tiffany, *Spiritualism Explained: Being a Series of Twelve Lectures Delivered Before the New York Conference of Spiritualists, by Joel Tiffany, in January, 1856*, 2nd ed. (New York: Graham and Ellinwood, 1856), 115; Clark, *Plain Guide*, 172. The formation of the New York Spiritualist Conference will be discussed in ch. 6.

48. *ST* 2 (24 December 1853): 135; Davis, *The Penetralia*, 341–42; idem, *Beyond the Valley*, 323–26; idem, *The Harmonial Man; or, Thoughts for the Age* (Boston: Bela Marsh, 1853), 17; Warren Chase, *The Gist of Spiritualism: Viewed Scientifically, Philosophically, Religiously, Politically, and Socially* (Boston: William White, 1865), 84, 96; Hughes and Allen, *Illusions of Innocence*, 17–20.

49. Davis, *The Great Harmonia*, 5 vols. (1850–59), III: 69; Hare, *Lecture on Spiritualism, Delivered Before an Audience of Three Thousand, at the Tabernacle, in the City of New York, in November, 1855* (New York: Partridge and Brittan, 1855), 14.

50. Emma Hardinge, *Questions Answered Extempore by Miss Emma Hardinge, at the Winter Soirées, Harley Street, London, January 22nd, 1866*), 7–8, in *Addresses and Questions* (London: T. Scott, 1865–1866); *ST* 6 (March 13, 1858): 374; Clark, *Plain Guide*, 170–71.

51. Hatch, *Democratization*, 35, 44; *JSW*, 1:2:234–35, 3:4:250, 4:1:164.

52. Capron, *Modern Spiritualism*, 197; *ST* 3 (August 5, 1854): 55.

53. *ST* 1 (July 31, 1852): 3; *ST* 3 (October 28, 1854): 101; *ST* 1 (January 29, 1853): 4.

54. Adin Ballou, *History of the Hopedale Community* (Lowell, Mass.: Vox Populi Press, 1897), 384–85. For Ballou's own view of the subject, see *PC* 18 (June 27, 1857): 17.

55. *ST* 8 (September 10, 1859): 235.

56. *ST* 6 (April 10, 1858): 407; *ST* 7 (May 29, 1858): 47.

57. The national Spiritualist organizations that eventually emerged during the late nineteenth and early twentieth centuries imposed few qualifications for clerical status.

58. *ST* 3 (June 3, 1854): 17; *ST* 7 (January 15, 1859): 377; Chase, *Life-Line*, 163, 170–71; Braude, *Radical Spirits*, 93. As Braude convincingly argues, women mediums stood to gain considerably from such arguments since their gender usually kept them from positions of public religious authority.

59. Braude, *Radical Spirits*.

60. *ST* 2 (February 4, 1854): 158; Braude, "News from the Spirit World: A Checklist of American Spiritualist Periodicals, 1847–1860," *Proceedings of the American Antiquarian Society* 99 (1989): 408; *SC* 1: 510.

61. *BJM* 3 (October 1851): 70–78, and 3 (December 1851): 33–45.

62. Clark, *Plain Guide*, 276–77.

4. The Structure of the Spirit World

1. Adams, *Letter*, 18, 26–27.

2. Hammond, *Light*, 251; Lehman, "Life of Spear," 234; Emma Hardinge, *Six Lectures on Theology and Nature* (1860), 52; Catherine L. Albanese, *Nature Religion in America: From the Algonkian Indians to the New Age* (Chicago: University of Chicago Press, 1990), 9; Hughes and Allen, *Illusions of Innocence*, 36. "Coming out," comments Albanese, involves a "natural freedom," a "separation from human society" and "a flight away to nature." Furthermore, Albanese points to Transcendentalist Convers Francis's likening of the universe to a temple as a "symbol of stability," a metaphor which Spiritualists frequently employed, as an important component of the mood of nature religion.

3. Davis, *Penetralia*, 287–317.

4. Clifford Geertz, "Religion as a Cultural System," 89. Transcendentalists, too, used the image of the circle to express their concern for wholeness; see Catherine L. Albanese, *Corresponding Motion: Transcendental Religion and the New America* (Philadelphia: Temple University Press, 1977), 116–17. The psychological significance of this symbol is considered in Zwelling, "Spiritualist Perspectives," 15.

5. Edmonds and Dexter, *Spiritualism*, I: 64, 109, 397, II: 378.

6. Albanese has interpreted Transcendentalism in terms of this "kinetic revolution" in *Corresponding Motion*. McDannell and Lang describe its effects on concep-

tions of the afterlife in the late eighteenth and nineteenth centuries in *Heaven,* 199–210, 276–87.

7. See Rothman, *The Discovery of the Asylum: Social Order and Disorder in the New Republic* (Boston: Little, Brown, 1971), 10–11. On the "great chain of being," see Arthur O. Lovejoy, *The Great Chain of Being: A Study of the History of an Idea* (Cambridge: Harvard University Press, 1964).

8. Andrew Jackson Davis, *The Philosophy of Special Providences: A Vision* (Boston: Bela Marsh, 1850), 45; Spear, *The Educator,* 154, 512–13.

9. Adin Ballou, *An Exposition of Views Respecting the Principal Facts, Causes and Peculiarities Involved in Spirit Manifestations: Together with Interesting Phenomenal Statements and Communications* (Boston: Bela Marsh, 1852), 69–70; Cora Hatch, *A Discourse on Faith, Hope, and Love. Delivered in New York, Sunday, April 23, 1857: To Which Is Added a Report of a Philosophical Investigation of the Nature of Mediumship* (New York: B. F. Hatch, 1858), 21.

10. Spear, *The Educator,* 63, 130, 163.

11. Davis, *Magic Staff,* 383. Catherine L. Albanese has argued that Davis increasingly identified God and Nature and conceived of Nature itself as "equal and active cause" with God. See Catherine L. Albanese, "On the Matter of Spirit: Andrew Jackson Davis and the Marriage of God and Nature," *Journal of the American Academy of Religion* 60 (1992): 7–9.

12. Davis was suspected by some of plagiarizing Robert Chambers's anonymously published deist tract *Vestiges of the Natural History of Creation* (London: J. Churchill, 1844), first published in the United States in 1845. On deism in antebellum America, see Albert Post, *Popular Freethought in America, 1825–1850* (Chicago: University of Chicago Press, 1943), and Turner, *Without God,* especially 73–167.

13. On the idea of "correspondence," see Signe Toksvig, *Emanuel Swedenborg, Scientist and Mystic,* 286ff., and George Trobridge, *Swedenborg: Life and Teaching,* 83–89. On the use of analogy by antebellum American scientists, see George Daniels, *American Science in the Age of Jackson,* 167–80.

14. Albanese, *Corresponding Motion,* 3ff.

15. "The New York Conference," *Telegraph Papers* 4 (February 28, 1854): 216; quoted in Moore, *White Crows,* 24.

16. Albanese has pointed out that a confusion about the relationship between spirit and matter pervaded many of the alternative religious ideologies of the mid- to late nineteenth century and was central to the "nature religion" of the period. Her comment about Phineas P. Quimby, ideological forerunner of Christian Science, could be applied to Spiritualists with equal accuracy: "as with Swedenborg and the Transcendentalists, matter shaded off into another realm"; see *Nature Religion,* 80–116. This aspect of Spiritualism lay at the heart of Moore's critique; see *White Crows,* 23ff.

17. Davis, *Spiritual Intercourse,* 39; Eliade, *The Sacred and the Profane,* 10.

18. See *SH* 1 (1852): 1, 57–72, 121–34, 239–49, 382–91.

19. Davis, *Spiritual Intercourse,* 102; *SM* 1 (October 16, 1852): 1; Davis, *The Principles of Nature,* 43. See also *SA* 1 (May 16, 1857). On the symbolic importance of Franklin, see Werner Sollors, "Dr. Benjamin Franklin's Celestial Telegraph, or Indian Blessings to Gas-Lit American Drawing Rooms," *American Quarterly* 35 (1983): 459–80.

20. Hardinge, *Modern American Spiritualism,* opp. 564; Davis, *Great Harmonia,* I: 282; Ballou, *Exposition of Views,* 7–8; Hare, *Experimental Investigation,* 362.

21. Spear, *The Educator,* 157–62, 328–32.

22. Davis, *Memoranda of Persons, Places, and Events; Embracing Authentic Facts, Visions, Impressions, Discoveries, in Magnetism, Clairvoyance, Spiritualism* (Boston: William White, 1868), 146. Werner Sollors has suggested in "Dr. Benjamin Franklin's

Celestial Telegraph" that through the spirit of Franklin, who "appeared in the role of a technological saint" (463), Spiritualists spiritualized technology, thus allowing them to cope with its troublingly rapid advance in what they feared was a materialistic culture.

23. Albanese, *Nature Religion*, 107–109; idem, "On the Matter of Spirit," 2.

24. On the early religious influences in Hare's life, see *ST* 5 (July 19, 1856) and (August 2, 1856).

25. Hare, *Experimental Investigation*, 35–55, 130, 131ff.; *Proceedings of the American Association for the Advancement of Science: first meeting, held at Philadelphia, September, 1848* (Philadelphia: John C. Clark, 1849), 76–78. Hare published a piece rejecting the spiritual origin of the manifestations in the July 27, 1853 issue of the *Philadelphia Inquirer*. On Hare's acquaintance with Holcombe, see Bruce Sinclair, *Philadelphia's Philosopher Mechanics: A History of the Franklin Institute* (Baltimore: Johns Hopkins University Press, 1974), 248n17.

26. Hare, *Experimental Investigation*, 25–29, 35–54, 159–65, 363–96, 432–60 (I have quoted from 25, 29, and 438); idem, *Lecture*; idem, *Dr. Hare's Letter to the Episcopal Clergy, Most Respectfully Offering to Submit to Their Consideration, New and Irrefragable Evidence of Human Immortality* (New York: Partridge and Brittan, 1855); Brittan to Hare, January 30, 1857, Hare Papers, American Philosophical Society.

27. On "esthetic spirituality" in American religion, see William Clebsch, *American Religious Thought* (Chicago: University of Chicago Press, 1973), xvi, 1. Spiritualists were somewhat different from other Americans of their time in the way they expressed this brand of religiosity. Whereas Clebsch accentuates unmediated contact between self and Other, Spiritualists retained notions of mediation and imagined a more elaborately architectured cosmos than that of Emerson, whom Clebsch considers the archetypal example of mid-nineteenth-century "esthetic" religion.

28. Lawton, *Drama of Life After Death*, 28, 33–36; *ST* 3 (July 1, 1854): 35; McLoughlin, *Revivals*, 20. Colleen McDannell and Bernhard Lang have persuasively argued in *Heaven* (181–227; see also 292–306) that Swedenborg's conception of the spirit world, focused on spirits, marked the beginning of a "modern" and anthropocentric heaven and a significant departure from earlier, more theocentric conceptions. On the other hand, the importance of theocentric ideas to Swedenborg's thought has been noted by Toksvig, *Swedenborg: Scientist*, 113.

29. Williams, "Bible Proof of Spirit Intercourse," 10–14, in *Three Pamphlets Bound Together* (Cincinnati: U. P. James, 1857); Davis, *Special Providences*, 48. On the problem of special providence in nineteenth-century America, see Turner, *Without God*, 38–40.

30. Edmonds and Dexter, *Spiritualism*, II: 329, 330, 332.

31. Ibid., II: 249, 250, 256, 257.

32. Hare, *Experimental Investigation*, 87, 88, 104, 113, 124–25.

33. Spear, *The Educator*, 425.

34. *JSW*, 2:1:103, 3:2:242.

35. T. Paul Verghese, *The Freedom of Man: An Inquiry into Some Roots of the Tension Between Freedom and Authority in Our Society* (Philadelphia: The Westminster Press, 1972), 46.

36. Hatch, *Democratization*. On this point, Spiritualist cosmology bore some resemblance to Mormon cosmology, which postulated the progressive apotheosis of the spirit. Klaus Hansen has remarked in *Mormonism and the American Experience* (Chicago: University of Chicago Press, 1981), 83, that Joseph Smith "out-Jacksoned the Jacksonians by proclaiming that the common man could become a god." Spiritualists did likewise in suggesting that spiritual advancement toward the deity was available to all as a necessary and inevitable result of divine law.

37. Hare, *Lecture*, 14; Mary Douglas, *Natural Symbols* (New York: Vintage Books, 1973).

38. Hare, *Experimental Investigation*, 117–18, 121, 139; Edmonds and Dexter, *Spiritualism*, I: 179.

39. Hatch, *Democratization*, 17–46; Arnold, "Democracy," in *Mixed Essays* (New York: Macmillan, 1879), 26.

40. *PC* 14 (February 25, 1854): 88. I am assuming that "Prisoner's Friend," who wrote this piece and quoted Hitchcock, was John Murray Spear. A close friend of Ballou, Spear and his brother Charles had produced a Boston weekly during the 1840s entitled *The Prisoner's Friend* and devoted to prison reform and the abolition of capital punishment.

41. E. W. Capron and Henry D. Barron, *Singular Revelations. Explanation and History of the Mysterious Communion with Spirits, Comprehending the Rise and Progress of the Mysterious Noises in Western New-York, Generally Received as Spiritual Communications*, 2nd ed. (Auburn, N.Y.: Capron and Barron, 1850), 33; Spear, *The Educator*, 517.

42. *SH* 1 (1852): 233–34; Adams, *Letter*, 45; Edmonds and Dexter, *Spiritualism*, II: 299; Davis, *Great Harmonia* II: 226, 286; Child, *The Progressive Life of Spirits After Death* (Boston: Bela Marsh, 1855), 15.

43. Adams, *Letter*, 38; Child, *ABC of Life* (Boston: William White, 1862), 22; idem, *Whatever Is, Is Right* (Boston: Berry, Colby, 1860), 16; *ST* 6 (June 13, 1857): 54; Hatch, *Discourse on the Immutable Decrees of God, and the Free Agency of Man, Delivered in the City Hall, Newburyport, Mass., Sunday, November 22, 1857* (New York: B. F. Hatch, 1858), 32; *ST* 2 (April 1, 1854): 189; *ST* 2 (April 29, 1854): 205.

44. *PC* 16 (November 17, 1855): 1st page–2nd page; *PC* 14 (April 8, 1854): 98; *PC* 18 (January 9, 1858): 74; *PC* 18 (October 17, 1857): 50; *ST* 6 (May 23, 1857): 30; *ST* 2 (May 14, 1853): 6–7; *SA* 1 (July 11, 1857): 42.

45. *PC* 14 (April 22, 1854); *PC* 15 (May 6, 1854); *PC* 15 (June 17, 1854).

46. Davis, *Great Harmonia*, II: 230 and III: 78–79; *PC* 18 (October 17, 1857): 50; *ST* 3 (September 16, 1854): 78; Williams, *Nature and the Bible*, 16; Adams, *Letter*, 44; *SA* 1 (July 11, 1857): 46; Waldo Beach, "Freedom and Authority in Protestant Ethics," *Journal of Religion* 32 (1952): 109. Though Moore has argued that Spiritualists paid little attention to divine sovereignty (*White Crows*, 51), discussions of divine sovereignty and its relationship with spirits' roles and the autonomy of the will in fact appeared with some frequency in Spiritualist publications.

47. The examples of Transcendentalists Orestes Brownson and Isaac Hecker further suggest how easily antebellum American religious seekers inclined toward spiritual individualism could become attracted to Catholicism. Antebellum Protestant attitudes toward Catholicism have recently been examined in Jenny Franchot, *Roads to Rome: The Antebellum Protestant Encounter with Catholicism* (Berkeley: University of California Press, 1994).

48. *JSW,* 1:4:99, 136.

49. On the Mercersburg theology, see James Hastings Nichols, *Romanticism in American Theology: Nevin and Schaff at Mercersburg* (Chicago: University of Chicago Press, 1961), and idem, ed., *The Mercersburg Theology* (New York: Oxford University Press, 1966). On "Catholic movements in American Protestantism," including the Mercersburg movement, see Ahlstrom, *A Religious History of the American People*, 615–632.

50. See *JSW,* 1:3:155–60, 1:4:136–47.

51. Lawton, *Drama of Life After Death*, 578; see also 168, 583–84.

52. Following sociologist Joachim Wach, Ellwood recognizes three forms of religious expression: the theoretical (conceptual and verbal expression in philosophy,

doctrine, and myth), the practical (praxis in worship, rite, prayer, etc.), and the sociological (styles of group, leadership, and interpersonal relations which the religion indicates). See Wach's *Sociology of Religion* (Chicago: University of Chicago Press, 1944), 17–34, and Ellwood, *Alternative Altars*, 32ff. Our concern here is with the theoretical dimension; we shall consider the "practical" and "sociological" dimensions of Spiritualist religion in ch. 6.

53. Robert S. Ellwood, *Alternative Altars*, ch. 2. The quotations in the text come from 26, 27, and 30.

54. Emma Hardinge, *Extemporaneous Addresses by Emma Hardinge* (London: T. Scott, 1866), 120; idem, *Six Lectures*, 52, 97; Hare, *Experimental Investigation*, 87–95 (the phrase "moral specific gravity," borrowed from physical science, appears on 116, 121).

55. David J. Rothman's *The Discovery of the Asylum* has shaped my interpretation of Spiritualist thought on this point. Spiritualist descriptions of the spirit world conformed to social scientist Erving Goffman's definition of a "total institution": "an environment in which a large number of like-situated individuals reside,... subjected to a common regime, often for the purpose of effecting a transformation in their identities." See Adam and Jessica Kuper, eds., *The Social Science Encyclopedia* (London: Routledge and Kegan Paul, 1985), s.v. "Institutions," by Roy Wallis, 399.

56. Rothman, *Discovery of the Asylum*, 191; Hare, *Experimental Investigation*, 92, 116.

57. T. Paul Verghese offers a relevant discussion in *The Freedom of Man*, 43–44. Rothman has noted the important influence of military models of discipline and controlled living on antebellum conceptions of ideal prisons and asylums; see *Discovery of the Asylum*, 105–108.

58. Child, *Progressive Life*, 7, 13; *SC* 1: 576; Hammond, *Light*, 102ff.; Edmonds and Dexter, *Spiritualism*, II: 440.

59. On Victorian comparisons between heaven and the home, see Ann Douglas, "Heaven Our Home: Consolation Literature in the Northern United States, 1830–1880," *American Quarterly* 26 (1974): 496–515; Ann Douglas, *The Feminization of American Culture*, 265–72; and Colleen McDannell, *The Christian Home in Victorian America, 1840–1900* (Bloomington: Indiana University Press, 1986), 50, 80, 83.

60. E. C. Henck, *Spirit Voices: Odes, Dictated by Spirits of the Second Sphere, for the Use of Harmonial Circles* (Philadelphia: G. D. Henck, 1853), 78; Chase, *Gist*, 41. Classic studies of the "cult of domesticity" in the antebellum period include Nancy F. Cott, *The Bonds of Womanhood*; Kathryn Kish Sklar, *Catharine Beecher: A Study in American Domesticity* (New Haven: Yale University Press, 1973); and Barbara Welter, "The Cult of True Womanhood, 1820–1860," *American Quarterly* 18 (1966): 151–74.

61. Davis, *Magic Staff*, 182; Adams, *Letter*, 5–6.

62. Ellwood, *Alternative Altars*, 36.

5. The Ministry of Spirits

1. Newton and Newton, *Answer to Charges*, 24, 26; idem, *"Ministry of Angels" Realized*, 23.

2. See Lawton, *Drama of Life After Death*, xii.

3. Braude, *Radical Spirits*, 57; Bednarowski, "Nineteenth Century American Spiritualism," 48–49.

4. Moore, *White Crows*, 52.

5. *SA* 1 (August 8, 1857): 59.

6. Newton and Newton, *"Ministry of Angels" Realized*, 7n; Post, *Voices*, xiii, 109; *JSW*, 2:3:23, 2:3:188; Williams, *Nature and the Bible*, 12.

7. *ST* 2 (March 18, 1854): 181; A. E. Newton, "What Does Spiritualism Teach?" *Tracts on Spiritualism* (Boston: Bela Marsh, 186-?), 3.

8. Edmonds and Dexter, *Spiritualism*, II: 130–31; Spear, *The Educator*, 280, 627.

9. Turner, *Without God*, 79, 82, 84; Bednarowski, Nineteenth Century American Spiritualism," 29–30; Lawton, *Drama of Life After Death*, xii, 28, 35, 423.

10. Ellwood, *Alternative Altars*, 27; Perry Miller, *Errand Into the Wilderness* (Cambridge: Belknap Press, 1975), 55; *SC* 1: 37; Child, *Progressive Life*, 6–7. While Spiritualists humanized their cosmos by emphasizing limited human spirits instead of God, Mormons did so by humanizing and limiting their God. On this aspect of Mormonism, see Bednarowski, *New Religions*, 22–24, 27.

11. McDannell and Lang, *Heaven*, 181–227, 292–306; Lawton, *Drama of Life After Death*, 35. Concerned with the nature of the afterlife rather than spirit communication, McDannell and Lang missed this important distinction between Swedenborg's and the Spiritualists' respective portrayals of spirits.

12. Otto, *The Idea of the Holy*, 15, 20, 26, 200.

13. Rabinowitz, *The Spiritual Self*, 178–88, 217. The quoted phrases in the text appear on 183 and 217 respectively.

14. Clark, *Plain Guide*, 156; Newton, *"Ministry of Angels" Realized*, 24.

15. *ST* 1 (July 31, 1852): 4; *PC* 17 (July 26, 1856): 4th page.

16. On this point, see Susan Juster, "'In A Different Voice': Male and Female Narratives of Religious Conversion in Post-Revolutionary America," *American Quarterly* 41 (1989): 56.

17. E. C. Henck, *Spirit Voices*, 78; Adams, *Letter*, 5–6; A. B. Child, *The Lily-Wreath of Spiritual Communications* (New York: Partridge and Brittan, 1855); idem, *The Bouquet of Spiritual Flowers* (Boston: Bela Marsh, 1856). I have quoted from *Lily-Wreath*, 100. The characteristics of male and female religious experience are sketched in Juster, "'In a Different Voice,'" 34–61.

18. Ann Douglas, *The Feminization of American Culture* (New York: Knopf, 1977). The themes discussed by Douglas have been applied to Spiritualism in Braude, *Radical Spirits*, 38–40.

19. A. B. Child, *An Address to Christian Churches* (Boston: Bela Marsh, 1856), 25; *SC* 1: 121.

20. *JSW*, 1:2:16, 1:4:151–52, 2:1:124; Chase, *Life-Line*, 156. On this point, see Douglas, *Feminization*, 240–72.

21. On the relationship between masculinity and Spiritualist ideology, see Bret E. Carroll, "The Religious Construction of Masculinity in Victorian America: The Male Mediumship of John Shoebridge Williams," *Religion and American Culture: A Journal of Interpretation* 7 (Winter 1997): 27–60.

22. *JSW*, 1:4:151, 2:3:36, 2:3:98–99, 3:3:83.

23. Coggeshall, *The Signs of the Times: Comprising a History of the Spirit Rappings in Cincinnati and Other Places* (Cincinnati: The Author, 1851), 33; Dellon Marcus Dewey, *History of the Strange Sounds or Rappings, Heard in Rochester and Western New York, and Usually Called the Mysterious Noises!* (Rochester: D. M. Dewey, 1850), 31–32; Clark, *Plain Guide*, 173.

24. *JSW*, 2:1:103, 3:2:242, 3:1:136; E. Anthony Rotundo, *American Manhood*, 172–74.

25. Spear, *The Educator*, 245–6; *JSW*, 2:1:4, 2:1:22, 2:1:127; Hare, *Experimental Investigation*, 54, 87–97, 104–11, 113–19.

26. Williams, "Bible Proof," 23; Newton and Newton, *"Ministry of Angels" Realized*, 24; Chase, *Life-Line*, 16–17, 28. On the growing absence of antebellum fathers from home life, see Rotundo, *American Manhood*, 28, and Robert L. Griswold, *Fatherhood in America: A History* (New York: Basic Books, 1993), 10ff.

27. Newton, *"Ministry of Angels" Realized*, 9, 10–11.

28. Ambler, *Spiritual Teacher*, 16, 54–55, 84; *SC* 2: 420; Hardinge, *Six Lectures*; *ST* 7 (May 8, 1858): 16; *ST* 2 (April 15, 1854): 199; Post, *Voices*, viii.

29. Hewitt, *Messages*, 146; Edmonds and Dexter, *Spiritualism*, II: 70; Hatch, *Discourse on Faith*, 21; *SH* 1 (1852): 7; Newton and Newton, *Answer to Charges*, 19. See also Lawton, *Drama of Life After Death*, 112, 112–13n90. Swedenborg himself had emphasized the spiritual equality between mortals and the spirits who influenced them. By following suit, Moore (*White Crows*, 22) slighted an important dimension of the Spiritualist ideology.

30. *SC* 1: 207; Edmonds and Dexter, *Spiritualism*, I: 352.

31. Edmonds and Dexter, *Spiritualism* I: 276, 288.

32. Newton, *"Ministry of Angels" Realized*, 18; Edmonds and Dexter, *Spiritualism*, I: 336.

33. *PC* 12 (November 8, 1851): 54. For Ballou's background see his *Autobiography*.

34. *ST* 6 (April 10, 1858): 407.

35. *ST* 7 (May 29, 1858): 47. Like Spiritualism, the "Christian" movement of the early nineteenth century involved an attempt to reduce emotional spiritual "exercises" to order; see Hughes and Allen, *Illusions of Innocence*, 119–21. Interestingly, Davis's desire for a more "feminine" religion led him to criticize Protestantism as excessively "masculine" and "less human" than Catholicism, with which Spiritualists had an ambiguous relationship. Despite his feeling that "the Catholic power" was the "exact antipode" of "true *Individualism*," he admitted that he thought the Church "beautiful in some of its features." See *ST* 7 (October 16, 1858): 244.

36. *ST* 6 (April 10, 1858): 407.

37. *ST* 7 (March 5, 1859): 446; *ST* 7 (November 20, 1858): 295; Hardinge, *Modern American Spiritualism*, 197–98, 525–26.

38. Ballou, *Exposition of Views*, 49; *SH* 1: 410.

39. *JSW*, 3:2:13; Edmonds and Dexter, *Spiritualism* II: 296; Hardinge, *Extemporaneous Addresses*, 114.

40. *ST* 7 (July 10, 1858): 102; Thomas Wentworth Higginson, *The Results of Spiritualism, A Discourse, delivered at Dodworth's Hall, Sunday, March 6, 1859* (New York: S. T. Munson, 1859), 20; Edmonds and Dexter, *Spiritualism*, II: 276–77. Ann Douglas has suggested in "Heaven Our Home," 509, that liberal ministers accepted Spiritualism because they could use the idea of spirit watching to reinforce their ebbing influence over their parishioners. But the fight over Spiritualism between Spiritualists and many liberal churches and clergy, the threat to clerical authority which Spiritualism often represented to those on both sides of the battle, and in many cases Spiritualists' own language, suggest that many followers of the new religion understood the spirits as surrogates for, rather than reinforcements of, ministerial authority and influence. R. Laurence Moore, meanwhile, has argued (*White Crows*, 60) that Spiritualists "turned away altogether from divine sanctions" in their search for order, but it is more accurate to say that they deemphasized deity in favor of mediating spirits.

41. David Pugh, *Sons of Liberty: The Masculine Mind in Nineteenth-Century America* (Westport, Conn.: Greenwood Press, 1983), 8; Douglas, *The Feminization of American Culture*, 8.

42. *SC* 1: 121; Ambler, *Spiritual Teacher*, 132.

43. *SC* 1: 524.

44. James Moorhead and Ruth Alden Doan have both suggested that these categories have been too rigidly applied to nineteenth-century American religious thought and culture. See "Between Progress and Apocalypse: A Reassessment of Millennialism in American Religious Thought, 1800–1880," *Journal of American History* 71 (1984): 524–42, and Doan, *Miller Heresy*, 14–15.

45. Davis, *Principles of Nature*, 17; *PC* 13 (March 26, 1853): 95; Brittan, "To the Reader," prospectus for the *Spiritual Telegraph* (n. d.). See Higham, *Boundlessness*, passim.; John L. Thomas, "Antislavery and Utopia," 265–66; Moore, *White Crows*, 71–101.

46. Michael Barkun, "'The Wind Sweeping Over the Country': John Humphrey Noyes and the Rise of Millerism," in Numbers and Butler, *The Disappointed*, 154; Williams, *Address*, 2.

47. See Frankiel, *California's Spiritual Frontiers*, 34; Logie Barrow, "Socialism in Eternity: The Ideology of Plebeian Spiritualists, 1853–1913," *History Workshop Journal*, issue 9 (spring 1980): 47; Robert A. Abzug, *Passionate Liberator: Theodore Dwight Weld and the Dilemma of Reform* (New York: Oxford University Press, 1980), 252; Moore, *White Crows*, 88. The concept of the "failure mechanism" has been developed in Leon Festinger, Henry W. Riecken, and Stanley Schacter, *When Prophecy Fails* (Minneapolis: University of Minnesota Press, 1956). On the Millerite strategy of "spiritualization," see Doan, *Miller Heresy*, 203–205, and Numbers and Butler, *The Disappointed*, xv.

48. *SH* 1 (1852): 75–80.

49. In addition to Chase's two autobiographical works, *Life-Line* and *Forty Years*, see Moore, *White Crows*, 91 92, and Isaacs, "A History," 53–54, 121–23, 241–42. This role of Spiritualism is examined from a psychological perspective in Zwelling, "Spiritualist Perspectives," 7.

50. Chase, *Life-Line*, 18–19, 84.

51. Ibid., 126–28; Chase, *Forty Years*, 179.

52. Chase, *Gist*, 70; idem, *Life-Line*, 168, 181.

53. Chase, *Life-Line*, 170, 171; idem, *Forty Years*, 70, 192; idem, *Gist*, 88–89; Zwelling, "Spiritualist Perspectives," 7.

54. On Spear's colorful career, see Lehman, "Life of Spear"; Moore, *White Crows*, 92–95; Spear, *The Educator*, 9–39; and idem, *Twenty Years on the Wing: Brief Narrative of My Travels and Labors as a Missionary Sent Forth and Sustained by the Association of Beneficents in Spirit Land* (Boston: William White, 1873).

55. Lehman, "Life of Spear," 108.

56. On this episode, see Spear, *The Educator*, 238–57; Hardinge, *Modern American Spiritualism*, 217–29; Lehman, "Life of Spear," 178–205; and Moore, *White Crows*, 94–95.

57. *SM* 2 (August 16, 1851): 16; Spear, *The Educator*, 35; idem, *Twenty Years*, 27.

58. Spear, *The Educator*, 241, 242. High Rock and the tower at its peak, like other mountains and pillars in religious literature, is an example of what Mircea Eliade has called a "cosmic axis" or point of contact between the spiritual and ordinary worlds (*The Sacred and the Profane*, 32–37). Spear used the language of electricity to describe the spiritual properties of this sacred spot.

59. Spear, *The Educator*, 245, 247; Hardinge, *Modern American Spiritualism*, 221.

60. Spear, *The Educator*, 248; Hardinge, *Modern American Spiritualism*, 222, 223. On martyrdom in American primitivism, see Hughes and Allen, *Illusions of Innocence*, 60–63.

61. *JSW*, 1:2:21, 2:4:137–44.

62. Ibid., 2:1:108; *ST* 7 (January 29, 1859): 397; Clark, *Plain Guide*, 169.

63. Davis, *The Principles of Nature*, iii.

64. Edmonds and Dexter, *Spiritualism*, I: 110; O'Sullivan, "A Harmony of Worlds," 107ff.; Bush, *Mesmer and Swedenborg*, 137.

65. New Church members shared Spiritualists' belief in what New Church leader Caleb Reed called the spirits' "influence in producing our affections and thoughts" [*NJM* 8 (1834–5): 243–45].

66. Newton and Newton, *"Ministry of Angels" Realized*, 13–14; *SA* 1 (September 12, 1857): 78.

67. *SC* 1: 139–40; *SC* 2: 51; Spear, *The Educator*, 424, 512.

68. Newton and Newton, *"Ministry of Angels" Realized*, 13; Spear, *The Educator*, 303, 425; *ST* 2 (August 20, 1853): 63; Williams, "Bible Proof," 23. Rudolf Otto has noted that religious experience involves "annihilation of the self" and a sense of "the transcendent as the sole and entire reality" (*The Idea of the Holy*, 21). To consider a specific example culturally and chronologically close to our own, Catherine L. Albanese has observed that in Transcendentalist mysticism, the "I" as an ego-based individual is replaced by the "I" of the cosmos; in other words, in Transcendentalist mysticism as in Spiritualist mediumship, the boundaries between subject and object, self and "other," are dissolved; see Albanese, *Corresponding Motion*, 153.

69. Ambler, *Spiritual Teacher*, 101–23; *SC* 1: 121.

70. Moore, *White Crows*, 7, 12, 19, 224; Fuller, *Mesmerism*, 72, 95ff.; Zwelling, "Spiritualist Perspectives," 21.

71. Davis, *Spiritual Intercourse*, 38; Coggeshall, *The Signs of the Times*, 12–13; Stebbins, *Upward Steps of Seventy Years* (New York: John W. Lovell, 1890), 262. This book is largely premised on my agreement with Fuller that scholarly focus on Spiritualism's sensationalistic aspects has obscured the "esthetic spirituality" which characterized its early phase (see *Mesmerism*, 95).

72. Fuller, *Mesmerism*, 56–57, 68.

73. *BJM* 1 (1849): 46, 321–30, 353–68, 412–25, 490–91; *BJM* 3 (1851): 80–81, 16–17; Coggeshall, *The Signs of the Times*, 108–10; Isaacs, "A History," 113.

74. On Sunderland, see Fuller, *Mesmerism*, 56, 83; Isaacs, "A History," 22ff. and 106ff.; and Swank, "The Unfettered Conscience," 186ff.

75. Sunderland, *Book of Psychology* (New York: Stearns, 1852), 20, 42–48; idem, *Human Nature*, 199–202, 217ff.

76. Fuller, *Mesmerism*, 81; Bush, *Mesmer and Swedenborg*, 69.

77. My discussion of character draws on Karen Halttunen, *Confidence Men and Painted Women: A Study of Middle-Class Culture in America, 1830–1870* (New Haven: Yale University Press, 1982), 4–5, 25–26, 33–55, and Doan, *Miller Heresy*, 143–51.

78. Halttunen, *Confidence Men and Painted Women*, 49, 50.

79. Davis, *Penetralia*, 253; *JSW*, 3:2:29, 4:1:185; Hare, *Lecture*, 15n.; idem, *Experimental Investigation*, 110, 121.

80. John Higham has argued that conservatives of the 1850s, unable to place great trust in internalized restraints of conscience as guarantors of social order, "were experimenting . . . with social control. They were exploring new possibilities for organizing and disciplining a culture of rampant individualism" (see *From Boundlessness to Consolidation*, 13–14, 26). The concept of spirit influence must be understood in this context.

81. *JSW*, 1:1:49, 1:4:153. This discussion of Williams's androgynous spirituality is developed more fully in Carroll, "The Religious Construction of Masculinity in Victorian America." Similarly, Susan Juster's analysis of conversion narratives of male and female evangelicals of the early nineteenth century has led her to postulate an "androgynous model of the conversion experience." See Juster, "'In a Different Voice'," 56.

82. LaRoy Sunderland, *Book of Human Nature*, 299, 314; Edmonds and Dexter,

Spiritualism, I: 314–15, 318–19; Davis, *Magic Staff,* 327, 346–47, 366, 370. The problem of Spiritualism and gender identity is explored at greater length and in a different context in Carroll, "The Religious Construction of Masculinity in Victorian America."

83. Post, *Voices,* 162; Davis, *Magic Staff,* 312.

84. Chase, *Gist,* 69–70; Clark, *Plain Guide,* 174; *JSW,* 3:2:32, 2:3:113, 1:4:237.

85. *ST3* (September 30, 1854): 85; *ST3* (June 10, 1854): 23; *ST3* (July 8, 1854): 39.

86. On Edmonds, see *SH* 1 (1852): 313–32; Brown, "Spiritualism," 83ff.; and Isaacs, "A History," 98ff. and 124ff.

87. Edmonds recounted his investigation in the introduction to *Spiritualism, I.*

88. Edmonds and Dexter, *Spiritualism,* I: 70, 319.

89. Hardinge, *Modern American Spiritualism,* 95, 99; *New York Times,* October 20, 1853; Isaacs, "A History," 99; *SH* I (1852): 325. It is noteworthy that Spear questioned his sanity; see Lehman, "Life of Spear," 117. Ruth Alden Doan has suggested that the followers of William Miller met with similarly intense opposition because they seemed to exemplify the "deviance" that Americans of the mid-nineteenth century defined against the internalized strength of purpose and self-willed discipline that constituted the cultural ideal of "character." See Doan, *Miller Heresy,* 54–82, 144ff. On Spiritualism, deviancy, and insanity, see Moore, *White Crows,* 98–100, 133–38, and Swank, "The Unfettered Conscience," 176–77. An excellent discussion of concepts of insanity and deviance in antebellum America appears in Rothman, *Discovery of the Asylum,* 109–29.

90. *ST* 7 (May 15, 1858): 26; *SM* 1 (October 16, 1852): 1; Rabinowitz, *The Spiritual Self,* 174; O'Sullivan, "Harmony of Worlds," 64, 245, 250; Ronald G. Walters, *American Reformers 1815–1860* (New York: Hill and Wang, 1978), 171; Sunderland, *Psychology,* 117. On the problem of anarchy in Protestantism, see Waldo Beach, "Freedom and Authority in Protestant Ethics," 108–18.

6. The Structure of Spiritualist Practice

1. Edmonds and Dexter, *Spiritualism,* I: iii, 144, II: 128.

2. Ibid., II: xvii, 531.

3. CFWP (the quotation in the text is from p. 8).

4. The following discussion of the New York Circle is drawn largely from Isaacs, "A History," 93–103, and Hardinge, *Modern American Spiritualism,* 73ff.

5. Hardinge, *Modern American Spiritualism,* 73ff.

6. Capron, *Modern Spiritualism,* 252, 253; [Anonymous,] *A History of the Recent Developments in Spiritual Manifestations, in the City of Philadelphia; By a Member of the First Circle* (Philadelphia: G. S. Harris, 1851), 22, 23, 24.

7. *History of the Recent Developments,* 5, 25; *Spiritual Instructions Received at the Meetings of One of the Circles Formed in Philadelphia, for the Purpose of Investigating the Philosophy of Spiritual Intercourse* (Philadelphia: Harmonial Benevolent Association, 1852), 11; Capron, *Modern Spiritualism,* 264–66; Henck, *Spirit Voices.*

8. James T. Richardson, "An Oppositional and Generational Conceptualization of Cult," unpublished paper read at the annual meeting of the Association for the Sociology of Religion (New York, 1976), 7 (cited in Ellwood, *Alternative Altars,* 18); Roy Wallis, "Ideology, Authority, and the Development of Cultic Movements," *Social Research* 41 (1974): 299–327.

9. The blending of old and new forms is characteristic of all religious revitalization movements; see McLoughlin, *Revivals,* 19.

10. Ellwood, *Alternative Altars*, 19.

11. Uriah Clark, *Spiritualist Register* (Auburn, N.Y.: Uriah Clark, 1860), 5.

12. Hardinge, *Modern American Spiritualism*, 101, 171, 195, 337, 350ff., 404; *History of the Recent Developments*, 3, 25, 37–38; Clark, *Plain Guide*, 34; Isaacs, "A History," 122; Turner, *Without God*, 164.

13. See Neil Harris, *Humbug: The Art of P. T. Barnum* (Chicago: The University of Chicago Press, 1973).

14. On the commodification of religion and its appeal to Americans' taste for mass entertainment, see Moore, *Selling God: American Religion in the Marketplace of Culture* (New York: Oxford University Press, 1994). He discusses nineteenth-century Spiritualism as an example on 125–27.

15. Davis, *Spiritual Intercourse*, 97, 121; *Spiritual Instructions*, 4, 34–35; Edmonds and Dexter, *Spiritualism*, I: 353. Moore's denial that the "goal of attendance" at a circle was "to achieve a higher plane of spiritual awareness" ("The Occult Connection?" 150) is by no means true of all séance-goers.

16. Clark, *Plain Guide*, 240; Coggeshall, *The Signs of the Times*, 6ff., 12–13, 24, 26; Hardinge, *Modern American Spiritualism*, 135, 375–76, 560; idem, *On the Road or The Spiritual Investigator. A Complete Compendium of the Science, Religion, Ethics, and Various Methods of Investigating Spiritualism* (Melbourne: George Robertson, 1878), 46–50.

17. *History of the Recent Developments*, 22, 23; Hardinge, *Modern American Spiritualism*, 270, 295.

18. Hardinge, *Modern American Spiritualism*, 310, 312, 319.

19. Ibid., 316, 322, 325. On the Koons spirit room, see Moore, *White Crows*, 16, and Isaacs, "A History," 127–29.

20. Fuller, *Mesmerism*, 73–80 (the quotation comes from 73).

21. *ST* 6 (April 10, 1858): 407; Clark, *Plain Guide,* ix, 247–48. This view of the séance confirms Robert C. Fuller's suggestion that revivalism's experiential thrust did not disappear with the waning of the Second Great Awakening after the 1830s but rather assumed new forms in the 1840s and 1850s beyond the confines of Christian orthodoxy and the mainline denominations. See Fuller, *Mesmerism*, 81.

22. Hardinge, *Modern American Spiritualism*, 283–84. Revivalist Charles G. Finney's scientific approach to conversion was a similar attempt to reduce revivalism's explosive potential to order. On the connection between Spiritualism and revivalism, see Moore, *White Crows*, 50–51, and Isaacs, "A History, 218–21.

23. On the religous functions of the Victorian home, see McDannell, *The Christian Home in Victorian America*.

24. J. B. Packard and J. S. Loveland, *The Spirit Minstrel; A Collection of Hymns and Music, for the Use of Spiritualists, in Their Circles and Public Meetings*, 2nd ed. (Boston: Bela Marsh, 1856), 87; Spear, *Twenty Years*, 19; idem, *The Educator*, 61.

25. George Lawton discusses Spiritualist religious practice in *Drama of Life After Death*, 135–372. Lawton's concern was Spiritualist practice circa 1930, and some of the elements of Spiritualist practice he described developed well after the 1850s; still, many of the essential elements were established, or at least present in embryonic form, during the 1850s.

26. McLoughlin, *Revivals*, 19, 104; Fuller, *Mesmerism*, xii–xiii. The structural nature of the circle is suggested implicitly, though not discussed in detail, in Isaacs, "A History," 111, 211ff. Like Ellwood, I reject Ernst Troeltsch's contrast between the unstructured nature of "cult" religions and the highly structured nature of "church" religions. Although antebellum Spiritualism lacked the institutional organization and permanence of what Troeltsch would call "church" religions, it showed tendencies toward structure and "routinization of faith." See Ellwood, *Alternative Altars*, 17–18.

27. See, for example, *History of the Recent Developments,* 28–40; Davis, *Spiritual Intercourse,* 96–125; idem, *Present Age,* 75–76; Clark, *Plain Guide,* 72; *Spiritual Instructions.* This last set of instructions, published by one of the circles that appeared in Philadelphia in the wake of Circle A's success, closely resembles those offered by Circle A. It was sold not only in Philadelphia but also in New York, Baltimore, and Cincinnati.

28. Braude, *Radical Spirits,* 23–24; Edmonds and Dexter, *Spiritualism* II: 374; Isaacs, "A History," 111.

29. Rabinowitz, *The Spiritual Self,* 204; Edmonds and Dexter, *Spiritualism,* II: 504; Henck, *Spirit Voices,* 57, 78. Sandra Sizer Frankiel has argued (*California's Spiritual Frontiers,* 43) that the "present experience of community" and "sense of connectedness" Spiritualists sought through communion with spirits did not usually translate into "community in a strong sense among fellow believers" and that "spiritual development itself remained individualistic." While she correctly notes that they generally "fragmented into small groups with no central leadership," she overlooks the fact that community could be quite strong within these groups.

30. Capron, *Modern Spiritualism,* 252; Davis, *Spiritual Intercourse,* 98–99; Henck, *Spirit Voices,* 7; Packard and Loveland, *Spirit Minstrel,* 87, 88; CFWP, 33.

31. Ellwood, *Alternative Altars,* 20, 21, 36ff., 39; *Spiritual Instructions,* 12; Edmonds and Dexter, *Spiritualism,* I: 401, 412, 463; CFWP, 33; Braude, *Radical Spirits,* 57.

32. Henck, *Spirit Voices,* 7, 57; Braude, *Radical Spirits,* 23–24; *Spiritual Instructions,* 3–4; *History of the Recent Developments,* 31.

33. *Spiritual Instructions,* 7, 34–35; Edmonds and Dexter, *Spiritualism* I: 343–44, 348, 353, II: 247, 384ff.

34. *Spiritual Instructions,* 65; Henck, *Spirit Voices,* 7; Davis, *Spiritual Intercourse,* 97; *History of the Recent Developments,* 36; Edmonds and Dexter, *Spiritualism* I: 324, 343, II: 245–46; Isaacs, "A History," 120.

35. *History of the Recent Developments,* 24; *JSW,* 1:1:138; CFWP, 40; Davis, *Spiritual Intercourse,* 97; Moore, "The Occult Connection?" 139–40, 146–47, 154–55.

36. *Spiritual Instructions,* 8, 9, 60–61, 72, 73–74, 78, 84–85; *History of the Recent Developments,* 24; Moore, "The Occult Connection?" 150 (Moore admits, however, that Spiritualists often did adopt practices of secrecy; see 152–54, 155). Like the religious functions of the séance, those of the home combined private and public dimensions; see McDannell, *The Christian Home in Victorian America,* xiv, 46–47.

37. Davis, *Spiritual Intercourse,* 98.

38. Ibid., 96, 97; Clark, *Plain Guide,* 171; *Spiritual Instructions,* 80; Edmonds and Dexter, *Spiritualism,* I: 308–309, II: 120; Newton and Newton, *"Ministry of Angels" Realized,* 8. Properly reverential behavior was also an important element of domestic religion; see McDannell, *The Christian Home in Victorian America,* 81.

39. Davis, *Magic Staff,* 383; Spear, *The Educator,* 63; Clark, *Plain Guide,* 172; Davis, *Spiritual Intercourse,* 96; *History of the Recent Developments,* 28, 30; Braude, *Radical Spirits,* 23–24.

40. Davis, *Spiritual Intercourse,* 97, 98, 99.

41. Rabinowitz, *The Spiritual Self,* 157; Davis, *Spiritual Intercourse,* 105.

42. Edmonds and Dexter, *Spiritualism,* I: 129, 242.

43. Braude, *Radical Spirits,* 20; Edmonds and Dexter, *Spiritualism* II: 128, 208; *SC* I: 472–74; Rabinowitz, *The Spiritual Self,* 153–65. On the importance of prayer to domestic religion see McDannell, *The Christian Home in Victorian America,* 77–82.

44. George P. Fisher, *Life of Benjamin Silliman* (New York: Charles Scribner,

1866), 100; Hare, *Experimental Investigation,* 362; *The Rambles and Reveries of an Art-Student in Europe* (Philadelphia, Thomas T. Watts, 1855), 13–14.

45. D. M. Dewey, *History of the Strange Sounds,* 31; Packard and Loveland, *The Spirit Minstrel,* 6, 21, 43, 51, 58, 87; Henck, *Spirit Voices,* iii, 9, 38, 39, 63, 78, 91, 100. On the importance of hymn singing to domestic religion, see McDannell, *The Christian Home in Victorian America,* 82–83.

46. *Spiritual Instructions,* 13, 79.

47. Coggeshall, *The Signs of the Times,* 32; Hardinge, *Modern American Spiritualism,* 80; Hare, *Experimental Investigation,* 21–22; *A History of the Recent Developments,* 30.

48. Davis, *Spiritual Intercourse,* 100.

49. Coggeshall, *The Signs of the Times,* 74; CFWP, 33; *A History of the Recent Developments,* 69; Henck, *Spirit Voices,* 7; Edmonds and Dexter, *Spiritualism,* I: 343–44.

50. Edmonds and Dexter, *Spiritualism,* I: 309.

51. Ibid., I: 314–15, 318–19, II: 91. Moore has commented (*White Crows,* 21) on the "sober" and "subdued" tone of Edmonds's writings, and on the "humdrum" nature of his visions.

52. Edmonds and Dexter, *Spiritualism,* I: 268.

53. Otto criticized Spiritualism for its routinization of religious experience; see Otto, *The Idea of the Holy,* 27, 62.

54. Rabinowitz, *The Spiritual Self,* 30–32, 157–59, 166–77 (the quoted phrase appears on 175).

55. Ellwood, *Alternative Alters,* 27; Sheldon R. Isenberg and Dennis E. Owen, "Bodies, Natural and Contrived: The Work of Mary Douglas," *Religious Studies Review* 3 (1977): 7–8.

56. This point has been made by Ann Braude in *Radical Spirits,* 82–98. Comparing Spiritualist religious practices with those of shamanism, Michael O'Sullivan commented that the shaman is not merely a "teacher" but "the conduit by way of which supernatural sanctions or reproofs are received by the community from the world of spirits" ("Harmony of Worlds," 250).

57. *JSW,* 3:3:125; Ambler, *Elements,* 51–52; *ST* 3 (June 3, 1854): 17.

58. Spear, *The Educator,* 293–95.

59. Newton and Newton, *"Ministry of Angels" Realized,* 13.

60. Otto, *The Idea of the Holy,* 32–33; Ellwood, *Alternative Altars,* 52.

61. Fuller, *Mesmerism,* 71–72.

62. *SA* I (May 9, 1857): 7; Braude, *Radical Spirits,* 95; Moore, *White Crows,* 113.

63. Spear, *The Educator,* 421–22, 642; idem, *Twelve Discourses,* 43 (the brackets in the text are Spear's); *JSW,* 3:1:125.

64. Sunderland, *Human Nature,* 406, 407; Ellwood, *Alternative Altars,* 33.

65. Spear, *The Educator,* 155, 159, 501; Hewitt, *Messages,* 160; *PC* XIV (February 11, 1854): 82; Moore, "The Occult Connection?," 152–53.

66. *ST* 3 (September 30, 1854): 85; *ST* 8 (July 16, 1859): 138.

67. Davis, *Present Age,* 82–127; Spear, *Twenty Years,* 14–15, 25–26; Lehman, "Life of Spear," 119–21; Spear, *The Educator,* 131.

68. Hardinge, *Modern American Spiritualism,* 219–20.

69. *ST* 7 (November 20, 1858): 297; *ST* 7 (December 11, 1858): 324; *ST* 7 (December 18, 1858): 332; *ST* 7 (December 25, 1858): 346–47; Lehman, "Life of Spear," 230–32, 277–80.

70. On the erosion of patriarchal authority in America, see Jay Fliegelman, *Prodigals and Pilgrims: The American Revolution Against Patriarchal Authority 1750–1800* (New York: Cambridge University Press, 1982).

71. *JSW*, 1:1:237, 2:4:64, 2:4:between 170 and 171, 2:4:215–16, 2:4:219–21, 3:1:117, 3:2:5, 3:2:189, 3:2:191.

72. See Braude, *Radical Spirits,* especially ch. 4.

73. Spear, *The Educator,* 64, 421–22.

7. The Structure of Spiritualist Society

1. Davis, *Principles of Nature,* 2; idem, *Magic Staff,* 204–20; *SH* I (1851): 411; *PC* 16 (May 5, 1855): 2nd page; Tiffany, *Spiritualism Explained,* 150; *ST* 7 (January 22, 1859): 381.

2. On Spiritualism's anti-institutional thrust, see Moore, *White Crows,* 13–14, and Braude, *Radical Spirits,* 163–73.

3. *JSW,* 3:1:77.

4. Eliade has pointed out that mountains, like pillars, may serve as "cosmic axes" that link the natural and spiritual worlds; see *The Sacred and the Profane,* 37.

5. Davis, *Present Age,* 82–127.

6. Spear, *The Educator,* 43–44, 46, 59, 60–61, 128, 131; idem, *Twenty Years,* 3, 22, 25–26.

7. *ST* 3 (September 30, 1854): 85; Spear, *The Educator,* 55–56; Ellwood, *Alternative Altars,* 27–28. The tendency of religious democratization to produce demagoguery and tightly bound religious groups is central to Hatch's *Democratization.*

8. *ST* 4 (September 15, 1855): 79.

9. *SC* I: 447–48; *SC* II: 321; Clark, *Plain Guide,* 276.

10. Elkins, *Fifteen Years in the Senior Order of Shakers: A Narrative of Facts, Concerning that Singular People* (Hanover, N. H.: Dartmouth Press, 1853), 60; Edmonds and Dexter, *Spiritualism,* II: 313; *ST* 5 (June 7, 1856): 41–42.

11. *JSW,* 2:1:41; *NI* 2 (August 12, 1854): 2; Thomas L. Nichols, *Forty Years of American Life,* 2 vols. (London: J. Maxwell, 1864), II: 66. On the Nicholses' involvement with Spiritualism and their subsequent conversion to Catholicism, see Spurlock, *Free Love,* 196–201 (I have quoted from 198).

12. *ST* 8 (September 10, 1859): 235; Spear, *The Educator,* 341.

13. There were 95 organized Spiritualist churches in 1870 and 334 in 1890, but only 17 in 1860. These few were relatively small in membership and as a result so poor that they relied on rented space for their services. See Brown, "Spiritualism," 153ff.

14. This separation of the "ministerial" function from mediumship, which characterized both the Spiritualist church and the public Sunday meetings discussed in the following paragraph, tended to accompany the formalization of Spiritualist practice. First developing during the 1850s, it became increasingly pronounced in the late nineteenth century. By 1930, the distinction between the function of the minister or lecturer, who delivered the sermon and attended to the minor items in the ritual, and that of the medium (who was often considered an "associate minister") or "message bearer," was clear; see Lawton, *The Drama of Life After Death,* 205–206. Braude suggests an inverse relationship between the trend toward organization and the prestige of the medium; see *Radical Spirits,* 162–73. See also Brown, "Spiritualism," 153ff., who discusses the increasing rigidity of the qualifications for becoming a Spiritualist minister (158–59).

15. See Hardinge, *Modern American Spiritualism,* 148, 170, and Isaacs, "A History," 213–14.

16. On the Spiritualist camp, see Lawton, *The Drama of Life After Death,* 293ff.;

Braude, *Radical Spirits*, 173–75; and Moore, *White Crows*, 67 (the quotation is from Moore).

17. Clark, *Plain Guide*, 202.

18. Moore, *White Crows*, 14; *ST* 3 (October 14, 1854): 95; Lehman, "Life of Spear," 213, 232ff.; *ST* 3 (October 14, 1854): 93.

19. *ST* 3 (July 1, 1854): 34.

20. *ST* 3 (November 25, 1854): 117.

21. See Braude, "News from the Spirit World," 404.

22. Isaacs, "A History," 100–101; see *SH* I (1851): 102–104.

23. Race, too, probably became a basis for Spiritualist community; common sense would suggest the existence of numerous African-American circles. On blacks and Spiritualism, see Braude, *Radical Spirits*, 28–30.

24. Braude, "News," 410. The circulation figure for the *Telegraph* comes from Brown, *"Spiritualism,"* 107.

25. Braude, "News," 409.

26. Braude, *Radical Spirits*, 163.

27. On the Mountain Cove community, see Isaacs, "A History," 243–47; Capron, *Modern Spiritualism*, 117–31; John Humphrey Noyes, *American Socialisms*, 568–76; Hardinge, *Modern American Spiritualism*, 207–17; *Encyclopedia of Occultism and Parapsychology*, 2nd ed. (Detroit: Gale Research, 1984), s.v. "Mountain Cove"; ibid., s.v. "Apostolic Circle." Another valuable source is the *Mountain Cove Journal and Spiritual Harbinger*, published weekly from 12 August 1852 through 20 October 1853; it is quite scarce and I have not seen a complete run.

28. Centralized authoritarianism and libertarian individualism, according to Michael Fellman, constituted the theoretical "boundaries" of nineteenth-century American utopian culture; see *The Unbounded Frame: Freedom and Community in Nineteenth-Century Utopianism* (Westport, Conn.: Greenwood Press, 1973), 3–19. As advocates of both individualism and order, Spiritualists participated in the entire spectrum of communitarian practice; they were attracted to both the libertarian Modern Times community and the rule-laden Hopedale community. Still, it is significant that both well known Spiritualist communities of the 1850s, namely Mountain Cove and Kiantone (see following note), tended toward authoritarianism.

29. Michael Fellman, *The Unbounded Frame*; Isaacs, "A History," 238ff.; Carl J. Guarneri, *The Utopian Alternative*, 348–53. On Hopedale, see Ballou, *History of Hopedale*; Edward K. Spann, *Hopedale: From Commune to Company Town* (Columbus: Ohio State University Press, 1992); and Philip Sidney Padelford, "Adin Ballou and the Hopedale Community." On Modern Times, see Roger Wunderlich, *Low Living and High Thinking at Modern Times, New York*. The only other significant Spiritualist community of the antebellum period was Kiantone, started in 1854 by John Murray Spear in western Pennsylvania; see Lehman, "Life of Spear," 206–46; Perry, *Radical Abolitionism*, 221; Russell Duino, "Utopian Theme with Variations: John Murray Spear and his Kiantone Domain," *Pennsylvania History* 29 (1962), 140–50; Ernest C. Miller, "Utopian Communities in Warren County, Pennsylvania," *The Western Pennsylvania Historical Magazine* 49 (1966), 301–17; and Isaacs, "A History," 249–54.

30. See Klaus Hansen, *Mormonism*, 32, 113–46; Noyes, *American Socialisms*, 617, 636–638; Lawrence Foster, "Had Prophecy Failed? Contrasting Perspectives of the Millerites and Shakers," in Numbers and Butler, eds., *The Disappointed*, 178; Priscilla J. Brewer, *Shaker Communities, Shaker Lives* (Hanover, N. H.: University Press of New England, 1986), 115–35.

31. Ballou, *History of Hopedale*, 228; idem, *Exposition of Views*, 49, 220–21, 225; *ST* 1 (May 22, 1852): 3rd page; Ballou, *Practical Christian Socialism: A Conversa-*

tional Exposition of the True System of Human Society (New York: Fowlers and Wells, 1854), ix, 108; Padelford, "Adin Ballou and the Hopedale Community," 277–80; Braude, *Radical Spirits*, 63–64; Spurlock, *Free Love*, 108, 113.

32. Moore has correctly pointed out that Spiritualism "was not a formative influence" on most of those communitarians who welcomed it, but he neglects the distinct Spiritualist variety of communitarian activity; see *White Crows*, 97. Lehman ("Life of Spear," 126) recognized a distinct Spiritualist communitarianism in noting that Spear's community "differed from all but a few others in that it used the Spiritualist philosophy as the basis for its quest for the perfection of humanity," but he did not explore the relationship between Spiritualist communitarianism and Spiritualist ideology.

33. See Isaacs, "A History," 260. Neither Moore nor Braude, who focus on Spiritualism's anti-institutional nature, devotes much attention to Spiritualist communitarianism.

34. Albanese, "On the Matter of Spirit," 4.

35. Hardinge, *Modern American Spiritualism*, 58ff., 207–208.

36. CFWP, 4, 13, 15, 17.

37. On Scott, see his *A Journal of a Missionary Tour through Pennsylvania, Ohio, Indiana, Illinois, Iowa, Wiskonsin and Michigan* (1843; reprint, Ann Arbor: University Microfilms, 1966).

38. Published semi-monthly, the paper ran from 20 February 1851 through 23 September 1851. The quotations come, respectively, from *Spirit Rapping in England and America: Its Origin and History* (London: H. Vizetelly, 1853), 103, and Capron, *Modern Spiritualism*, 118.

39. Noyes, *American Socialisms*, 568–71.

40. *MCJ* 1 (December 30, 1852): 63; *MCJ* 1 (January 13, 1853): 67; Spear, *The Educator*, 69, 140. Most pieces in the *Journal* were not signed. I assume that most of its unsigned material was written either by Scott or Harris, or had at least been approved by them for publication.

41. Capron, *Modern Spiritualism*, 111; *MCJ* 1 (January 13, 1853): 67. The connection between Millerism and Mountain Cove has been briefly discussed in Michael Barkun, *Crucible of the Millennium: The Burned-Over District of New York in the 1840s* (Syracuse: Syracuse University Press, 1986), 45.

42. Thomas Lake Harris, *The Morality of Religion* (New York: Fowler and Wells, 1850), 4; *ST* 1 (May 15, 1852): 1; *MCJ* 1 (April 21, 1853): 99; *MCJ* 1 (September 23, 1852): 23. Communitarian culture involves a movement from idealistic conceptions of absolute truth to attempts to realize those conceptions in practice; see Fellman, *The Unbounded Frame*, xv, 3.

43. See Robert W. Delp, "The Southern Press and the Rise of American Spiritualism, 1847–1860," *Journal of American Culture* 7 (1985), 90.

44. Capron, *Modern Spiritualism*, 119, 121, 123–24; *ST* 1 (October 16, 1852): 4 (emphasis in original). Spear made similar claims to authority at Kiantone; see Perry, *Radical Abolitionism*, 220–21.

45. *ST* 2 (July 2, 1853): 35; *MCJ* 1 (January 13, 1853): 67.

46. Noyes likewise instructed his followers at Oneida that a communal spirit orchestrated by a strong leader (which he called a "medium") representing social unity and God's authority was essential to the success of his utopian experiment. "All assertions of individualism," says Fellman, "had to be subordinated to this collective spirit. Only the agreed upon primacy of the group will could guarantee communal survival. . . . Those who entered Noyes's communities had to surrender all claims to self-governance and to submit to the discipline of the dictatorially led group." At both Oneida and Mountain Cove, "spiritual relations" were to be substituted for "merely natural ones"; see Fellman, *The Unbounded Frame*, 50–51.

47. *MCJ* 1 (May 5, 1853): 98–99; Noyes, *American Socialisms,* 568–71.

48. Capron, *Modern Spiritualism,* 123–24, 128–29.

49. *MCJ* 1 (April 21, 1853): 99; his lecture was delivered in St. Louis in March 1853 and published as *Lecture on Spiritual Manifestations, Past, Present, and Future, Delivered in the People's Theater, Saint Louis, Mo., Sunday Evening, March 24, 1853* (Boston: George C. Rand, 1853).

50. *ST* 2 (July 2, 1853): 35.

51. The text of the May 1852 epistle appears in Capron, *Modern Spiritualism,* 124–27.

52. These powers are described in Revelation 11: 5–6. Hughes and Allen allude to this feature of American primitivism in Hughes and Allen, *Illusions of Innocence,* 103.

53. Capron, *Modern Spiritualism,* 130–31.

54. Hyatt was Capron's "informant"; see Hardinge, *Modern American Spiritualism,* 214–16. His periodical appeared semi-monthly between 5 June 1851 and 11 November 1851.

55. *ST* 1 (October 16, 1852): 4.

56. *ST* 1 (October 16, 1852): 4; *ST* 2 (July 2, 1853): 35.

57. *ST* 1 (October 16, 1852): 4; *ST* 2 (July 2, 1853): 35.

58. *ST* 2 (July 2, 1853): 35; *ST* 2 (August 6, 1853): 55; Noyes, *American Socialisms,* 567, 576. Other attempts to marginalize the Mountain Cove episode include Hardinge, *Modern American Spiritualism,* 207–13; Capron, *Modern Spiritualism,* 131; and *ST* 7 (November 13, 1858): 286. As we have seen, Spear was similarly marginalized. My argument against such attempts is similar to that in Lehman, "Life of Spear," 18.

59. Spear proved no better able to hold Kiantone together. Lehman has pointed to his authoritarian tendencies and to the tension at Kiantone between charismatic authority and individualism; see "Life of Spear," 358, 370, 383, 404, 456.

60. On Spiritualism's changing ideological content, see Braude, *Radical Spirits,* 162–91. Spiritualist communities of the post-Civil War years are discussed in Robert S. Fogarty, *All Things New: American Communes and Utopian Movements, 1860–1914* (Chicago: University of Chicago Press, 1990).

61. *ST* 3 (June 3, 1854): 17.

Conclusion

1. Moore, *White Crows,* 231; Hatch, *Democratization,* 222; Paul E. Johnson, "Democracy, Patriarchy, and American Revivals, 1780–1830," *Journal of Social History* 24 (summer 1991): 849.

2. Mary F. Davis, *Danger Signals: An Address on the Uses and Abuses of Modern Spiritualism* (New York: A. J. Davis, 1875), 28.

3. Braude, *Radical Spirits,* 162–73.

4. See ibid., 175, 181–82, and Brown, "Spiritualism," 192ff.

SELECTED BIBLIOGRAPHY

＋

Primary Sources

Newspapers and Periodicals

(only the years consulted are listed)
Banner of Light (Boston, 1857–59)
Buchanan's Journal of Man (Cincinnati, 1849–56)
Christian Spiritualist (New York, 1854–56)
Mountain Cove Journal and Spiritual Harbinger (Mountain Cove, Va., 1852–53)
New England Spiritualist (Boston, 1855–56)
New Era (Boston, 1853–56)
Nichols' Journal (New York, 1853–54)
Practical Christian (Hopedale, Mass., 1851–57)
Sacred Circle (New York, 1854–56)
Shekinah (Bridgeport, Conn., 1851–53)
Spirit Messenger (Springfield, Mass., 1850–53)
Spiritual Age (New York, 1857–59)
Spiritual Philosopher (Boston, 1850)
Spiritual Telegraph (and Fireside Preacher) (New York, 1852–59)
Univercoelum and Spiritual Philosopher (New York, 1847–49)

Books, Pamphlets, and Manuscript Collections

Adams, J. S. *A Letter to the Chestnut St. Congregational Church, Chelsea, Mass., in Reply to its Charge of Having Become a Reproach to the Cause of Truth, in Consequence of a Change in Religious Belief.* Boston: Bela Marsh, 1854.
———. *A Rivulet from the Ocean of Truth: An Authentic and Interesting Narrative of the Advancement of a Spirit from Darkness to Light.* Boston: Bela Marsh, 1854.
Ambler, R. P. *Elements of Spiritual Philosophy; Being an Exposition of Interior Principles.* Springfield, Mass.: R. P. Ambler, 1852.
———. *The Spiritual Teacher; Comprising a Series of Twelve Lectures on the Nature and Development of the Spirit.* New York: R. P. Ambler, 1852.
Ballou, Adin. *Autobiography of Adin Ballou.* William S. Heywood, ed. Lowell, Mass.: Vox Populi Press, 1896.
———. *An Exposition of Views Respecting the Principal Facts, Causes and Peculiarities Involved in Spirit Manifestations: Together with Interesting Phenomenal Statements and Communications.* Boston: Bela Marsh, 1852.
———. *Practical Christian Socialism: A Conversational Exposition of the True System of Human Society.* Hopedale, Mass.: Community Press, 1854.

Brittan, S. B. *A Discourse on War, or the Duties and Obligations of the Individual, as Connected with the Rights of the Civil Government.* Albany: J. Munsell, 1847.

Brittan, S. B., and B. W. Richmond, *A Discussion of the Facts and Philosophy of Ancient and Modern Spiritualism.* New York: Partridge and Brittan, 1853.

Buchanan, J. R. *Society As It Is and Society As It Should Be; Being a Report of Two Lectures, Delivered by Public Request, in the Tabernacle, cor. 7th and John Streets, Cincinnati, March 19–20, 1846.* Cincinnati: [n.p.], 1846.

Burns, J., ed. *Letters and Tracts on Spiritualism by Judge Edmonds.* London: J. Burns Progressive Library and Spiritual Institution, 1874.

Bush, George. *Mesmer and Swedenborg; or, the Relation of the Developments of Mesmerism to the Doctrines and Disclosures of Swedenborg.* New York: John Allen, 1847.

———. *Prof. Bush's Reply to Emerson on Swedenborg.* New York, 1846.

Capron, Eliab Wilkinson. *Modern Spiritualism: Its Facts and Fanaticisms, Its Consistencies and Contradictions.* New York: Partridge and Brittan; Boston: Bela Marsh, 1855.

——— and Henry D. Barron. *Singular Revelations. Explanations and History of the Mysterious Communion with Spirits, Comprehending the Rise and Progress of the Mysterious Noises in Western New York.* 2nd ed. Auburn, N.Y.: Capron and Barron, 1850.

Chase, Warren. *Forty Years on the Spiritual Rostrum.* Boston: Colby and Rich, 1888.

———. *The Gist of Spiritualism: Viewed Scientifically, Philosophically, Religiously, Politically, and Socially.* Boston: William White, 1865.

———. *The Life-Line of the Lone One; or, Autobiography of the World's Child.* Boston: Bela Marsh, 1857.

———. *Three Lectures on the Harmonial Philosophy.* Cleveland: L. E. Barnard, 1856.

Child, A. B. *ABC of Life.* Boston: William White, 1862.

———. *An Address to Christian Churches.* Boston: Bela Marsh, 1856.

———. *The Bouquet of Spiritual Flowers; Received Chiefly through the Mediumship of Mrs. J. S. Adams.* Boston: Bela Marsh, 1856.

———. *The Lily-Wreath of Spiritual Communications: Received Chiefly through the Mediumship of Mrs. J. S. Adams.* New York: Partridge and Brittan, 1855.

———. *The Progressive Life of Spirits After Death.* Boston: Bela Marsh, 1855.

———. *Whatever Is, Is Right.* Boston: Berry, Colby, 1860.

Clark, Uriah. *Plain Guide to Spiritualism.* 4th ed. Boston: William White, 1863.

———, ed. *The Spiritualist Register for 1859. Facts, Philosophy, Statistics of Spiritualism.* Auburn, N.Y.: U. Clark, 1859.

Coggeshall, William Turner. *The Signs of the Times: Comprising a History of the Spirit-Rappings in Cincinnati and Other Places.* Cincinnati: The Author, 1851.

Davis, Andrew Jackson. *Beyond the Valley; A Sequel to the Magic Staff: An Autobiography.* Boston, Colby and Rich, 1885.

———. *Death and the After-Life.* New York: A. J. Davis, 1866.

———. *The Great Harmonia.* 5 vols. 1850–59.

———. *The Harmonial Man; or, Thoughts for the Age.* Boston: Bela Marsh, 1853.

———. *The Magic Staff: An Autobiography.* New York: J. S. Brown, 1857.

———. *The Penetralia; Being Harmonial Answers to Important Questions.* Boston: Bela Marsh, 1856.

———. *The Philosophy of Special Providences: A Vision.* Boston: Bela Marsh, 1850.

———. *The Philosophy of Spiritual Intercourse: Being an Explanation of Modern Mysteries.* New York: Fowler and Wells, 1851.

———. *The Present Age and Inner Life; A Sequel to Spiritual Intercourse.* New York: Partridge and Brittan, 1853.

———. *The Principles of Nature, Her Divine Revelations, and a Voice to Mankind.* New York: S. S. Lyon and W. Fishbough, 1847.

Dewey, Dellon Marcus. *History of the Strange Sounds or Rappings, Heard in Rochester and Western New York, and Usually Called the Mysterious Noises!* Rochester, N.Y.: D. M. Dewey, 1850.

Edmonds, John W., and George T. Dexter. *Spiritualism.* 2 vols. New York: Partridge and Brittan, 1853–55.

Elkins, Hervey. *A Discourse on Modern Spiritualism, Delivered at Burlington, Vt., March 17, 1858.* Burlington, Vt.: Stacy, 1858.

Emerson, Ralph Waldo. "Swedenborg; or, the Mystic." In *Selected Essays, Lectures, and Poems of Ralph Waldo Emerson.* Ed. Robert E. Spiller. New York: Washington Square Press, 1965, 129–156.

Fish, William H. *Orthodoxy versus Spiritualism and Liberalism.* Hopedale, Mass.: Community Press, 1857.

Forster, Thomas Gales. *What Is Spiritualism?* Boston: William White, 1868.

Hallock, Robert T. *The Child and the Man: or, Anniversary Suggestions, by Dr. R.T. Hallock.* New York: Ellinwood and Hills, 1856.

———. *The Road to Spiritualism.* New York: Spiritual Telegraph Office, 1858.

Hammond, Charles. *Light from the Spirit World; The Pilgrimage of Thomas Paine, and Others, to the Seventh Circle in the Spirit World.* Rochester: D. M. Dewey, 1852.

———. *Philosophy of the Spirit World: Communicated by Spirits, through the Mediumship of Rev. Charles Hammond.* New York: Partridge and Brittan, 1853.

Hardinge [Britten], Emma. *Extemporaneous Addresses by Emma Hardinge.* London: T. Scott, 1866.

———. *Modern American Spiritualism. A Twenty Years' Record of the Communion Between Earth and the World of Spirits.* New York: The author, 1870.

———. *On the Road or The Spiritual Investigator. A Complete Compendium of the Science, Religion, Ethics, and Various Methods of Investigating Spiritualism.* Melbourne: George Robertson, 1878.

———. *Six Lectures on Theology and Nature.* [Chicago?]: n.p., 1860.

Hare, Robert. *Dr. Hare's Letter to the Episcopal Clergy, Most Respectfully Offering to Submit to Their Consideration, New and Irrefragable Evidence of Human Immortality; To Which Is Subjoined a Brief Sketch of the Spirit-World, and of the Moral Influence of Spiritualism; Also, Heaven and Hell, as Described by Scripture and by Spiritualism, Contrasted.* New York: Partridge and Brittan, 1855.

———. *Experimental Investigation of the Spirit Manifestations, Demonstrating the Existence of Spirits and Their Communion with Mortals.* New York: Partridge and Brittan, 1855.

———. *Lecture on Spiritualism, Delivered Before an Audience of Three Thousand, at the Tabernacle, in the City of New York, in November, 1855, Comprising an Account of the Manifestations which Induced the Author's Conversion to Spiritualism, and Confirmed His Hope of Immortality.* New York: Partridge and Brittan, 1855.

Harris, Thomas Lake. *Lecture on Spiritual Manifestations, Past, Present, and Future, Delivered in the People's Theater, Saint Louis, Mo., Sunday Evening, March 24, 1853.* Boston: George C. Rand, 1853.

———. *The Morality of Religion.* New York: Fowlers and Wells, 1850.

Hatch, Cora. *A Discourse on Faith, Hope, and Love. Delivered in New York, Sunday, April 23, 1857: To Which Is Added a Report of a Philosophical Investigation of the Nature of Mediumship.* New York: B. F. Hatch, 1858.

———. *A Discourse on the Immutable Decrees of God, and the Free Agency of Man, Delivered in the City Hall, Newburyport, Mass., Sunday, November 22nd, 1857.* New York: B. F. Hatch, 1858.

———. *Lecture by Mrs. Cora Hatch on the Nature of the Life After Death and a Description of the Spiritual World.* Syracuse: [n.p., 1857].

Henck, E. C. *Spirit Voices: Odes, Dictated by Spirits of the Second Sphere, for the Use of Harmonial Circles.* Philadelphia: G. D. Henck, 1853.

Hewitt, S. C. *Messages from the Superior State; Communicated from John Murray, through John M. Spear.* Boston: Bela Marsh, 1853.

Higginson, Thomas Wentworth. *The New Revolution: A Speech Before the American Anti-Slavery Society, at Their Annual Meeting in New York, May 12, 1857.* Boston: R. F. Wallcut, 1857.

———. *The Rationale of Spiritualism. Being Two Extemporaneous Lectures Delivered at Dodworth's Hall, December 5, 1858.* New York: T. J. Ellinwood, 1859.

———. *The Results of Spiritualism, A Discourse, Delivered at Dodworth's Hall, Sunday, March 6, 1859.* New York: S. T. Munson, 1859.

———. *The Unitarian Autumnal Convention, A Sermon by Thomas Wentworth Higginson.* Boston: Benjamin B. Mussey, 1853.

A History of the Recent Developments in Spiritual Manifestations, in the City of Philadelphia; By a Member of the First Circle. Philadelphia: G. S. Harris, 1851.

Newton, A. E. *Tracts on Spiritualism.* Boston: Bela Marsh, [186-?].

Newton, A. E., and Sarah J. Newton. *Answer to Charges of Belief in Modern Revelations, Etc., Given Before the Edwards Congregational Church, Boston, by Mr. and Mrs. A. E. Newton.* Boston: Bela Marsh, 1856.

———. *The "Ministry of Angels" Realized. A Letter to the Edwards Congregational Church, Boston.* 3rd ed. Boston: A. E. Newton, 1853.

Packard, J. B., and J. S. Loveland, *The Spirit Minstrel; A Collection of Hymns and Music, for the Use of Spiritualists, in Their Circles and Public Meetings.* 2nd ed. Boston: Bela Marsh, 1856.

Post, Isaac. *Voices from the Spirit World, Being Communications from Many Spirits, by the Hand of Isaac Post, Medium.* Rochester: C. H. McDonell, 1852.

Spear, John Murray. *The Educator: Being Suggestions, Theoretical and Practical, Designed to Promote Man-Culture and Integral Reform with a View to the Ultimate Establishment of a Divine Social State on Earth.* A. E. Newton, ed. Boston: Office of Practical Spiritualists, 1857.

———. *Twelve Discourses on Government: Purporting to Have Been Delivered in Boston, Mass., December 1853, by Thomas Jefferson, of the Spirit World, through John M. Spear, Medium.* Hopedale, Mass.: Community Press, 1857.

———. *Twenty Years on the Wing. Brief Narrative of My Travels and Labors as a Missionary Sent Forth and Sustained by the Association of Beneficents in Spirit Land.* Boston: William White, 1873.

Spiritual Instructions Received at the Meetings of One of the Circles Formed in Philadelphia, for the Purpose of Investigating the Philosophy of Spiritual Intercourse. Philadelphia: Harmonial Benevolent Association, 1852.

Sunderland, LaRoy. *Book of Human Nature: Illustrating the Philosophy (New Theory) of Instinct, Nutrition, Life; with their Correlative and Abnormal Phenomena, Physiological, Mental, Spiritual.* New York: Stearns, 1853.

———. *Book of Psychology.* New York: Stearns, 1852.

———. *Pathetism: Man Considered in Respect to His Form, Life, Sensation, Soul, Mind, Spirit.* Boston: White and Potter, 1847.

Tiffany, Joel. *Spiritualism Explained: Being a Series of Twelve Lectures Delivered Before the New York Conference of Spiritualists, by Joel Tiffany, in January, 1856.* 2nd ed. New York: Graham and Ellinwood, 1856.

Williams, John Shoebridge. *An Address to the Officers and Citizens of the United States, Recomending a Manifestation in Favor of the Bible.* Baltimore, Sherwood, 1854.

———. Manuscripts on Spiritualism. State Historical Society of Wisconsin.

———. *Nature and the Bible Have One Author, Demonstrated by Their Coincidences and Common Sense, Without Reference to History or the Opinions of Men.* Cincinnati: Wrightson, 1861.

———. *The Patriarchal Order, or True Brotherhood.* Cincinnati: Longley Bros., 1855.

———. *Three Pamphlets Bound Together.* Cincinnati: U. P. James, 1857.

Secondary Sources

Ahlstrom, Sydney E. *A Religious History of the American People.* New Haven: Yale University Press, 1972.

Albanese, Catherine L. *Nature Religion in America: From the Algonkian Indians to the New Age.* Chicago: University of Chicago Press, 1990.

———. "On the Matter of Spirit: Andrew Jackson Davis and the Marriage of God and Nature." *Journal of the American Academy of Religion* 60 (1992): 1–17.

Barrow, Logie. *Independent Spirits: Spiritualism and English Plebeians, 1850–1910.* London: Routledge and Kegan Paul, 1986.

———. "Socialism and Eternity: The Ideology of Plebeian Spiritualists, 1853–1913." *History Workshop Journal* 9 (1980): 37–69.

Beach, Waldo. "Freedom and Authority in Protestant Ethics." *Journal of Religion* 32 (1952): 108–18.

Bednarowski, Mary Farrell. *New Religions and the Theological Imagination in America.* Bloomington: Indiana University Press, 1989.

———. "Nineteenth-Century American Spiritualism: An Attempt at a Scientific Religion." Ph.D. diss., University of Minnesota, 1973.

———. "Spiritualism in Wisconsin in the Nineteenth Century." *Wisconsin Magazine of History* 59 (1975): 2–19.

Bitton, Davis. "Mormonism's Encounter with Spiritualism." *Journal of Mormon History* 1 (1974): 39–50.

Block, Marguerite Beck. *The New Church in the New World: A Study of Swedenborgianism in America.* New York: Holt, Rinehart, and Winston, 1932.

Braude, Ann. "News from the Spirit World: A Checklist of American Spiritualist

Periodicals, 1847–1900." *Proceedings of the American Antiquarian Society* 99 (Oct. 1989): 399–462.

———. *Radical Spirits: Spiritualism and Women's Rights in Nineteenth-Century America.* Boston: Beacon Press, 1989.

———. "Spirits Defend the Rights of Women: Spiritualism and Changing Sex Roles in Nineteenth-Century America." In *Women, Religion, and Social Change.* Ed. Ellison Findly and Yvonne Haddad. Albany: State University of New York Press, 1985, 419–31.

Brewer, Priscilla J. *Shaker Communities, Shaker Lives.* Hanover, N.H.: University Press of New England, 1986.

Broadway, J. William. "Universalist Participation in the Spiritualist Movement of the Nineteenth Century." *Proceedings of the Unitarian Universalist Historical Society* 19, part I (1980–81): 1–15.

Brown, Burton Gates. "Spiritualism in Nineteenth-Century America." Ph.D. diss., Boston University, 1972.

Brown, Slater. *The Heyday of Spiritualism.* New York: Hawthorn Books, 1970.

Butler, Jon. "The Dark Ages of American Occultism, 1760–1848." In *The Occult in America: New Historical Perspectives.* Ed. Howard Kerr and Charles L. Crow. Urbana: University of Illinois Press, 1983, 58–78.

———. *Awash in a Sea of Faith: Christianizing the American People.* Cambridge: Harvard University Press, 1990.

Carroll, Bret E. "Spiritualism and Community in Antebellum America: The Mountain Cove Episode." *Communal Societies* 12 (1992): 20–39.

———. "The Religious Construction of Masculinity in Victorian America: The Male Mediumship of John Shoebridge Williams." *Religion and American Culture: A Journal of Interpretation* 7 (Winter 1997): 27–60.

———. "Unfree Spirits: Spiritualism and Religious Authority in Antebellum America." Ph.D. diss., Cornell University, 1991.

Cross, Whitney. *The Burned-Over District: The Social and Intellectual History of Enthusiastic Religion in Western New York, 1800–1850.* Ithaca, N.Y.: Cornell University Press, 1950.

Cuthbert, Arthur A. *The Life and World-Work of Thomas Lake Harris.* New York: AMS Press, 1975.

Darnton, Robert. *Mesmerism and the End of the Enlightenment in France.* Cambridge: Harvard University Press, 1968.

de Grazia, Sebastian. "The Principle of Authority in Its Relation to Freedom." *Educational Forum* 15 (1951): 145–55.

Delp, Robert. "American Spiritualism and Social Reform, 1847–1900." *Northwest Ohio Quarterly* 44 (Fall 1972): 85–99.

———. "Andrew Jackson Davis and Spiritualism." In *Pseudo-Science and Society in Nineteenth-Century America.* Ed. Arthur Wrobel. Lexington: University Press of Kentucky, 1987, 100–21.

———. "Andrew Jackson Davis: Prophet of American Spiritualism." *Journal of American History* 54 (1967): 43–56.

———. "Andrew Jackson Davis's *Revelations,* Harbinger of American Spiritualism." *New York Historical Society Quarterly* 55 (1971): 211–34.

———. "The Harmonial Philosopher: Andrew Jackson Davis and the Foundation of

Modern American Spiritualism." Ph.D. diss., George Washington University, 1965.

———. "The Southern Press and the Rise of American Spiritualism, 1847–1860." *Journal of American Culture* 7 (1985): 88–95.

Doan, Ruth Alden. "Millerism and Evangelical Culture." In *The Disappointed: Millerism and Millenarianism in the Nineteenth Century*. Ed. Ronald L. Numbers and Jonathan M. Butler. Bloomington: Indiana University Press, 1987, 118–38.

———. *The Miller Heresy, Millennialism, and American Culture*. Philadelphia: Temple University Press, 1987.

Douglas, Ann. *The Feminization of American Culture*. New York: Alfred A. Knopf, 1977.

———. "Heaven Our Home: Consolation Literature in the Northern United States, 1830–1880." *American Quarterly* 26 (1974): 496–515.

Duino, Russell. "Utopian Theme with Variations: John Murray Spear and His Kiantone Domain." *Pennsylvania History* 29 (1962): 140–50.

Ekirch, Arthur. *The Idea of Progress in America, 1815–1860*. New York: Columbia University Press, 1944.

Ellwood, Robert S., Jr. *Alternative Altars: Unconventional and Eastern Spirituality in America*. Chicago: University of Chicago Press, 1979.

———. "The American Theosophical Synthesis." In *The Occult in America: New Historical Perspectives*. Ed. Howard Kerr and Charles L. Crow. Urbana: University of Illinois Press, 1983, 111–34.

Farrell, James J. *Inventing the American Way of Death*. Philadelphia: Temple University Press, 1980.

Fellman, Michael. *The Unbounded Frame: Freedom and Community in Nineteenth-Century American Utopianism*. Westport, Conn.: Greenwood Press, 1973.

Foster, Lawrence. "Had Prophecy Failed? Contrasting Perspectives of the Millerites and Shakers." In *The Disappointed: Millerism and Millenarianism in the Nineteenth Century*. Ed. Ronald L. Numbers and Jonathan M. Butler. Bloomington: Indiana University Press, 1987, 173–88.

Frankiel, Sandra Sizer. *California's Spiritual Frontiers: Religious Alternatives in Anglo-Protestantism, 1850–1910*. Berkeley: University of California Press, 1988.

Fuller, Robert C. *Mesmerism and the American Cure of Souls*. Philadelphia: University of Pennsylvania Press, 1982.

Goldfarb, Russell M. and Clare R. Goldfarb. *Spiritualism and Nineteenth-Century Letters*. Rutherford, N.J.: Fairleigh Dickinson University Press, 1978.

Guarneri, Carl. *The Utopian Alternative: Fourierism in Nineteenth-Century America*. Ithaca, N.Y.: Cornell University Press, 1991.

Hansen, Klaus. *Mormonism and the American Experience*. Chicago: University of Chicago Press, 1981.

Hatch, Nathan O. *The Democratization of American Christianity*. New Haven: Yale University Press, 1989.

Higham, John. *From Boundlessness to Consolidation: The Tranformation of American Culture, 1848–1860*. Ann Arbor: William L. Clements Library, 1969.

Homer, Michael W. "Spiritualism and Mormonism: Some Thoughts on Similarities and Differences." *Dialogue: A Journal of Mormon Thought* 27 (1994): 171–94.

Hovenkamp, Herbert. *Science and Religion in America, 1800–1860*. Philadelphia: University of Pennsylania Press, 1978.

Isaacs, Ernest Joseph. "A History of Nineteenth-Century American Spiritualism as a Religious and Social Movement." Ph.D. diss., University of Wisconsin, 1975.

———. "The Fox Sisters and American Spiritualism." In *The Occult in America: New Historical Perspectives*. Ed. Howard Kerr and Charles L. Crow. Urbana: University of Illinois Press, 1983, 79–110.

Judah, J. Stillson. *The History and Philosophy of the Metaphysical Movements in America*. Philadelphia: Westminster Press, 1967.

Kerr, Howard. *Mediums, Spirit-Rappers, and Roaring Radicals: Spiritualism in American Literature, 1850–1900*. Urbana: University of Illinois Press, 1972.

——— and Charles L. Crow, eds. *The Occult in America: New Historical Perspectives*. Urbana: University of Illinois Press, 1983.

Lawton, George. *The Drama of Life After Death: A Study of the Spiritualist Religion*. New York: Henry Holt, 1932.

Lehman, Neil B. "The Life of John Murray Spear: Spiritualism and Reform in Antebellum America." Ph.D. diss., Ohio State University, 1973.

Lewis, I. M. *Ecstatic Religion*. Hammondsworth: Penguin Books, 1971.

McDannell, Colleen. *The Christian Home in Victorian America, 1840–1900*. Bloomington: Indiana University Press, 1986.

——— and Bernhard Lang. *Heaven: A History*. New Haven: Yale University Press, 1988.

Miller, Ernest C. "Utopian Communities in Warren County, Pennsylvania." *The Western Pennsylvania Historical Magazine* 49 (1966): 301–17.

Moore, R. Laurence. *In Search of White Crows: Spiritualism, Parapsychology, and American Culture*. New York: Oxford University Press, 1977.

———. *Religious Outsiders and the Making of Americans*. New York: Oxford University Press, 1986.

———. "Spiritualism and Science: Reflections on the First Decade of the Spirit Rappings." *American Quarterly* 24 (1972): 474–500.

———. "The Occult Connection? Mormonism, Christian Science, and Spiritualism." In *The Occult in America: New Historical Perspectives*. Ed. Howard Kerr and Charles L. Crow. Urbana: University of Illinios Press, 1983, 135–61.

Nelson, Geoffrey K. *Spiritualism and Society*. London: Routledge and Kegan Paul, 1969.

Noyes, John Humphrey. *History of American Socialisms*. New York: J. P. Lippincott, 1870.

Oppenheim, Janet. *The Other World: Spiritualism and Psychical Research in England, 1850–1914*. New York: Cambridge University Press, 1985.

O'Sullivan, Michael A. "A Harmony of Worlds: Spiritualism and the Quest for Community in Nineteenth-Century America." Ph.D. diss., University of Southern California, 1981.

Owen, Alex. *The Darkened Room: Women, Power, and Spiritualism in Late Victorian England*. Philadelphia: University of Pennsylvania Press, 1990.

Perry, Lewis. *Radical Abolitionism: Anarchy and the Government of God in Antislavery Thought*. Ithaca, N.Y.: Cornell University Press, 1973.

Podmore, Frank. *Modern Spiritualism: A History and a Criticism*. 2 vols. London: Methuen, 1902.

Prothero, Stephen. "From Spiritualism to Theosophy: 'Uplifting' a Democratic Tradition." *Religion and American Culture* 3 (1993): 197–216.

Rabinowitz, Richard. *The Spiritual Self in Everyday Life: The Transformation of Personal Religious Experience in Nineteenth-Century New England.* Boston: Northeastern University Press, 1989.

Rothman, David J. *The Discovery of the Asylum: Social Order and Disorder in the New Republic.* Boston: Little, Brown, 1971.

Saum, Lewis O. *The Popular Mood of Pre–Civil War America.* Westport, Conn.: Greenwood Press, 1980.

Schneider, Herbert and George Lawton, *A Prophet and a Pilgrim.* New York: Columbia University Press, 1942.

Sollors, Werner. "Dr. Benjamin Franklin's Celestial Telegraph, or Indian Blessings to Gas-Lit American Drawing Rooms." *American Quarterly* 35 (1983): 459–80.

Spirit Rapping in England and America: Its Origin and History. London: H. Vizetelly, 1853.

Spurlock, John C. *Free Love: Marriage and Middle-Class Radicalism in America, 1825–1860.* New York: New York University Press, 1988.

Stein, Stephen J. "Liberty, Equality, and Community: Shakerism and Republicanism in the Early Republic." Unpublished paper presented at 1991 annual meeting of the Organization of American Historians, Louisville, Kentucky.

———. *The Shaker Experience in America.* New Haven: Yale University Press, 1992.

———. "Shaker Gift and Shaker Order: A Study of Religious Tension in Nineteenth-Century America." *Communal Societies* 10 (1990): 102–13.

Swank, Scott Trego. "The Unfettered Conscience: A Study of Sectarianism, Spiritualism, and Social Reform in the New Jerusalem Church, 1840–1870." Ph.D. diss., University of Pennsylvania, 1970.

Thomas, John L. "Antislavery and Utopia." In *The Antislavery Vanguard: New Essays on the Abolitionists.* Ed. Martin Duberman. Princeton: Princeton University Press, 1965, 240–69.

———. "Romantic Reform in America, 1815–1865." *American Quarterly* 17 (1965): 656–81.

Turner, James. *Without God, Without Creed: The Origins of Unbelief in America.* Baltimore: Johns Hopkins University Press, 1985.

Tyler, Alice Felt. *Freedom's Ferment: Phases of American Social History from the Colonial Period to the Outbreak of the Civil War.* Minneapolis: University of Minnesota Press, 1944.

Walters, Ronald G. *American Reformers, 1815–1860.* New York: Hill and Wang, 1978.

Welter, Barbara. "The Feminization of American Religion: 1800–1860." In *Clio's Consciousness Raised: New Perspectives on the History of Women,* ed. Mary S. Hartman and Lois Banner. New York: Octagon Books, 1976.

Wilson, John B. "Emerson and the 'Rochester Rappings.'" *New England Quarterly* 41 (1968): 248–58.

Zwelling, Shomer. "Spiritualist Perspectives on Antebellum Experience." *Journal of Psychohistory* 10 (1982): 3–25.

INDEX

✛

Abzug, Robert A., 184*n*28

Adams, John Quincy, 3

Adams, John S., 49, 50, 60, 78, 79, 84, 109; withdrawal from Congregational church, 48

African Americans: and Spiritualism, 205*n*23

Ahlstrom, Sydney, 6, 26

Albanese, Catherine L., 61, 69, 164, 191*n*2, 191*n*6, 192*n*11, 192*n*16, 199*n*68

agnosticism, 88

Albro, Stephen, 35

Ambler, R.P., 40, 41, 45, 47, 55, 67, 95, 97, 101, 110, 144

American Association for the Advancement of Science (AAAS): response to Spiritualism, 70

American Revolution, 3, 35, 116; meaning for Spiritualists, 9, 36, 52–53, 54–55, 177

Andrews, Stephen Pearl, 163

Arnold, Matthew, 76

atheism, 88, 111, 127

Auburn Circle, 166, 168, 169, 170, 172

Bacon, Francis, 97, 120, 142; symbolic meaning to Spiritualists, 67–68, 141

Baconianism, 28, 186*n*29. *See also* empiricism

Ballou, Adin, 41, 47, 64, 68, 78, 79, 90, 99, 117, 147, 152, 154, 161, 194*n*40; and Hopedale community, 42–43, 55, 102, 152, 163, 164; biographical background, 42–43, 47, 97; conversion to Spiritualism, 42–43, 97

Barkun, Michael, 102

Barnum, P.T., 125

Barrett, B.F., 31, 32

Barrow, Logie, 12

Bednarowski, Mary Farrell, 6, 88, 181*n*9, 182*n*10

Benedict, Ann, 166, 168, 169, 170

Bercovitch, Sacvan, 181*n*10

Braude, Ann, 11, 14, 21, 47, 57, 150, 182*n*10, 182*n*13, 190*n*36, 191*n*58, 204*n*14, 206*n*33

Brisbane, Albert, 20

Brittan, Samuel Byron, 9, 35–36, 40, 49, 67, 79, 87, 96, 99, 103, 106, 121, 145, 152, 157; as Spiritualist editor and publicist, 70, 121–22, 161; biographical background, 20, 47; break with Spiritualism, 179; conversion to Spiritualism, 20; early involvement with Spiritualism, 19–20

Brown, Mrs. H.F.M., 161

Brownson, Orestes, 81, 194*n*47

Buchanan, Joseph Rodes, 27, 58, 113; biographical background, 111; investigation of Spiritualism, 111–12

Bush, George, 108–109, 113; belief in spirit communication, 29; critique of Spiritualism, 32, 78; early enthusiasm for Spiritualism, 20, 32

Bushnell, Horace, 62

Bushnell, Mrs. G.B., 139

Butler, Jon, 4, 8, 10, 13

Calvinism, 21, 93; Spiritualists' opposition to, 45, 75; Spiritualism's resemblance to, 101

Capron, Eliab Wilkinson, 55, 166, 168, 169, 207*n*54; early involvement with Spiritualism, 55

Catholicism, 166; Spiritualists' aversion to, 40, 57, 79, 81, 156, 176; Spiritualism's resemblance to, 79–81; Spiritualists' attraction to, 80–81, 156, 194n.47, 197n.35

character, 200*n*89; Spiritualists' concern with, 113–15

Chase, Warren, 43, 53, 57, 83, 91, 106, 117; activities of, 57, 104–105; attraction to Spiritualism, 104–105; biographical background, 21, 57, 103–104; conversion to Spiritualism, 104

Child, Asaph Bemis, 77, 78, 82, 88, 90, 91

Christianity, 4, 17, 21, 24, 32, 39, 40, 42, 43, 55, 58, 62, 70, 85, 100, 105, 107, 115, 201*n*21; Spiritualism as expression of, 8–10, 19, 40, 44, 110, 137–39, 157, 167. *See also* Christian Spiritualism

"Christian" movement, 43, 45, 46, 197*n*35

Christian Science, 10, 123, 179, 192*n*16. *See*

ences of, 72, 73, 116, 141–42

Edmonds, Laura, 83, 120, 132

electricity, 70, 102, 106, 111, 112, 127, 198*n*58; and Spiritualist conceptions of deity, 68–69; and Spiritualist cosmology, 68–69, 132; and Spiritualist religious ritual, 135–37, 140

Eliade, Mircea, 10, 67, 198*n*58, 204*n*4

Elkins, Hervey, 155

Ellwood, Robert S., 81, 123, 144, 145, 185*n*15, 194–95*n*52, 201*n*26

Emerson, Ralph Waldo, 29, 39, 51, 54, 59, 119, 193*n*27; attitude toward Spiritualism, 28; interpretation of Swedenborg, 26–28

empiricism, 2, 11, 27–28, 66, 110–11, 137, 141, 143. *See also* Baconianism

Enlightenment, 2, 9, 17, 18, 19, 87, 88

ether, concept of, 68; and Spiritualist cosmology, 68, 70

evangelicalism, 49, 98, 111, 127, 189*n*30. *See also* revivalism; Second Great Awakening

Evans, Frederick W., 155, 185*n*15. *See also* Shakers

"excursus" religion: Spiritualism as example of, 81, 84, 88, 131, 144, 147

Fellman, Michael, 205*n*28, 206*n*46

Finney, Charles G., 112, 137, 141, 201*n*22

First Harmonial Association of New York, 179

Fish, William, 41, 42, 47

Fishbough, William, 20, 21, 42

Fourier, Charles, 18, 20, 163, 165

Fourierism, 130; contribution to Spiritualist ideology, 18–19. *See also* Fourier, Charles

Fowler family, 121

Fox, George, 52, 147

Fox sisters, 3, 21, 28, 44, 47, 51, 55, 121, 125, 138, 166

Frankiel, Sandra S., 103, 202*n*29

Franklin, Benjamin, 93, 94; symbolic meaning for Spiritualists, 37, 38, 68, 69, 192–93*n*22

Fuller, Robert C., 43, 110, 111, 145, 199*n*71, 201*n*21

Garrett, Clarke, 46

Garrison, William Lloyd, 57–58

Geertz, Clifford, 62, 182*n*11

Gender, 191*n*58, 199*n*81; and Spiritualist communitarianism, 169–70; and Spiritualist concept of selfhood, 115; and Spiritualist cosmology, 64–65, 94,115, 135, 150; and Spiritualist religious ritual, 135, 136; and Spiritualists' conception of spirits, 84, 90–94, 100–101

Giles, Chauncey, 30

Goffman, Erving, 195*n*55

Gray, John B., 121

Gray, John F., 98, 128

Greene, Harriet N., 90, 161

Grimes, James Stanley, 19

Hall, Abby T., 38, 82–83, 88, 91, 101, 110, 120

Hallock, Robert T., 37, 38, 40, 45, 49, 53, 87, 121

Halttunen, Karen, 114

Hammond, Charles, 44, 45, 47, 60, 83, 93, 138

Hansen, Klaus, 193*n*36

Hardinge, Emma, 54, 60–61, 68, 82, 99, 100, 122, 128, 139, 148, 157, 164, 176; as Spiritualist historian, 8, 22, 126; biographical background, 126; conversion to Spiritualism, 126

Hare, Robert, 54, 68, 73–74, 75, 76, 82, 94, 114, 138, 139, 143; scientific background, 70, 193*n*25; scientific investigation of Spiritualism, 28, 69–71

Harmonial Benevolent Society of Philadelphia, 122, 132, 158

harmonial religion, 6, 130, 140

harmonial philosophy, 20, 21, 32, 121–22, 166, 179; emergence of, 19

Harris, Thomas Lake, 53, 57, 144, 161; and Mountain Cove community, 32, 162, 164, 166, 167, 168, 169, 171, 172, 173, 174, 175, 176, 206*n*40, 207*n*49; biographical background, 20–21, 32, 47, 166; early involvement with Spiritualism, 20–21, 32, 166

Hatch, Cora, 64, 78, 96, 146, 157

Hatch, Nathan O., 25, 54, 76, 147, 182*n*13

healing, spiritual, 18, 19, 20, 101, 105, 109, 110, 112–13, 148

heaven: conceptions of, 88–89, 191–92*n*6, 193*n*28

Hecker, Isaac, 81, 194*n*47

hell: rejected by Spiritualists, 22, 78, 128; Swedenborg's conception of, 18

Henck, E.C., 123

Hewitt, Simon Crosby, 47, 106, 158, 161

Heywood, William S., 38, 41, 102

leadership in, 169–70; property arrangements in, 170–71, 174; spirits' perceived role in, 168–69, 172–73; Spiritualists' criticisms of, 164, 173, 175

Mountain Cove Journal and Spiritual Harbinger, 167, 168, 173, 205*n*27, 206*n*40

mysticism, 10, 19, 112–13; Spiritualist mediumship distinguished from, 110, 142; Spiritualist mediumship compared to, 110–11, 199*n*68

National Association of Spiritualists (NAS), 178

natural law, 2, 9, 19, 36, 37, 77, 79, 82, 86, 87, 138; applied to spirit world, 65–71

nature, Spiritualist concept of, 26, 65–67, 86, 192*n*11

Neoplatonism, 62

"nature religion," 61, 69, 191*n*2, 192*n*16

New Church: *see* Church of the New Jerusalem

New Era, 92, 93, 161

New Era movement, 46; and spirit communication, 31, 32–33; attitude toward Spiritualism, 33; compared with Spiritualism, 31–32; contrasted with Spiritualism, 32–33

"new motor," 106–107, 117, 135, 153

New Thought, 10

Newton, Alonzo E., 27, 43, 85, 87, 90, 94–95, 97, 106, 109, 135, 145, 158, 161; withdrawal from Congregational church, 48–49, 85

Newton, Isaac, 68, 94

Newton, Sarah, 85, 94–95, 106; withdrawal from Congregational church, 48–49, 85

New York Circle, 122, 123, 130, 133; activities of, 121–22, 134; formation of, 121

New York Spiritualist Association, 179

New York Spiritual Conference, 53, 56, 87, 98, 190*n*47; formation of, 121

Nichols, Mary Gove, 44, 80, 156

Nichols, Thomas Lowe, 44, 80, 156

Nord, David, 159

North American Fourierist Phalanx, 104

Noyes, John Humphrey, 52; attitude toward spirit communication, 163; compared with Spiritualist mediums, 150, 206*n*46; criticism of Mountain Cove community, 175

Oneidans, 9, 46, 163, 206*n*46. *See also* Noyes, John Humphrey

Oppenheim, Janet, 11

organization: Spiritualists' attitude toward, 7, 39–40, 123, 152–62, 178

Orton, J.R., 53, 56, 71

Otto, Rudolf, 10–11, 89, 142–43, 199*n*68, 203*n*53

Owen, Alex, 11, 182*n*10

Paine, Thomas, 37, 45, 48, 74, 83

pantheism, 67, 71, 86

Partridge, Charles, 41, 42, 56, 70, 121, 127, 145, 156, 161

patriarchy, 91, 92, 149–50, 169–70

periodicals, Spiritualist, 21, 57–58, 69, 159–61

Philadelphia Harmonial Circle A, 123, 124, 130, 132, 133, 134, 140, 141, 202*n*27; activities of, 122–23, 124, 126, 138, 158; formation of, 122

phrenology, 4, 104, 111, 112–13, 121, 125

Poe, Edgar Allan, 20

Post, Amy, 47, 55, 56

Post, Isaac, 47, 50, 55, 56, 87, 96, 116

postmillennialism, 102

prayer, 120; in Spiritualist ritual, 137–38; in Spiritualist churches, 157

premillennialism, 102, 168

primitivism, Protestant, 9–10; Spiritualism as example of, 9–10, 40, 43, 44, 50, 53, 61, 173

Prothero, Stephen, 182*n*13

providence, concept of, 72, 88

psychology, 20, 27, 121; Spiritualism and emergence of, 111–13

Puritanism, 9, 37, 38, 78, 113, 133, 146

Quakers, 4, 22, 47, 80; contribution to Spiritualist ideology, 19; criticized by Spiritualists, 154–55; Spiritualism's resemblance to, 50, 55, 56, 57, 156; Spiritualists' departure from, 87. *See also* Congregational Quakers; Hicksite Quakers

Quimby, Phineas P., 192*n*16

Rabinowitz, Richard, 89, 119, 143

Randolph, P.B., 159

rationalism, 8–9, 43, 48, 50, 57, 70, 71, 87, 158; connection to Spiritualism, 4. *See also* deism

Reed, Caleb, 29, 199*n*65

reform. *See* Spiritualism, and antebellum reform

republican ideology, 3, 4, 5, 9, 14, 64, 73–74,

BRET E. CARROLL
is visiting assistant professor of history at the
University of Texas at Arlington.

www.ingramcontent.com/pod-product-compliance
Lightning Source LLC
Chambersburg PA
CBHW070447100426
42812CB00004B/1225